# Nature, culture and gender

# Nature, culture and gender

*Edited by*

## CAROL P. MacCORMACK

*Ross Institute*
*London School of Hygiene and Tropical Medicine*
*University of London*

*and*

## MARILYN STRATHERN

*Girton College, Cambridge*

## CAMBRIDGE UNIVERSITY PRESS

*Cambridge*
*London    New York    New Rochelle*
*Melbourne    Sydney*

Published by the Press Syndicate of the University of Cambridge
The Pitt Building, Trumpington Street, Cambridge CB2 1RP
32 East 57th Street, New York, NY 10022, USA
296 Beaconsfield Parade, Middle Park, Melbourne 3206, Australia

First published 1980

Printed in the United States of America

*British Library Cataloguing in Publication Data*

Nature, culture and gender
1. Sex role
2. Culture
3. Nature
I. MacCormack, Carole P
II. Strathern, Marilyn
301.2    GN479.65    80-40921
ISBN 0 521 23491 3  hard covers
ISBN 0 521 28001 X paperback

# Contents

# Plates

# Preface

The book was conceived in Swansea at the 1977 meeting of the Association of Social Anthropologists. We listened to Harris's paper in which she mentioned that married couples were the social category considered fully cultural in Laymi society. Chatting afterward about the assumption that nature is to culture as female is to male, one of us (MacCormack) mentioned that on the basis of her field work, the gender part of the equation did not seem universally valid. The other (Strathern) made the more radical suggestion that on the basis of her field work, she could not subscribe to the putative universality of the nature—culture categories themselves. We had been stimulated by ideas in important articles by Ardener, and Ortner, in which the nature—culture and female—male analogy was explicitly, though very differently, developed. Why were we so fascinated by those theoretical propositions? Jordanova, then a research fellow in history and philosophy of science, gave us insights into some of the assumptions of our own intellectual tradition. On another occasion, while co-examining a pile of student scripts with Maurice Bloch, and wishing to talk about anything but the chore before us, we turned to nature, culture and Rousseau. Jean Bloch, a lecturer in French, then added her valuable perspective.

In addition to this process of 'cultural self-analysis', we felt the need for a 'second opinion' from ethnographers interested in folk definitions of nature and gender. Jane Goodale had long ago raised a query about the Ortner paradigm, a query she elaborates here. Gillian Gillison worked in the same geographical region as Marilyn Strathern, but among people whose cultural constructs could not be more different from those in Strathern's Mt Hagen area. Our thinking had also been influenced by Nicole-Claude Mathieu's 1973 article in *L'Homme*, and we were disappointed when the pressure of work precluded her contributing a chapter to the book.

Our invitation to the various contributors was simply to reflect upon the manner in which anthropologists especially have used the concepts of nature and culture in the exegesis of other peoples' gender symbolism. While we have been concerned to bring together a collection of essays focussed on a single theme, this has not been a collective endeavour, and no single line of argument has been imposed on the contributions. Indeed, in the first place each was written largely independently of the others. They thus represent the meeting of diverse interests; at the same time most at one point or other relate their own arguments to the monumental works of Lévi-Strauss, as well as the inspiration of Ardener on the one hand and Ortner on the other. Although the resultant and numerous citations might give the impression that we are treating these authors' writings as some kind of 'text', we would rather be understood to be using them as exemplars. The ideas of nature and culture, though employed with varying intention, are encountered in their works as explicit analytical devices. If they have drawn, as anthropology must, on philosophical constructs embedded in our own cultural tradition, they have also — unwittingly or no — stimulated an easy acceptance of the conclusion that to illuminate other people's thought systems in such terms yields an ultimate insight into what other 'cultures' imagine they are all about.

That it is necessary to go over again ground long traversed by other disciplines, and by anthropology itself in the old nature–nurture debate, comes directly from the current interest in conceptualisations of gender which has followed the discovery of 'women' as an analytical category. This is not of course restricted to anthropology — far from it; anthropology thrives on and in turn feeds widespread contemporary concern with gender studies. One theme which emerges quite strongly from these essays is the self-consciousness of our own culture about its 'culture' in antithesis to nature, in the same way as many attempts at feminist analysis are predicated upon a self-consciousness about the category 'woman', in antithesis to man. Indeed, these two concerns may be brought into explicit conjunction. So although this book is framed in a largely anthropological idiom, by asking how and to what end we sometimes resort to notions of nature and culture in our explication of gender formulations, it touches on issues much more widely located in the world we inhabit.

The Women in Society Research Seminar at Cambridge organized by Elena Lieven and Marthe Macintyre commented constructively on three of the chapters. We also wish to thank members of anthropology seminars at Cambridge, the London School of Economics, Oxford, Sussex, UCLA, and the Collège de France for commenting on some of these chapters. Our ideas are our own responsibility, but the lively response from colleagues gave the encouragement necessary to see the task through.

Carol P. MacCormack
*London*

Marilyn Strathern
*Cambridge*

## References

Ardener, Edwin. 1975 [1972]. 'Belief and the problem of women', and 'The problem revisited' in *Perceiving Women*, ed. by Shirley Ardener, pp. 1–18 and 19–28. London: Malaby.

Harris, O. 1978. 'Complementarity and conflict: an Andean view of women and men' in *Sex and age as principles of social differentiation*, ed. by J. La Fontaine, ASA 17. London: Academic Press.

Mathieu, Nicole-Claude. 1973. 'Homme culture et femme nature?', *L'Homme* 13:101–41.

Ortner, Sherry B. 1974. 'Is female to male as nature is to culture?' in *Woman, culture and society*, ed. by M.Z. Rosaldo and L. Lamphere, pp. 67–88. Stanford: Stanford University Press.

# 1 Nature, culture and gender: a critique

CAROL P. MacCORMACK

## I

*Categories and transformations*

This is an exploration of the belief that human beings differ from animals and its corollary that culture is distinct and contrasted with nature. We are also concerned with the question of metaphoric transformations of the nature—culture contrast into raw—cooked or wild—tame. More controversially, we will explore the possibility that the female—male contrast can be understood as a further metaphoric transformation of an allegedly universal nature—culture contrast (Ortner 1974 and Ardener 1975). However, we are not only concerned with stark categories or metaphoric clusters of contrasts standing in wooden opposition to each other, but will also consider how we conceive of nature becoming culture; the process by which we feel we became human. Or, as formulated by Rousseau, how we passed from a state of nature to become beings with language and culture.

Following Rousseau, Lévi-Strauss attributes this transition to our capacity for culture rather than to the manifestations of culture itself (Wokler 1978:126). From our capacity to make discriminations, such as between 'us' as a kin category and 'other', and our ability to know rules of incest avoidance and marriage exogamy, we are capable of the Rousseauesque social contract in which we give up a state of nature, which means incest and the social isolation of small kin groups, for reciprocating kin ties and social contracts with others (Badcock 1975). To exist as a species we must eat, copulate, and meet other basic animal needs. To do so is 'natural' in that it is necessary for all animals. Whereas most basic human needs must be met or the *individual* will die, and they can be satisfied individually, procreative sex is not necessary to maintain the life of individuals but of *societies*, and that need cannot be met individually but requires paired

I wish to express gratitude to Meyer Fortes, Christine Hugh-Jones, Stephen Hugh-Jones, Jenny Teichman, and Marilyn Strathern. I have not always followed their intelligent advice, but respect their points of view profoundly.

1

opposites: male and female. Sexuality is natural but becomes cultural with incest prohibitions and rules of marriage exogamy (Lévi-Strauss 1969a:30).

From the rule to give 'us' (siblings) and receive 'other' (spouse) follows further patterned exchanges in persons, goods and services, and information. Exchanges which manifest the structure of human society give clues to the structure of an ultimate human code. The foundation of an ultimate structure is the human ability to make binary distinctions (Lévi-Strauss 1978:22–3). By perceiving opposites or contrasts the mind builds up its perceptions of the world. One does not perceive light without knowing darkness, nor unvoiced fricatives without knowing voiced ones. But isolated contrasts are not an end in themselves, for the human mind seeks analogies with other contrastive phenomena and upon finding them encompasses the analogies into its system of classification. On a conscious level people are aware of concrete manifestations rather than the relations themselves, but for structuralists the unconscious tendency to perceive relations is fundamental to the mind.[1]

The first distinction all new-born humans make is that between self and nurturing other. Then, as children develop they begin to discern phonetic contrasts, expanding the scope of logical operations inherent in the nature of their minds. Animals have no sense of kin boundaries; have no incest taboo or other socially-transmitted rules. The capacity to know rules binding upon all individuals is essential for the formation of human society, and from this capacity to know and formulate rules comes marriage, social alliances, language, and reciprocities of all kinds (Lévi-Strauss 1969a:32–3). The original transformation from nature to culture is repeated as societies perpetuate themselves by their cultural rules.

## Unconscious and conscious

Structuralists proceed upon the basis of belief that there is a single basic structure of binary thinking underlying all human mental functioning and behaviour, which can be discovered through orderly analysis informed by techniques of linguistic analysis. Once that structure is known it can help us understand the whole of human behaviour despite its manifest diversity. When the coding of the mind is known we will be able to decode the products of minds (Scheffler 1970:58).

Structuralist theory is inspired by linguistic theory, particularly by the work of de Saussure, who described language as a set of signs which could be studied in isolation from other cultural products. Language could be broken down into discrete elements, then one could examine the way the elements were combined to produce meaning. De Saussure expanded his

---

1   See Gardener (1976) for further discussion of this point, especially with reference to Lévi-Strauss and Piaget.

enquiry to include forms of etiquette, military signals, rituals and other systems of meaning. In all these, one could develop abstract formal models of underlying structure.

Following from de Saussure, Lévi-Strauss sought the cause of kinship, myth and totemic classification in our intellectual nature which, at its deepest and most pan-human level, is largely unconscious, just as comprehension of phonetic opposites is systematic and rational even though we are unaware of them. Kinship and myth are analogous in structure to language and function as codes.[2]

Lévi-Strauss is not an Idealist for whom the mind embodies fundamental logical categories and final truths. He does indeed have a Kantian unconscious which combines and categorizes, but it is a categorizing system homologous with nature or is nature itself (Lévi-Strauss 1969a:11). It is located in the physical brain, with its capacity to constitute codes which we call culture (Lévi-Strauss 1978:8).

For Lévi-Strauss, 'the unconscious . . . is always empty — or more accurately it is akin to mental images as the stomach is to food which passes through it. As the organ of a specific function the unconscious merely imposes structural laws upon inarticulate elements which originate elsewhere' (Lévi-Strauss quoted in Jenkins 1979:14). The brain functions at this unconscious level to generate ordered systems of representations by placing the perceptions which pass through it into relations of contrast and opposition.

One of the great difficulties with Lévi-Strauss's structuralism is the nature of the link between these unconscious functions of the brain and the 'reality' structuralism is meant to explain. Lévi-Strauss locates fundamental structure at the deep level of unconscious function, and gives it an ontological status, or existence, of its own. But what is the exact relationship between the organizing work of the unconscious and the conceptual domain of social structure, political relations, and so forth? On this latter conscious level concepts and operational categories do their work of giving meaning to empirical perceptions. Either we can leave the relationship between the physical brain's function and the mind's work of conceptual model building unexplained, or we can unify them in one of two possible ways.

We might opt for a biological reductionism in which the emphasis is placed on the role of the physical brain. Indeed, much of Lévi-Strauss's thinking is reductionist. He uses nature in two senses; the phenomenological world as we perceive it, excluding culture. Nature then is the residual category of everything outside culture (Badcock 1975:98). But it is also human nature to which cultural codes are reduced and, as Leach has pointed

---

2 Lévi-Strauss (1978:53) has stated that myth and music are not merely analogous with language but are derived from language.

out, Lévi-Strauss is caught in paradox. If he succeeds in identifying facts such as the incest taboo and rules of exogamy as universally true for humans, they must be natural. However, he assumes that the unique cultural quality of humanity rests on that which is not natural; on that which is socially transmitted and arbitrary in the way that symbol is to meaning in language (Leach 1970:121 and 1973:39). Thus, in one sense Lévi-Strauss reduced culture to biology; culture is nature, the physical brain and human nature. But in his later work, he suggested that the nature— culture contrast was an artificial creation of culture (1969a:xxxix), and was only a methodological device (1966:247).[3]

Schneider pushed the pendulum the rest of the way; culture is not nature, but nature is entirely a cultural concept (1972). We might regard all representations of structure as *concepts* of structure formulated at a conscious level through the process of model building (Jenkins 1979:36– 7). In this book we are not concerned with an unknowable unconscious but with folk models of nature, culture and gender which are consciously expressed in particular societies. That is not to say that every member of the society in question can express a complete, coherent model. The observer must build it up from explicit statements, myths, symbols, modes of classification, and other observations (see chapter 8). Nor is there a single model which characterizes the thought of all people in a society. If we think of a model as a plan for action, for example in making marriage alliances, there may be different plans for action held by different groups with varying degrees of political power in the society. Or, we may think of normative and pragmatic models which actors hold simultaneously.

Scheffler has argued that all formal models should have three qualities: (1) simplicity, (2) consistency, and (3) they should be judged adequate and appropriate by the local people in question (1970:67). Lévi-Strauss dismisses the question of adequacy and correspondence with conscious models, regarding the conscious as a screen which may hide the deep structure (1963:281). Nutini has attempted to find a middle ground, suggesting that unconscious models and conscious models are not different in kind but in degree, and that we are dealing with a single model which is revealed by the most careful, detailed field work possible (1970:82). Leach has commented that when we begin the study of another culture we rapidly formulate a model with which to explain it, but the model is largely shaped by our own presuppositions and may not correspond at all to the conscious model in the minds of the native people. But as months go by and we learn

---

3  See Badcock (1975) for a fuller discussion, and a comparison of Lévi-Strauss's biological reductionism with that of Freud. In his later work, Lévi-Strauss writes of the ambiguity of nature. It is subcultural, but it is also the means through which man hopes to contact ancestors, spirits and gods. Thus, nature is also 'supernatural' (1977:320).

the language and the thought patterns of the people, we radically revise the model. Those who work at a distance, from published ethnographic literature, and ethnographers who already 'know' the salient categories and their meaning before going to the field, are likely to give attention only to the phenomena that fit their presuppositions. Leach rejects Lévi-Strauss's definition of social anthropology as a branch of semiology with the internal logical structure of the meanings of sets and symbols as its central concern, looking instead for meaning in the actual social behaviour of human beings (1970:105).

Structuralist theory gives comprehensive explanations, but because it refers to the unconscious it is difficult to validate, while more empirically based theory is easy to validate but offers explanations which are less satisfying and often tautologous. Some observers have suggested that structurally-oriented social scientists model themselves after natural scientists, observing, describing, then constructing formal models with which to draw conclusions about the significance of that which they observed (Gardener 1976:4–7). Leach, however, speculates that Lévi-Strauss started at the other end by first asking himself: 'how is it and why is it that men, who are part of nature, manage to see themselves as "other than" nature even though, in order to subsist, they must constantly maintain "relations with" nature'? (1970:129). Lévi-Strauss observes that such things as the incest taboo or cooking are widespread, but not necessary to maintain life in the animal world. Therefore these things must be symbols 'by which culture is distinguished from nature in order that men might reassure themselves that they are not beasts' (Leach 1970:129). Others have also commented that Lévi-Strauss's method is not inductive but primarily deductive. He hypothesizes that in every myth he should find a structuring binary opposition which is not specific for only one version of the myth. Indeed, he does find it and often complementary pairs of oppositions as well (Pettit 1975:87–8).

## 'Nature' and 'culture' as cultural constructs

We do not wish to deny that binary contrasts are vital to human thought; it is the allegedly universal meanings given to some category nouns which concern us. Since the structuralist method seeks to reduce data to their symbolic structure, symbols are more real than the phenomena; the signifier is more important than the signified (Scholte 1974:428). But symbols such as nature or female have meanings attached to them which are culturally relative. Douglas, and Kirk, insist that content cannot be ignored; different versions of a myth, for example, cannot be reduced to a single structure (Douglas 1967:66 and Kirk 1970:78). Structuralist analysis should explain with reference to a particular myth how its meanings are

produced and therefore explanation requires an understanding of the culture in which the myth arises.[4]

Thus, although Lévi-Strauss has attempted to cast the nature—culture
contrast in a timeless, value-free model concerned with the working of the
human mind, ideas about nature and culture are not value free. The 'myth'
of nature is a system of arbitrary signs which relies on a social consensus
for meaning. Neither the concept of nature nor that of culture is 'given',
and they cannot be free from the biases of the culture in which the concepts were constructed (see chapters 2, 3). Our European ideas about
nature and culture are fundamentally about our origins and evolution. The
'natural' is that which is innate in our primate heritage and the 'cultural'
is that which is arbitrary and artificial. In our evolutionary history we have
improved and constrained ourselves by creating our own artificial rule-
bound order.

Our minds structure myth, and in a feedback loop myth instructs our
perceptions of the phenomenological universe. Genesis, for example, sets
humans in opposition to nature and promises us dominion over nature.
With Protestantism, we come to take individual responsibility for the
rational understanding and harnessing of nature. The myth in its present-
day form reflects the faith of industrial society that society is produced by
enterprising activity. Sahlins has expressed the opinion that 'development
from a Hobbesian state of nature is the origin myth of Western capitalism'
(1976a:52—3).[5] We allocate honour and prestige to people of science and
industry who excel in understanding and controlling the powerful domain
of nature. We also honour people who overcome animal urges, curbing
these urges in accordance with moral codes. When women are defined as
'natural' a high prestige or even moral 'goodness' is attached to men's
domination over women, analogous to the 'goodness' of human domination of natural energy sources or the libidinal energy of individuals. It
seems quite logical for us now, in our Judaeo-Christian and industrial tradition, to link nature with wildness and with femaleness (Ardener 1975).
However, even our own specific European intellectual history has not consistently linked the natural with wildness.

In the eighteenth century, nature was that aspect of the world which
had been revealed through scientific scrutiny to have its predictable laws,
but also that which was not yet mastered. Women were the repository of
'natural laws' and 'natural morality', but also that which was emotional
and passionate, needing constraint within social boundaries (see chapters 2,
3). The opposed categories of nature and culture (or society) arose as part of

4    See Lévi-Strauss (1978:26ff.) for response to this criticism.
5    Sahlins (1976a:53) commented: 'So far as I know, we are the only
    people who think themselves risen from savages; everyone else believes
    they descended from gods.'

a historically particular ideological polemic in eighteenth-century Europe; a polemic which created further contradictions by defining women as natural (superior), but instruments of a society of men (subordinate) (see chapter 2).

By the mid nineteenth century, evolutionary ideas provided a 'natural' explanation of gender differences. In 1861 Bachofen posited an ancient period of 'mother right' in which women ruled the state as well as the household, but were subdued by vigorous Roman patriarchy in classical times. McLennan in 1865 wrote of the stage in history when men captured and exchanged women, stressing the need for rules of exogamy and marriage alliance if human society was to be peaceful. Morgan in 1877 elaborately developed a matrilineal stage of human history, superseded by male control, a theme Engels took up in *The Origin of the Family, Private Property and the State* in 1884 (Lowie 1937:40ff.). Eighteenth-century ambiguity and contradictions persist into the twentieth century, and the simple nineteenth-century unilineal evolutionary model has been set aside. With this ambiguity and complexity at the heart of our European definitions, how can we agree that the following set of metaphors represent universal human cognative structure?

| nature | : | culture |
|--------|---|---------|
| wild | : | tame |
| female | : | male |

Structural models are dynamic in that they are concerned with becoming and transforming. Europeans have a concept of history, of literate accumulation, of progressive change over time, and a notion of genesis as the one and only beginning. We have the concept that one category can transform into another, with nature becoming culture, children through socialization becoming adults who marry exogamously, wild becoming domesticated, and raw becoming cooked. To a great extent, meaning for us depends upon 'becoming' (Wagner 1975). But our meanings are not found to be universally true, and some societies conceive of 'nature' as an immutable category incapable of transformation (see chapter 8). Lévi-Strauss stressed not just becoming, but dominating, with the social dominating the biological and the cultural dominating the natural (1969a:479). The slightly scrambled sequence of events in Genesis, for example, move from seething nature to man's dominion over nature, in accordance with moral rules.

Using a linguistic idiom, the passage from nature to culture is a greatly abbreviated syntagmatic chain of mythic units, forming a metonymic axis from left to right. Reading from top to bottom we have paradigmatic associations, or metaphoric transformation (Leach 1976:25−7):

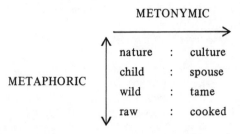

If we add gender to this set we achieve a non-sequitur:

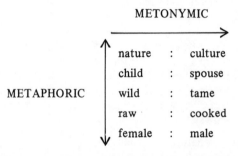

In our European thought system gender provides two obvious categories of social differentiation but lacks the dynamic potential for transformation that other paired contrasts have. On the metonymic axis, in what sense can female become male as nature becomes culture? None, if we are to regard genders as immutable categories 'in nature'. But a case can also be made for gender categories 'in culture'. That is, they are socially constructed (Mathieu 1978). However, in cases where individuals choose to change their social identity it is not only females who take on male identity, but some males move to femaleness.

On the metaphoric axis we have already noted that at some periods of European history female was not exclusively identified with wild but with the harmonious repository of nature's laws. Ardener, in his account of the Bakweri, stresses the metaphor nature=wildness=female. But he tells us men are also associated with nature and wildness, in hunting and ritual, highlighting the problem of knowing which units of mythic text or observed behaviour are to be selected as manifestations of underlying structure.[6]

6   Ardener (1975:14): Men 'hunt on the mountain top away from all villages and farms, this is ritually expressed in the men's elephant dance'. We might conclude that the beast is in all of us, not just women, and the non-social=non-human=the wild=nature is a powerful metaphor for *human* contemplation. Ardener acknowledges La Fontaine's observation that men's wild usually stands for death and destruction while women's wild stands for agriculture and fertility (1975:16).

Some writers, following Lévi-Strauss, seem to be giving a greater weight of 'truth' to metaphoric associations than the concept of metaphor will bear. Words such as 'nature' are polysemic, having many implicit meanings. Metaphor is based upon a figurative, not a literal meaning of a word, thus the meaning of a word can be shaped or extended through metaphor. Menstruating women have cyclicity as nature does, therefore they are wild and untamable. But wildness can also be an implicit meaning of maleness. Because metaphor is based upon the polysemic and open nature of words it has great potential for both contradiction and for 'redescribing reality' and must not be taken as truth in any literal sense (Ricoeur 1978:169ff.). As Harris explains, although the Laymis of Bolivia make a series of associations that may lead us to conclude that wild is identified with female, Laymis themselves do not make that association. 'To apply "logical" procedures . . . is to forget that what are being compared are complex concepts, and that in each identification it is different and specific characteristics of these phenomena that are selected for comparison' (see chapter 4).

Much of the ethnographic literature suggests that rather than viewing women as metaphorically in nature, they (and men) might better be seen as mediating between nature and culture, in the reciprocity of marriage exchange, socializing children into adults, transforming raw meat and vegetable into cooked food, cultivating, domesticating, and making cultural products of all sorts.[7]

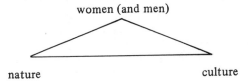

women (and men)

nature          culture

If we took an extreme position of defining women but not men as socializers, cultivators, cooks — as mediators between nature and culture — and if we viewed them in the structure of kinship as mediators between exogamous social groups, then we must look more closely at the attributes structuralists confer upon mediators. Because they can merge and reconcile opposites, mediators are deity or messiah and at the same time clown and trickster (Lévi-Strauss 1978:32–3). This definition is quite at odds with some structuralists' definition of women as simple, passive objects in kinship systems, pointing to yet another logical inconsistency in structuralist models.

The ethnographic literature does not justify the extreme position of

---

7  Ortner (1974) builds a theory of female as nature, but retreats from the extreme position by acknowledging women's role in mediating between nature and culture. See also Lévi-Strauss (1966:128).

defining women but not men as mediators between nature and culture, nor does it uniformly equate women's attributes exclusively with those of nature. In the Mount Hagen area of Papua New Guinea, for example, people do not conceive a nature–culture contrast in the way Europeans do, and they attribute qualities to both men and women which Western structuralists would classify as natural and cultural (see chapter 8). Rather than concepts of nature and culture as we understand them, Hageners think with the categories of 'planted' (*mbo*) and 'wild' (*rømi*). 'Planted' refers to crops, breeding pigs and human beings rooted in clan territory; 'wild' refers to that which is solitary, exotic and non-human. Male–female categories are not consistent secondary discriminators. Hageners do use gender categories, with male representing that which is prestigious (*nyim*) and female that which is rubbish (*korpa*), but those categories are not explained by the difference between the planted and the wild.

Within the Hagen folk model nature does not become culture. The 'wild' is encountered and dealt with, but is not dominated, nor is it incorporated within culture, explained by 'natural' laws, robbed of its powers. It does not become with human 'progress' an ever-shrinking residual category. The power of the wild can be brought to bear on human activity precisely because it is antithesis to *mbo*. Similarly, in the Gimi area of Papua New Guinea nature is not devalued. Male essence is identified with the wild, its spirits and birds. *Kore* means forest, afterlife, and an honorific title of address for high status males. Gender distinctions are not so much the cold rational process of category discrimination Lévi-Strauss emphasizes, as the highly emotive matters of sexuality, birth, nurturing, eating and women's releasing men's spirit essence back into the forest as spirit/flute/bird; a matter ultimately concerned with men's dependence on women (see chapter 7).

There is no way to absolutely verify that the nature–culture opposition exists as an essential feature of universal *unconscious* structure, and there is ethnographic evidence to suggest that in the form in which Europeans now conceive it, the contrast is not a universal feature of consciously-held folk models. If we use the categories 'nature–culture' merely as a methodological device for ordering folk concepts which roughly approximate European meanings, then gender categories are not necessarily linked to them. Goodale's description of the Kaulong of New Britain gives the following metaphoric set (see chapter 6):

| animal | : | human | | |
|---|---|---|---|---|
| reproduction | : | production | | |
| forest | : | garden | : | hamlet |

The Kaulong do not have a strongly defined sexual division of labour. Both men and women develop their social identity by growing produce and acquiring other goods for exchange. Both are at the centre of their own network of cognatic kin, and trading partners. By contrast, reproduction is relatively non-social, requiring only one partner. The married must live away from the hamlet, in gardens, and are marginalized by residence and other taboos.

For the Laymis of Bolivia it is not the married, but the unmarried, who are marginal (see chapter 4):

| incomplete | | complete |
|---|---|---|
| division | : | division |
| of labour | | of labour |
| | | |
| unmarried | : | married |

With a clearly defined sexual division of labour, unmarried men and women are not complete in the socio-economic sense. In Laymi thought, that which is fully cultural is the unity of man and woman in marriage, and even spirits in 'nature' have their spouse.

Sherbros of West Africa resemble the Kaulong in that women transact in goods and services and are important in cognatic kin groups, but resemble the Laymis with a clearly defined sexual division of labour. Socialization is viewed as a process which transforms proto-social children into initiated adults who understand and vow to live by ancestral laws (culture). But females are as carefully and completely socialized as males. Female officials, female imagery and ancestresses are as important in the ritual process as their male counterparts (see chapter 5):

| 'nature' | : | 'culture' |
|---|---|---|
| proto-social | : | initiated |
| children | | adults |

## Gender attributes in models of kinship

Although Lévi-Strauss clearly states that structure does not lie at the level of empirical reality (1977:79), he appeals to empirical 'reality' in constructing a model of human society in which women are simple passive objects of male activity (1963:47).[8] His model of human society has the basic premise that it is 'the men who own and the women who are owned ... wives who are acquired and sisters and daughters who are given away' (1969a: 136). For him, men and women are interchangeable and equal from a formal point of view, but they are not from the social point of view. A sister changes her role to that of a wife through the transactions men make, and

8  In the analysis of social structure, Lévi-Strauss follows in the Rousseavian tradition of defining men as active and women as passive and controlled (see chapter 2). In the analysis of myth, he works with a rich variety of qualities attributed to women and does not consistently link female to nature as Ortner and Ardener do.

he chooses not to acknowledge that men also undergo role changes embedded within marriage transactions, most markedly with uxorilocal residence following marriage. Structuralists using the Lévi-Straussian model of kinship thus define men as actors and women as acted upon; men as subject and women as object. Although Lévi-Strauss has overtly used empiricism to construct the gender aspect of his model, when cases of matrilineal dowry systems in which men move between groups are noted (Junus 1964), or cases of societies where women have formal decision-making roles are noted (MacCormack 1972; 1974; 1976; 1979), structuralists retreat behind a screen of indifference to 'surface manifestations' which mask the deep structure (Lévi-Strauss 1963:281; 1977:78).[9] Is it simply a matter of one man's empiricism being another's 'apt examples', or do those ethnographic observations reveal false models which mask true structure? If that is the case, why do societies hide their fundamental structures with screening models? Nutini has suggested that some conscious models are more accurate than any that could be built up by the anthropologist and, even if there are deceptions, those very errors constitute the social facts under study (1970:73 and 82).

The model of kinship formulated by Lévi-Strauss is a logical construct based upon the allegedly universal rule of incest avoidance and a set of rules for marriage exogamy. It is ambivalent about the far more complex level of what men and women actually do. The logic of the model as constructed denies or is disinterested in observations that women are active in courtship (see chapters 6 and 4), sometimes act as matchmakers, and share in the wealth of affine's labour and goods in marriage transactions. The model has no provision for women who do not marry, nor for divorce and the active role women take in making their subsequent marriages. If we believe the model, then the above behaviour, which may be statistically significant (Bledsoe 1980), is conceptually aberrant, if not 'unnatural'. However, that behaviour might be seen as a healthy adaptation to the physical and social conditions in which women find themselves. Might our own Western cultural assumptions about the natural world being acted upon, and our notions of property, predispose the model makers to view male as subject and female as passive object?

Furthermore, limiting women to passive objectivity limits the explanatory power of the model. As the model stands, sisters (and daughters) are

9  In 'The Meaning and Use of the Notion of Model' (1977) Lévi-Strauss cautions against confusing a theoretical analysis of models with an actual description of data as they appear to the empirical observer. 'Many Southeast Asian societies make the useful and often true statement that women circulate, not men; this does not invalidate the truth (to be covered by a generalized model) that nothing would be changed in the formal properties of the structure if the situation were described the other way around, as some tribes actually do' (p. 78).

denied to men by the incest taboo and are given away by them to become other men's wives (Lévi-Strauss 1969a:136). Thus, the following set of metaphoric transformations:

nature : culture
incest : rules of exogamy
sister : wife

But if we return to first principles, that procreative sexuality requires the binary set of male and female, must not both categories in that set undergo role changes as a concomitant of the incest taboo? When women reach sexual maturity they are indeed regarded by their 'brothers' as other men's wives and, in a balanced way, when men reach sexual and social maturity they must be regarded by their 'sisters' as other women's husbands. The set of metaphors might be reformulated as:

nature : culture
incest : rules of exogamy
sibling : spouse

The reader is probably thinking: of course we know that for the incest taboo and rules of exogamy to do their work of initiating reciprocities and integrating social groups both men and women experience role changes. This is so obvious that it does not need to be stated. Is it then a component of the one 'true' structure, and have Lévi-Strauss and others thrown up a screening model which hides the deep structure?

For prescriptive marriage systems to do their work of interweaving consanguineous groups together into a human society women cannot be simply passive. Some women object to an arranged marriage and manage to cause enough trouble to disrupt the complex pattern of reciprocities over time inherent in alliance systems. Others actively agree to marriage, enabling a brother to marry a wife from a reciprocating group. By agreeing to marry, a woman in a sense provides her brother with a wife, laying a claim upon him to give assistance to her and her children for the rest of his life (Van Baal 1975:76). On the level of myth and ritual, men's and women's ritual associations may exist in balanced reciprocity, each needing the other to make a complete conceptual system (MacCormack 1981). But even in societies where there are men's associations only, men must have the active cooperation of women to provide a terrorized audience to confirm the terror of the gods, or an uninitiated group to confirm the secrets of the initiated (Van Baal 1975:72).

The attributes we assign to gender categories are based upon our perceptions of what men and women do. Ardener has suggested that men move about more widely in social and geographical space than women, becoming aware of others more frequently than do women. They are therefore more likely to develop 'metalevels of categorization' that enable them to conceptually bound themselves and their women off from other men and their women (1975:6). However, women are not universally restricted to the closed domestic sphere. Some Third World women of low class and caste travel widely to find wage employment (Boserup 1970:79–80). Women migrate in large numbers to some urban areas (Little 1973: chapter 2). Some women traders cover hundreds of miles (MacCormack 1976). Even Ardener describes Bakweri women as having long travelled from stranger quarter to stranger quarter (1975:13). Because the set of behavioural manifestations which reveal putative deep structure is not 'given', any behaviour may or may not be selected by the anthropologist as revealing that structure.

Women seem most restricted in societies with patrilineal descent groups where they enter into bridewealth marriages and do not trade or seek wages. But even in this type of society it is usually the women who actually go and live with their husband's kin group. They are aware in childhood that this will be their fate (Paulme 1963:6–7). Unless we want to deny women a potential for intelligence and intellectual curiosity equal to men's, we logically cannot deny them conceptual models for making sense of their own existence. If they 'giggle when young, snort when old, reject the question, laugh at the topic, and the like' (Ardener 1975:2), might they not be reacting to the cultural assumptions unconsciously biasing the investigator's questions? Does the status difference between a European in a colonialized country and the village woman not predictably shape the kind of responses one can expect within particular cultural contexts (Goody 1978)?

Much of the published literature on social structure which some structuralists use for data reflects the power of an earlier model, Radcliffe-Brown's 'jural model'. The idea of descent is equated with the transmission of rights, duties, power and authority. Jural rules, too often enunciated by male informants, stress male authority roles. However, the folk models of most societies stress a far more complex pattern of male and female interaction than the jural model can accommodate (James 1978:145). In matrilinially organized kin systems, for example, if we look beyond the authority role of mother's brother, we find women controlling the regeneration of lineage identity for both males and females, centrally placed within a structure of reciprocal obligations. Women control items of great cultural significance, and in the Trobriand case control the cosmic cycle itself, 'leaving men to create, through women, artificial extensions of their own historically bounded time' (Weiner 1976:23). Even within patrilinially organized societies men ritually express anxiety about their dependence on women as regenerators of life (see chapter 7), and there is ample evidence that folk concepts of descent and continuity acknowledge the vital attributes of women (Singer 1973; James 1978:155ff.). Within a single society the investigator often receives very different definitions of 'woman' depending upon whether he or she asks about woman-as-mother, or woman-as-wife.

## Gender attributes in models of economic exchange

If we shift from the consideration of kinship reciprocities to economic reciprocities, we might look closely at the exchange of goods and services. With the possible exception of advanced industrial societies where machines replace labour and cause an 'unemployment problem', can we attribute to women as passive a role in production and exchange of goods and services as has been assigned to them in kinship transactions?

Most societies have a division of labour based upon gender categories which might be seen as a metaphor for procreative sex. As both male and female are required for sexual reproduction of society, so they are also required for production of goods and services to sustain and integrate it. Logically, both male and female participate in the same cognitive model, each playing by the same set of rules, each dependent upon the other. In some societies women are prodigious producers of goods, and in all societies they provide services (Boserup 1970). Whether the activity of providing goods and services takes place in domestic space or public space has no bearing on the quantity of those goods and services. Domestic production should not be deleted from economic calculations, and if it cannot be reckoned in money terms then better economic models must be devised. Sexually immature children provide services for kin bounded by the incest taboo, but with sexual maturity and marriage they provide services for those in another group outside the boundary of the incest taboo, their affines. In societies with patrilineal institutions, husbands (and their close kin) may give bridewealth and labour defined by affinal obligation, and wives give children and labour defined by affinal obligation:

| | | |
|---|---|---|
| nature | : | culture |
| kin bounded by the incest taboo | : | affines |
| goods and services for 'us' | : | goods and services for 'other' |
| boys and girls | . | men and women |

To restrict the definition of men to giver and women to given is to deny the model of a kind of symmetry and balance that must necessarily exist.

But is there a qualitative difference between goods and services exchanged by men and those exchanged by women? In many societies men unquestionably have more power and appropriate the product of women's labour, commanding more goods with which to initiate alliances. If to marry out is better than to be killed out, then alliances initiated with men's wealth might be given positive value (Lévi-Strauss 1969a:43). Alliances integrate groups, and in most societies men are more active in the political domain which unifies social units while women are more active in domestic groups which are fragments of the society. In this sense we can assess a high value to men who transcend and unify (Ortner 1974:79), if we ignore the fact that those who unify through politics also divide and destroy through war.

Economic exchange is concerned with services as well as goods. If we consider the full range of goods and services exchanged in human society, can we be confident that the goods men command and bestow necessarily rank above the services women command and bestow? As Lévi-Strauss focussed the analysis of exchange on the biological dictum of 'marry out or be killed out', might we also ask, on a biological level, is Homo sapiens more likely to survive as a species because of the 'high level' exchanges men tend to engage in, or the domestic production, sharing and pro-creation by women? Domestic services are devalued in advanced industrial societies where 'work' is defined as wage labour and is separated from domestic space, and where a 'population problem' is perceived. But those are the biases of our own culture and are not universally valid.

## Nature, culture and biological reproduction of society

Ortner has proceeded in the Lévi-Straussian manner of asking a question about humanity, then setting out to answer it. She asks: how might we account for universal female subordination? Moving quickly to a biological reductionist argument, she sees that 'woman's body seems to doom her to mere reproduction of life; the male in contrast, lacking natural creative functions, must (or has the opportunity to) assert his creativity externally, "artificially", through the medium of technology and symbols. In doing so he creates relatively lasting, eternal, transcending objects, while the woman creates only perishables — human beings' (1974:75). This view, which originates with de Beauvoir (1953:239), is remarkable for its ethnocentri-city. A vast number of societies, and particularly the totemic societies Lévi-Strauss has used for analysis, have lineage systems which exist, by definition in perpetuity. Each human who is born fits into a great social chain of being, ensuring the immortality of both self and group. Houses rot, villages are moved, empires fall, but the great faith is that the lineage, including the 'real' company of ancestors, will endure forever.

Is there anything more intrinsically natural about women's physiology than men's? In most societies men's procreative role is seen as being as essential as women's for the continuity of social groups. Both men and women procreate, eat, defecate and satisfy other survival needs. To do so is natural, but the etiquette of eating, the time, place and position for defecation, and indeed the rules prescribing time, place and position for ejaculation or parturition are cultural. Fertility and birth are guided by definitions of symptoms and technological modifications brought about by chemical and mechanical therapy in virtually all societies and cannot be used as the single characteristic for defining women as 'natural' (Mac-Cormack 1981).

The statement that women are doomed by their biology to be natural, not cultural, is of course a mythic statement, and both Ortner and Lévi-Strauss retreat from it. Of course woman cannot be consigned fully to the category of nature 'for it is perfectly obvious that she is a full-fledged human being endowed with human consciousness just as man is; she is half the human race, without whose cooperation the whole enterprise would collapse' (Ortner 1974:75–6). Or, as expressed by Lévi-Strauss, 'women could never become just a sign and nothing more, since even in a man's world she is still a person, and since insofar as she is defined as a sign she must be recognized as a generator of signs' (1969a:496). Thus, Lévi-Strauss's fundamental paradox reappears in metaphoric transformation:
(1) Culture transcends nature, but is grounded in the human mind (brain) which is nature.
(2) Men transcend nature with their mentality, but are in nature as procreated, procreators, and possessors of human minds.
(3) Women transcend nature with their mentality, but are in nature as procreated, procreators, lactators, and possessors of human minds.
Or, two and three might be combined to read:
(4) Men and women transcend nature with their mentality, but are in nature as procreated, procreators, nurturers, and possessors of human minds.
Might we then conclude that both men and women are nature and culture, and there is no logic compelling us to believe that at an unconscious level women, because of their naturalness, are opposed and subordinate to men?

## Ideology and the adequacy of models

Ortner states that 'everywhere, in every known culture, women are considered in some degree inferior to men' (1974:69). But she does not say by whom they are considered to be so. By men? By women? By how many? In field work I have talked with women chiefs, women heads of descent groups, heads of women's secret societies, and women household heads who would not agree with the sweeping thesis as it stands. They would say that women are inferior to men in some ways and men are inferior to women in some ways, giving productive tasks in the division of labour as examples. There would not be the social ferment over gender roles in Western industrial societies today if a substantial number of men and women did not subscribe to the thesis of universal female subordination. The methodological problem is this: can structural models stand without reference to consciously-held folk models and actual statistical descriptions? Scheffler opts for models which are judged adequate and appropriate by the people in question (1970:67), and Lévi-Strauss mis-trusts the people's own assessment as a possible screen hiding deep structure (1963:281).

Ardener's position regarding models of nature, culture and gender is ambiguous. On the one hand, he sees reality in the conscious folk model, alleging that Bakweri women perceive themselves as being in nature.[10] As with Lévi-Strauss and Ortner, he does not attempt to put women entirely within the domain of nature, but sees them bounding themselves with both nature and culture while men bound themselves off from nature. But he also sees validity in metaphorically linking female and nature at the level of unconscious structure.[11] However, in the familiar pattern of structuralist reasoning, he ultimately reduces the argument to biology, saying 'since women are biologically not men, it would be surprising if they bounded themselves against nature in the same way as men do' (1975:5).

But the link between nature and women is not a 'given'. Gender and its attributes are not pure biology. The meanings attributed to male and female are as arbitrary as are the meanings attributed to nature and culture (Mathieu 1973). Those who have developed the nature—culture—gender thesis root femaleness in biology and maleness in the social domain (de Beauvoir 1953:239; Ortner 1974:67—88; Ardener 1975:5; Lévi-Strauss 1969a:482). However, if men and women are one species and together constitute human society then, logically, analysis of intrinsic gender attributes must be made with reference to the same domain. Equally in error is the formulation of sociobiologists who root male gender attributes excessively in biology, thus explaining the 'naturalness' of men's political dominance over women.[12]

10   In an account of a Bakweri story and associated ritual, Ardener explains: 'Bakweri women themselves bound their world as including the wild that Moto [men] exclude . . . Although the men bound off "mankind" from nature the women persist in overlapping into nature again' (pp. 7 and 8). 'Bakweri women define the boundary of their world in such a way that they live as women in men's definition of wild, as well as partially within the men's world inside the village fence' (p. 13).

11   Ardener interprets the initiation stage of the *liengu* (water spirit) rite to be women's 'final incorporation in the wild, outside the fence of the village' (p. 12). Using 'methods of the type used by Lévi-Strauss in *Mythologiques*', Ardener reveals an unconscious model linking women and nature through structural analysis of the rite (p. 8).

12   See for example, E.O. Wilson (1975: chapter 27). However, socio-

In his conclusion, Ardener seems to return to the level of the conscious model; the dominant male model in which 'some features of women' do not fit within the boundaries of human society as men define it (p. 23). Bakweri women themselves, he tells us, are not confused by the male model, but acquiesce to it because they are subordinate and made 'mute' by male domination (p. 24).

We are now brought to a relativistic point of view where men think one thing, women know another, but are not allowed a hearing because European investigators turn to men as the authoritative spokesmen. We are no longer dealing with putative universal categories but with a political problem in which women are kept from speaking by men who constitute the political power elite, and we are left to ponder our own European cultural history to discover why some anthropologists consider the conscious models which colonialized men give them to be so satisfying.

Although structuralist models apply to the synchronic dimension of social phenomena, Lévi-Strauss and others are interested in the diachronic dimension of social change as well. As de Saussure made a distinction in his work on linguistics between the science of *langue* (code) and the science of *parôle* (message), so Lévi-Strauss uses both a synchronic structuralism and a marxist dialectic, the latter explaining social change and the final social causes of particular cultural codes. When women garden and weave, their activity is conceived as being within the order of nature. When men appropriate the same type of activity and interpose culture in the form of complex machinery in the process, the male activity is within the order of culture (Lévi-Strauss 1977:321). Presumably women, as poorly paid or unpaid labour, are viewed by men as a cheap natural resource in the productive process. On the topic of Third World development, Lévi-Strauss reasons that societies are not 'underdeveloped' through their own doing, but because capitalistic societies have extracted wealth from them since the sixteenth century. Conquests which yielded gold from the New World, slaves from Africa, and other wealth, link the non-industrial and the industrial countries into a common system with a common history. The relationship between colonialist and colonialized, and the relationship between capitalist and proletarian in industrial societies, are manifestations of the same process: 'the mute slavery of the New World was needed as a cornerstone on which the covert slavery of Europe's wage earners was built' (quoted by Lévi-Strauss 1977:315):

| colonialist | : | colonialized |
| capitalist | : | proletarian |

---

biologists cannot spell out the mechanisms by which the genes instruct humans to the specific behaviour attributed to each gender, especially given the cultural variability of 'natural' attributes. See Sahlins (1977) for a general critique.

For Lévi-Strauss, the creation and very reality of industrial society is found in the irreversible historical condition of oppression, and he criticizes Malinowski for considering development to result from the impact of a higher and more active culture on a simpler and more passive one. ' "Simplicity" and "passivity" are not intrinsic properties of these societies, but the result of the development's action upon them from its very beginnings; a situation created by brutality, pillage, and violence, without which the historical conditions of this very development would not have been brought together' (Lévi-Strauss 1977:316).

Although he acknowledges Engels in his analysis of colonialization and proletarianization, Lévi-Strauss does not acknowledge Engels's analysis of the process by which women as a category have become the 'proletariat' to men, the 'bourgeoisie', through the rise of private property and the privatization of women's labour (Engels 1942:48ff.):

|  |  |  |
|---|---|---|
| colonialist | : | colonialized |
| capitalist | : | proletarian |
| male | : | female |

If Lévi-Strauss insists that simplicity and passivity are not intrinsic properties of the colonialized and proletarianized, then logically he must insist that they are not intrinsic properties of females, but the result of a historical process which leaves women marginalized and powerless. We suggest that it is as important to understand the 'message' of property relations as the 'code' of naturalness if we are to understand accounts of women's marginality in human societies.

## II

These remarks are a prologue. The following two chapters turn to the constructive task of deepening our understanding of European concepts of nature, human society and gender. In the latter part of the book we examine those concepts in a more comparative frame.

During the Enlightenment the concept of nature was crucial to both political discourse and the rise of scientific enquiry. Maurice and Jean Bloch ground the idea of nature in a political dialectic which opposed 'natural law' to the doctrine of divine right of kings. Later, Rousseau shaped 'nature' to mean the very source by which corrupt society reformed and purified itself. This concept of nature was crucial to Rousseau's radical advocacy of sovereignty of the people and the legitimacy of democracy. The concept of nature takes its meaning in part from that to which it is opposed; divine kings, pre-society, corrupt society, and so forth. Since 'nature' has been opposed to different doctrines at different points in history, its meaning shifts accordingly.

Rousseau set up a further dialectic between the idea of nature as guide and teacher for reformed society, and nature associated with women's emotions and domesticity. Eighteenth-century ideas of social and political reform did not extend to women. Although they were more purely natural than men, women were socially defined as passive, dependent and politically inferior to men. This contradiction is preserved in Lévi-Strauss's vision of social structure, and constitutes part of the dialectic on gender to which this book contributes.

In the eighteenth century, nature was both that part of the world which had not yet been penetrated, and that part of the world which men understood, mastered, and made their own. Jordanova explains how scientific enquiry paralleled political discourse in assigning contradictory attributes to women. They were the repositories of natural law; the founder of human society was the mother of a family. Through the scientific unveiling of women, nature could be revealed and understood. But women were also the repositories of passions which needed to be contained and controlled. By the mid eighteenth century, a well-established bio-medical tradition observed and defined humans, hardening the conceptual division between unique feminine and unique masculine attributes. A biological determinism 'explained' women, but men were defined more by their social acts, an attitude of enquiry which persists in some present-day literature on gender.

Broadening our scope of enquiry, we might return to the relationship between European colonial powers and the Third World. In discourse on the meaning of culture and society, European concepts might be seen as a 'dominant code' (Ardener) which universalizes our European vision of the world. As Harris points out, we are then less likely to hear 'muted codes'. But social scientists must guard against the tendency to use the dominant discourse of European culture to universalize our categories, thus rendering ourselves deaf to alternative ways of structuring the world. Chapters by Harris, MacCormack, Goodale, Gillison and Strathern painstakingly explore some of those alternative structures. Although the peoples considered use binary constructs contingent upon nature or gender, none of the resulting symbolic equations can be reduced to a simple nature:culture::female:male analogy. Strathern's concluding chapter is both a theoretical overview and a searching ethnographic exploration.

## Bibliography

Ardener, Edwin. 1975 [1972]. 'Belief and the Problem of Women', and 'The Problem Revisited' in *Perceiving Women*, ed. by Shirley Ardener, pp. 1—18 and 19—28. London: Malaby.

Badcock, C.R. 1975. *Lévi-Strauss: Structuralism and Sociological Theory*. London: Hutchinson.

Bledsoe, Caroline. 1980. *Women and Marriage in Kpelle Society*. Stanford: University Press.

Boserup, Esther. 1970. *Woman's Role in Economic Development*. London: George Allen and Unwin.

de Beauvoir, Simone. 1972 [1949]. *The Second Sex*. New York: Knopf.

Douglas, Mary. 1967. 'The Meaning of Myth' in *The Structural Study of Myth and Totemism*, ed. by E.R. Leach, pp. 49—70. London: Tavistock.

Engels, Frederick. 1942 [1884]. *The Origin of the Family, Private Property, and the State*. New York: International Publishers.

Gardener, Howard. 1976. *The Quest for Mind: Piaget, Lévi-Strauss and the Structuralist Movement*. London: Quartet Books.

Goody, Esther N. 1978. 'Toward a Theory of Questions' in *Questions and Politeness*, ed. by E.N. Goody, pp. 17—43. Cambridge: Cambridge University Press.

James, Wendy. 1978. 'Matrifocus on African Women' in *Defining Females*, ed. by Shirley Ardener, pp. 140—62. London: Croom Helm.

Jenkins, Alan. 1979. *The Social Theory of Claude Lévi-Strauss*. London: Macmillan.

Junus, U. 1964. 'Some Remarks on Minangkabau Social Structure', *Bijdragen tot Taal- Land- en Volkenkunde* **120**, 293—326.

Kirk, G.S. 1970. *Myth*. Cambridge: Cambridge University Press.

Leach, Edmund. 1970. *Claude Lévi-Strauss*. New York: Viking Press.
1973. 'Structuralism in Social Anthropology' in *Structuralism: An Introduction*, ed. by David Robey, pp. 37—56. Oxford: Clarendon Press.
1976. *Culture and Communication*. Cambridge: Cambridge University Press.

Lévi-Strauss, Claude. 1963 [1958]. *Structural Anthropology*, vol. 1. New York: Basic Books.
1966 [1962]. *The Savage Mind*. Chicago: University of Chicago Press.
1969a [1949]. *The Elementary Structures of Kinship*. Boston: Beacon.
1969b [1964]. *The Raw and the Cooked*. New York: Harper.
1977 [1973]. *Structural Anthropology*, vol. 2. London: Allen Lane.
1978. *Myth and Meaning*. London: Routledge and Kegan Paul.

Little, Kenneth. 1973. *African Women in Towns*. Cambridge: Cambridge University Press.

Lowie, Robert A. 1937. *The History of Ethnological Theory*. New York: Holt, Rinehart and Winston.

MacCormack, Carol P. (Carol P. Hoffer). 1972. 'Mende and Sherbro Women in High Office', *Canadian Journal of African Studies* **6**, 151—64.

1974. 'Madam Yoko: Ruler of the Kpa Mende Confederacy' in *Woman, Culture and Society*, ed. by M.Z. Rosaldo and L. Lamphere, pp. 173–88. Stanford: Stanford University Press.

1976. 'The Compound Head: Structures and Strategies', *Africana Research Bulletin* 6, 44–64.

1979. 'Sande: The Public Face of a Secret Society' in *The New Religions of Africa*, ed. by B. Jules-Rosette, pp. 27–38. Norwood, N.J.: Ablex.

1981. 'Health, Fertility and Childbirth in Southern Sierra Leone' in *Ethnography of Fertility and Birth*, ed. by Carol P. MacCormack. London: Academic Press.

Mathieu, Nicole-Claude. 1973. 'Homme–culture et femme–nature?', *L'Homme* 13, 101–41.

1978. *Ignored by Some Denied by Others: The Social Sex Category in Sociology*. London: Women's Research and Resources Centre Publications.

Nutini, Hugo. 1970. 'Some Considerations on the Nature of Social Structure and Model Building' in *The Anthropologist as Hero*, ed. by E.N. Hayes and T. Hayes, pp. 70–107. Cambridge, Mass.: MIT Press.

Ortner, Sherry B. 1974. 'Is Female to Male as Nature is to Culture?' in *Woman, Culture and Society*, ed. by M.Z. Rosaldo and L. Lamphere, pp. 67–88. Stanford: Stanford University Press.

Paulme, Denise. 1963 [1960]. *Women of Tropical Africa*. Berkeley: University of California Press.

Pettit, Philip. 1975. *The Concept of Structuralism: A Critical Analysis*. Dublin: Gill and Macmillan.

Ricoeur, Paul. 1978. *The Rule of Metaphor: Multi-disciplinary Studies of the Creation of Meaning in Language*. London: Routledge and Kegan Paul.

Sahlins, Marshall. 1976. *Culture and Practical Reason*. Chicago: University of Chicago Press.

1977. *Use and Abuse of Biology*. London: Tavistock.

Scheffler, Harold W. 1970 [1966]. 'Structuralism in Anthropology' in *Structuralism*, ed. by Jacques Ehrmann, pp. 56–78. Garden City, N.J.: Anchor Books.

Schneider, David. 1972. 'What is Kinship All About?', in *Kinship Studies in the Morgan Centennial Year*, ed. by P. Reining. Washington, DC: Anthropological Society of Washington.

Scholte, Bob. 1974. 'Structural Anthropology as an Ethno-logic' in *The Unconscious in Culture*, ed. by Ino Rossi, pp. 424–54. New York: Dutton.

Singer, Alice. 1973. 'Marriage Payments and the Exchange of People', *Man* 8, 80–92.

Van Baal, J. 1975. *Reciprocity and the Position of Women*. Amsterdam: Van Gorcum.

Wagner, Roy. 1975. *The Invention of Culture*. Englewood Cliffs, NJ: Prentice-Hall.

Weiner, Annette B. 1976. *Women of Value, Men of Renown: New Perspectives in Trobriand Exchange*. Austin: University of Texas Press.

Wilson, E.O. 1975. *Sociobiology*. Cambridge, Mass.: Harvard University Press.
Wokler, Robert. 1978. 'Perfectable Apes in Decadent Cultures: Rousseau's Anthropology Revisited', *Daedalus* **107**, 107–34.

# 2 Women and the dialectics of nature in eighteenth-century French thought

MAURICE BLOCH and JEAN H. BLOCH

## I

Ortner stresses that any link-up between nature and women 'is a construct of culture rather than a fact of nature' (1974:p. 87). She notes, following Lévi-Strauss, that 'the culture nature distinction is itself a product of culture'. The implications of that statement, in the context of this book, are quite complex. If the distinctions we examine in other cultures are the product of a specific historical and cultural transformation they must be examined with great caution in their own right without too hasty an assumption that we are in every case dealing with the same phenomena. The article by Strathern in this volume shows how easy it is to slip into unwarranted assumptions. Secondly, the terms we use ourselves cannot be assumed to identify straightforwardly a genuine analytical focus and so we must therefore also examine the formation of European concepts in the specific historical process which has brought them about in order to understand *their* ambiguities and their social implications. This is what we want to do in this chapter.

As MacCormack comments, Lévi-Strauss more than anyone else reintroduced into social and cultural anthropology the opposition between nature and culture, both as an analytical dichotomy to understand the passage from a state of nature to a state of culture, as for example in *The Elementary Structures of Kinship*, and as an organizing principle of human thought, especially in the fields of myth and symbolism as in *The Savage Mind*. Lévi-Strauss bewilderingly, but intentionally, slips from one concern to the other, thereby stressing the unity of his speculations with those of the people he studies. He chooses to trace his approach back very specifically to Rousseau, and more particularly to the Rousseau of the *Discourse on Inequality* (Lévi-Strauss, 1962:142–6). This is understandable since Rousseau is probably the first writer to make the opposition between nature and something else, whether it be 'society' or the 'arts and sciences',

We would like to thank Professor J.S. Spink for his helpful comments on this article during its preparation. We are, of course, entirely responsible for the interpretations and emphasis given in this chapter.

a central tool for thinking out the human condition; so an examination of his ideas and others around him is particularly revealing of the kind of concepts with which we are dealing. Rousseau was nonetheless working within a tradition well established long before his time and which caught fire in the eighteenth century in such countries as France and Britain as part of the search for new legitimacies for a new emerging order. This was the tradition stemming from classical times of understanding human beings in terms of a before — nature — and an after — society — the turning point being one or more contracts.

During the seventeenth century the natural law philosophers, Grotius and Pufendorf, like Hobbes and Locke in England, drew on the concept of a hypothetical state of nature and elaborated the theory of the foundation of society through the acceptance of the social contract. Such theories were intended in the first instance to combat the doctrine of the divine right of kings, but when they spread into France in the first half of the eighteenth century they became focussed on the notion of the right of the people to resist abuse of power by the sovereign. Rousseau's position was, however, much more radical than that of his predecessors. Whereas Hobbes, Grotius and Pufendorf were ready to use such arguments to support the legitimacy of absolute or, at best, 'limited' monarchy, Rousseau used it to argue the inalienable sovereignty of the people and the legitimacy of democracy (Derathé 1950). But whether it was to combat the traditional attitude of the Church over the divine right of kings, or to resist political tyranny, the repeated recourse to the concept of the state of nature in the seventeenth and eighteenth centuries can be understood as representing an obvious attempt to outflank the mere historical legitimacies of states and systems of domination.

This means that in tracing back the opposition of nature and culture we are looking more at the dynamics of an ideological discourse than seeking fixed definitions. It also means that we must first and foremost see how this discourse is embedded in the intellectual and political context of its time. Only when this is done can we be clear about the implications of carrying it on to discuss the thought of other cultures in other times as anthropologists have once again begun to do.

The Enlightenment, especially the French Enlightenment, is necessarily of interest to anthropologists in a way which has often been pointed out (e.g. Duchet 1971), since from it originate many of the theoretical positions of modern social science. In the mechanistic theories of such writers as La Mettrie and Helvétius we have the 'vulgar materialism' of the cultural ecologists or of the sociobiologists. In the voluntarism of Locke we have the origins of the liberal individualist theories of transactional analysis, while in Rousseau's insistence on the need for the citizen to think of himself as part of a whole in contrast with his notion of man before society we have ideas which Durkheim rightly or wrongly regarded as precursors of his notion of society and the social fact. Furthermore, in Rousseau's insistence on the potentially exploitative nature of the foundation of society through the legitimizing of inequality we have a clear, though largely unacknowledged, predecessor of Marx (Coletti, 1972:187–93). In going back to the French eighteenth century here, however, and in focussing on the relation of such notions as nature, culture and gender, we intend to do more than simply trace back the origins of theoretical concepts. We shall also look at the ideas of that period as an ethnographic case.

One interesting aspect of the eighteenth-century debate on nature is that we find it entangled with pre-existing ideological notions about the naturalness or otherwise of women versus men: notions which are only partly examined by the writers of the eighteenth century but which are the source of many contradictions and problems for the new views which the philosophers of the time were trying to forge. It is this conflict of ideas and the dialectic that is set up between nature as pre-society or as guide and teacher for reformed society and nature as associated with women, their hysterics and domesticity, which will be outlined below.

The eighteenth-century debate provides an ethnographic example of changing ideology coming into conflict with other perhaps more fundamental notions based on unchallenged inequalities. When, furthermore, we realize that it is this complex debate, with all its contradictions, both social and intellectual, which is at the source of tools with which we try to illuminate similar problems in other societies and other times, our attitude to them and their value must inevitably be modified.

## II

There seems little doubt that the Enlightenment is a period when the notion of opposition between nature and the state of society or of education suddenly gains a great prominence. It is also clear that the status of 'nature' becomes much higher in this period than it had been in more traditional dialectics, where it was associated with the fall, savages and the failure of education. This dramatic reversal, however, was far from absolute, and understanding it is made all the more problematical by the variety of notions covered by the terms used, especially the term 'nature' itself (see Cassirer 1951). For present purposes we can distinguish four main areas of meaning.

In the first, the state of nature refers to a chronologically pre-social state. In the second, nature means the internal processes of the human body, especially instincts and emotions but also reproductive processes. Thirdly 'nature' is taken to mean the universal order which implies the harmonious co-existence of human nature and the external world of plants, animals and the countryside. Fourthly, nature is used to qualify the way of life of primitive peoples whether real, imaginary or a mixture of the two. This is not an exhaustive list but these four 'natures' are the most significant for our present purpose and are also intricately intertwined one with another. Indeed, these four areas are not separated in this way in the work of any of the writers we consider; neither do we wish to imply that the order in which they are presented has any chronological significance. We attempt here to present these ideas as closely as we can to the way the writers under discussion did themselves. We have retained their own terms as far as possible to give the flavour and perhaps the ambiguities of their thought. In particular, we have retained their use of the word 'man' to mean human beings as this not only reflects their usage, but shows significantly the ideological context in which they were working.

The first meaning, nature as a pre-social-contract state, is, as we have noted above, a notion of great antiquity in political philosophy. However, renewed interest in the idea of the social contract, or of the passage from a state of nature to a state of society, came to eighteenth-century France in large part through the writings of those two antithetical Englishmen Locke and Hobbes. Their main concern was with the contract itself and how far it was permanently binding. This was in part because of the direct relevance of these problems for the nature of the English constitution before and after the Glorious Revolution and much of their speculations follow from this. For example, Hobbes's famous remark about the brutishness of the state of nature was only intended to emphasize what man had been saved from by the contract and how, therefore, the contract could not be the result of an agreement between people and sovereign which could be changed by either party. When we look at Rousseau, however, the main continental heir of this controversy, we find the idea of the contract and of the associated contrast between nature and society becoming something very different: the central tool for an understanding of Man in a very general way (cf. Derathé 1950).

Rousseau's starting point is the opposite of his predecessors' and indeed of many of his contemporaries in that he argues that the alleged progress of culture in contemporary society, a culture much vaunted by, for example, Voltaire, is in fact a mask and encourages vice. Rousseau suggests in the *Discourse on the arts and sciences* (1750) that culture (in the sense of the arts and technology) has created *false* knowledge which supports corrupt society and which contrasts with the truth discovered by the great scientists, Bacon, Descartes and Newton. In the later *Discourse on Inequality* (1755) he goes further by contrasting social man (man created by man), whom he sees as depraved, enslaved and unhappy, with man in the 'State of Nature' (which includes group life on the family level) whom he believed would have been good, free and happy. Though he in no way envisaged a return to the 'State of Nature', which he presented in the *Discourse on Inequality* as an intellectual abstraction or norm, and although he argued that there is an essential difference in kind between 'natural'

man (who is self-sufficient and independent of others) and 'social' man
(who is necessarily only a fraction of the total society and dependent on
others within the community for his well being), Rousseau nevertheless
suggests in his later works that something of the 'natural' still remains in
man and that this needs to be reconciled with his now inevitable social role.
Like his contemporary, the naturalist Buffon, he attempted to distinguish
everything in man that comes from nature from what he has acquired from
culture in its widest sense.

For the first time, therefore, in the contrast between 'nature' and
society, society comes off worse, although this is only to lead to the pro-
posal in a later work, the *Social Contract* (1761), of a better society which
would harmonize the apparent contradiction between the natural and
social states.

A second area of meaning given to the notion of nature by French
writers in the eighteenth century was that of man as a natural being, and
concerned the value or otherwise to be accorded to bodily processes,
instincts and senses. Medical theory of the time seems to have been divided
on how intractible the natural element in man was and how much it could,
or should, be controlled by society. In many ways disagreement seems to
cut across the more explicit divisions between such schools as mechanists
and vitalists who disagreed on how far the soul was simply a bodily function.

One trend, which is associated with the 'mechanist' La Mettrie, was the
positive evaluation of spontaneous impulse and instincts which he saw as
natural and the devaluation of that false 'nature' which is formed by education and which imposes limits on nature. For La Mettrie it is society
which has established rules and conditioned the individual. Something like
the label adultery, for example, is an arbitrary sign placed on a physical
phenomenon and could, therefore, be changed. Man could rediscover
happiness in spontaneous acts by reinventing instinct. La Mettrie saw
medical philosophy as entirely different from moral and social philosophy
and sought only to concern himself with biological explanations. Later,
however, the *philosophes*, especially Diderot, were to pick up important
notions from La Mettrie's mechanistic physiological theory and to en-
tangle themselves in an attempt to unite them with social and moral considerations.

A particular tendency which developed from the same source is that of
'sensationalism', which has been so called because sensationalists believed
that ideas came directly from sensation and the senses. It is a kind of
materialist behaviourism in which man can be seen as totally moulded by
experience and where an opposition between a natural core and a cultural
overlay is meaningless since human nature consists entirely of the ability
to be moulded, though in its concept of 'ideas' as representation by the
imagination, it in fact goes beyond the sphere of vulgar behaviourism. This
view is important for such a writer as d'Holbach, who believed that a scien-

tific study of human behaviour in society could provide a rational model of human nature. It is especially important for Helvétius who stressed the supreme importance of cultural phenomena on the individual. His sensationalist psychology states that ideas are formed as the result of sense experience, but instead of assuming, as Rousseau does, that the better the training of the senses, the better our ideas will be, he assumes that all well-constituted human beings have sufficient sensitivity to form all ideas equally well; it is differences of environment and education which produce intellectual inequality.

In a way this conclusion is almost the opposite of that of La Mettrie but both agree in the fundamental point that culture and education are acceptable insofar as they accord with nature.

This view is developed much more clearly in the work of Rousseau on education and here we enter the third major area of nature. In his book *Emile* (1762), a strange mixture of novel and philosophical treatise, Rousseau postulates an ideal system of education which his pupil, Emile, undergoes. This education is to be both 'natural' (i.e. not contaminated by notions and needs which have only developed within the social group) and, at the same time, to prepare the young man for life in society, which is necessarily 'unnatural'.

In order to preserve the natural innocence which Rousseau believed exists in the child before contact with society, his imaginary pupil is removed from the corrupting influence of eighteenth-century French society and educated in isolation by his tutor. Rousseau declares education to be an art, therefore man-made or cultural, but an art which can be handled to educate man in accordance with what appears to be nature's aim. By means of constant watchfulness, vice (which is the product of society) can be prevented from reaching the child, while the physical and intellectual aptitudes which the child has received from nature are to be developed to the full according to the capacities of his age. The result is to be a young man, free from prejudice and error, adaptable, independent and humane, a member of the human race in which, physical inequalities apart, all should be equal in their quality as members. The method of this education is to be the perfect harmonizing of art and nature with the intentions of nature (and not those of man) taken as a guide.

In such a theory, nature reaches perhaps its most exalted role. It is no longer just a hypothetical pre-social better state but has become a guide for future society, a rejuvenating and purifying source which is able to develop man's essential 'nature' and harmonize it with environmental physical nature in the sense of our third area of meaning as the environment of geography, plants and animals.

Finally we turn to the fourth area of nature, that of the primitives. The use made of information about exotic peoples by Enlightenment writers has been thoroughly explored by M. Duchet (1971) but it is worth emphasizing some of the main points again here. Rousseau saw primitive peoples and even peasants as less corrupt and more natural than the society of the towns and the courts but, even so, for him they were far from natural. It was Diderot who made these savages examples of the virtue of natural society. For his purposes he found some of the reports of real primitives awkward, and so he invented imaginary savages in a fictional supplement to the travels of the explorer Bougainville, which supposedly describes Tahitian society. He presents Tahiti as a more natural society in which bodily instinct is properly respected and handled. Tahiti would seem to be presented by Diderot as a model by means of which man might regain happiness. Diderot emphasizes the sensitivity and innocence of the body in contrast to the pernicious 'unnatural' effects of 'legislated' sex in Europe which he sees as a false extension of the notions of private property. Indeed Diderot suggests that law and domination of all sorts would be unnecessary if, like the Tahitians, man followed the law of nature: a total reversal of the traditional position where authority, morality and religion are seen as necessary for virtue in order to regulate 'the old Adam'.

This review of differing areas of meaning of the notion of 'nature' in Enlightenment writers is brief and cursory in the extreme, yet the overall picture it gives is clear enough. In spite of the many important differences these various writers have among themselves, indeed in spite of the inconsistencies of their different ideas, a common position comes through. Nature is no longer something to be despised as low; it is rather to be cherished, and, above all, it is the source whereby society, morals, education, even medicine, are to be reformed and purified. The radical implication of such an idea for a society where legitimacy was supposed to come from God through monarch and church can hardly be over-emphasized, and, although it had been foreshadowed, it implies a real intellectual revolution, the accepted original source of 'right' is replaced by an antecedent and therefore superior basis for morality and society: 'nature'. Such a reversal, whether or not it influenced the bourgeois revolutions which followed, cannot but be seen as heralding them.

Another observation which follows from viewing the 'nature' of the French Enlightenment in this way is that the general and ambiguous nature of the concept comes from the fact that it is mainly defined in opposition to something else, but that this 'something else' is extremely varied. In the short survey (given here) nature has been opposed to society in general, to corrupt society, particularly French society, to the arts and sciences, to law, to culture in the sense of the manners of the upper class, to culture in the sense the word is used by the anthropologist, and to civilization. This is because nature is at bottom a category of challenge rather than an element in a stable binary contrast.

## III

If the writers of the Enlightenment reverse the valuation of nature in most fields there is an area of the conceptualization of the natural where they are, by contrast with their general radicalism, conservative. This area is the relation of nature to the particular status of women. This is no accident. If these writers saw themselves as reformers of the social and political order, they did not in their mind extend this to the position of women except in so far as they envisaged a better society resulting from the proper exercise by women of their domestic and maternal functions (Bloch 1979). In the medical ideology to which the French eighteenth-century writers were heirs, women and nature were seen to be in a peculiarly close relationship, particularly with regard to childcare. Although by the seventeenth century the traditional, basically naturalistic philosophy stretching back to classical times had become modified by the new concept that human reason could improve on nature and that even something as natural as breast-feeding could be replaced by bottle-feeding, there was still very strong support for the belief that nature had intended women to breast feed and that human interference in this was a violation of nature (Mercier 1961; Bloch 1974). Furthermore, this close relationship of women and nature was given as a reason for their exclusion from the political domain and generally as an explanation of their inferiority. The acceptance, more or less consciously, of this notion by the writers under consideration meant that either they had to negate their valuation of nature in order to accommodate the position of women, or accept the superiority of women, something which they ultimately rejected. In many ways this was an insoluble problem, so long as they were unwilling to include in their reforming scheme a significant reform of the position of women. As they did not, this had a profound limiting effect on their thought, as it inevitably affected their use of nature as a liberating concept. The contradiction to which the new view of nature led with regard to women is interesting both as an intellectual problem and as something which clearly reveals the limitation of the reform of society their work implied. These contradictions can be seen in three of the meanings of nature we have considered so far: the notion of nature as human physiology, the notion of environmental nature as a guide to man, and even in the ideal existing society of natural men which Diderot invented on Tahiti. In all three the contradictions lead to inconsistencies and *ad hoc* arguments to deal with them.

The traditional view which the philosophers accepted was that woman was closer to nature than man because of her physiological role in sex and motherhood. This basic assumption, however, took many forms. The medical theory of the times had been moulded in part by such writers as the German Stahl, who held that the soul's ultimate purpose was to preserve the body in order to achieve its own goal of mental activity. In woman, however, this ultimate purpose is subordinate to motherhood which seeks the continuation of the species in order to achieve the ultimate goal of mental activity. For Stahl, woman has a more stable temperament than man and is less exposed to accidents of race, climate and environment. She is governed by three fundamental 'affections' which correspond to her ultimate purpose: (i) pleasure, which corresponds to her need to be impregnated; (ii) fear, which ensures care for the embryo; (iii) inconstancy, because she must be able to dispense affection to *all* the children she conceives. She unconsciously and spontaneously chooses a quiet, protected life which is suited to her ultimate purpose of procreation (*Vraie théorie médicale* in Stahl (1863—4)).

Stahl's ideas, which were taught in the medical school in Montpellier, were developed further in eighteenth-century France by the doctor Roussel, who argued that it would be wrong for women to engage in intellectual activity. 'Let women leave to men the doubtful benefit that they seek in this dangerous enterprise [intellectual work] : nature has done enough for them already and it would be an offence against her if through such an activity women were to lose the lustre of the precious gifts which she has bestowed.'[1] (For a detailed discussion of eighteenth-century physiological theories concerning women see Hoffman 1977.)

In this type of writing we find the often noticed association of woman and nature justified by notions of biological maternity and of the female bodily processes. In spite of the playful tone of the above quotation this association is used in a variety of ways as justification for subordination in the political and intellectual spheres, a position with which anthropologists are familiar in the ideology, especially the religious ideology, of peoples throughout the world (for which Ortner (1974) gives ample evidence). But it is also worth noting how well such a position accords with a pervasive ideology which devalues nature generally as being something to be conquered and mastered. With such a position the association of women—nature—subordination can be said to be 'in harmony'. It is therefore somewhat surprising that this view of women is maintained not simply by doctors such as Roussel but also by radical French writers who had elsewhere changed the status of nature.

Nevertheless, this is precisely what we find again and again. Some of the *philosophes* of the French Enlightenment drew their physiological notions from La Mettrie, perhaps the most potentially radical of all the eighteenth-century authors in his denial of the soul and the rehabilitation of instinct, but when it comes to women even he argues: 'Among the fair sex their

1 'Qu'elles abandonnent aux hommes la vaine fumée qu'ils cherchent dans cette acquisition dangereuse: la nature a assez fait pour elles: ce serait un attentat contre elle [la nature] de flétrir les dons précieux, qu'elles lui doivent' (Preface to the *Système physique et moral de la femme*, 1784).

spirit accords with the delicacy of their temperament, hence this tender-
ness, this affection, this vivacity of feeling based more on passion than on
reason; hence too these prejudices, these superstitions whose stronghold
can hardly ever be loosened.'[2]

La Mettrie sees female behaviour as though it were due simply to the
closeness of woman to organic nature. More spontaneous than man and
more obedient to nature's impulses she affords at the same time an example
of the workings of nature and of mental weakness. But surely closeness to
nature for a writer who argues elsewhere that the hindering of instincts is
unlawful would, if followed through, imply that woman should offer a
guide to the new uninhibited natural man and would be superior to him.
In fact up to a point La Mettrie suggested such a conclusion but ultimately
negated it for his successors by a strange overstatement. What La Mettrie
gives as examples of woman's closeness to nature and lack of inhibition is
above all her 'wild' desires during pregnancy, in particular the occasional
occurrence of cannibalism which offers a strange fascination for him.
Although La Mettrie does not seem to object to such practices but uses
them as 'scientific' evidence, he ensured by emphasizing them, whether
consciously or not, that in this area the implication of his work would be
negated by overstatement.

Less strange, but equally illuminating, is the case of Helvétius, who ran
into a problem with his sensationalist philosophy. If knowledge was to be
obtained through the senses and if one believed that the senses as natural
powers were more developed in women because of their greater physical
sensitivity, it would follow that women would be wiser. Helvétius actually
considers this disturbing conclusion, the product of the ideological inconsistency we have been considering, only to wriggle out of it. In his book
*On Man* (*De l'Homme*, I, pp. 128–9) he observes:

Empirical observation . . . does not accord here with our argument. It does
indeed show that we owe our ideas to our senses, but it does not show that
our degree of intelligence is related to a greater or lesser degree to discern-
ment by our senses. Women, for example, who, because they have finer
skin than men and therefore a finer sense of touch, are not cleverer than a
Voltaire.[3]

We are left to decide which piece of 'evidence' came first.

2  'Dans le beau sexe l'Ame suit encore la délicatesse du tempérament:
   de là cette tendresse, cette affection, ces sentimens vifs, plutôt fondés
   sur la passion que sur la raison; ces préjugés, ces superstitions, dont la
   forte empreinte peut à peine s'effacer' (*L'Homme-machine*, 1966
   edition).

3  'l'Expérience . . . n'est pas sur ce point d'accord avec le raisonnement.
   Elle démontre bien que c'est à nos sens que nous devons nos idées,
   mais elle ne démontre point que l'esprit soit toujours en nous pro-
   portionné à la finesse plus ou mous grande de ces mêmes sens. Les
   femmes, par exemple, dont la peau plus délicate que celle des hommes,

To be fair, Helvétius, apart from this aside, explains the inferiority of women elsewhere as simply due to their poor education, but when he turns to the positive role they might play in society, the association of women and natural processes again produces a quaint suggestion: that women could be the source of morality by being judicious suppliers of man's greatest pleasure, sexual satisfaction, as rewards for public-spirited behaviour. He fails to notice however that in the process women would appear to lose their autonomy while men would not. As with the other writers, bringing in 'natural' women forces him into contradictions and retractions.

This, however, is nowhere clearer than in the case of Rousseau. His position was profoundly radical, even paradoxical to his contemporaries, on a wide range of subjects, but when he turns to women he is not only orthodox but even conservative.

Basing himself on some of the biological arguments of the day, and mainly on Buffon, he argues that in everything that is not associated with sexual differentiation men and women are demonstrably the same: everything they have in common relates to the species, everything that is different relates to sex. He then supposes that it can be demonstrated that physiological differences influence the *moral* being. For Rousseau this pre-empts all possible discussion concerning the superiority of one sex or the other *and* all discussion concerning the equality of the sexes. Nature has made them different but perfect each in their own way. They are obviously intended to complement one another and in what they do not have in common they cannot be compared. From this starting point he provides a biological basis for his subsequent analysis, which argues that the male is necessarily strong and active and the female weak and passive; that consequently woman is made to please man and that if man needs to please too, it is by dint of the fact that he is strong. Rousseau takes this to be the law of nature. He also argues that because of woman's power to excite man's desire to a greater degree than it can be satisfied, she is in fact in the stronger negotiating position and it is through this 'natural' hold over man that she too can affect moral regeneration by inspiring man to virtuous and heroic acts. She can do this even more for the next generation but this only by the proper carrying out of her natural condition which Rousseau states to be that of motherhood. In book I of *Emile* he maintains that a return to maternal breast-feeding alone could bring about total reform (p. 258).

Even Rousseau's most cherished premise, that of man's natural goodness (innocence), is compromised when he thinks of woman: 'It is right that this sex should share in our ills of which it is the cause',[4] an obvious

leur donne plus de finesse dans le sens du toucher n'ont pas plus d'espirit qu'un Voltaire.'
4 'il est juste que ce sexe partage la peine des maux qu'il nouse a causés' (Pléiade IV p. 709).

reference to Eve's fault, remarkable in a writer who had rejected original sin elsewhere.

In this type of writing one seems to be far away from Rousseau's bold and adventurous theorizing and so it is particularly interesting to see what happens when the two meet. They meet indeed in a particularly explicit manner in *Emile*. There the young hero, having kept to the path of virtue by avoiding the corrupt society of his time, needs nevertheless a proper and worthy mate when he reaches maturity. Rousseau therefore supplies him with a female equivalent: Sophie. One would have thought that for Sophie to be suitable to share life with Emile she would have needed a similar education. This turns out to be far from the case because of Rousseau's view of women, but the matter reaches an even greater degree of contradiction over the role of nature. Nature for Emile had been a guide to be sought to enable him to become a free man; for Sophie, however, nature is already there and seems to be the reason for her subjugation. Whereas Emile's 'natural' education was to emphasize freedom and independence, Sophie's must emphasize dependence and constraint in order to prepare her for her future natural dependence on man for her continuing existence.

Whereas Rousseau argued that society necessarily denatures humanity, yet believed that he could envisage a 'new' man who would harmonize the claims of both nature and society or a new society which would respect and harmonize the claims of both the natural and the social in man, he tried to argue that Sophie must stay close to nature within the unnatural order which is society. And this because he shared the belief with many of his contemporaries that the mother is Nature herself and that woman must not be turned away from her.

Emile is to pay no attention to public opinion, Sophie is to be judged by it; Rousseau argues that a woman must be held to be faithful to her husband (p. 702). Emile must develop towards his potential state through education while remaining true to his essence but for Sophie it is simply a matter of remaining true to her essence. Maturation is not necessary for girls and Rousseau makes the point that women remain as children, shown by the fact that their voice does not break, a notion and an argument which anthropologists have reported from many parts of the world. Rousseau, who had gone completely against most of the accepted notions of his time in his analysis of nature and society and the implications of this for education, when it came to the precise question of the condition, role and education of Sophie becomes repressive and reactionary precisely because of the natural character of women and especially mothers. He seems to forget that this Sophie is to be a match to an Emile who has been liberated precisely by being placed in accord with nature. In some ways in bringing in Sophie at the last moment Rousseau puts in question the whole edifice he has built, because in introducing woman he reintroduces all the assumptions he elsewhere tried to destroy.

Finally we can turn to that other area of meaning of the concept nature which was concerned with savages and return to our example of Diderot's *Supplement to the journey of Bougainville*. His description of Tahiti, this utopia of freedom, reasonableness and happiness is much concerned with women, as is inevitable given the place the discussion of sexual morality has in the work. There women, like men, are not bounded by laws in their sexual and material activity but follow their natural inclinations joyfully. The women of Tahiti 'stand up straight, are healthy, fresh and beautiful', they are able to produce strong healthy children and are proud to excite desire in man. In Tahiti the free expression of bodily instinct resulting in procreation is shown as the basis of 'natural' affections, such as love of children, and is contrasted to the thwarting of nature in iniquitous 'civilized' society through marriage, the 'art' of love, celibacy, etc.

This, however, turns out to be a two-edged state of affairs. On the one hand it gives women a freedom which is remarkably powerfully expressed. Diderot says that anybody, man or woman, has the right to join in sexual union with whoever and whenever they wish, because to forbid this is 'contrary to nature since it assumes that a thinking, feeling and free being could be the property of another similar being'. 'Can't you see,' says the Tahitian elder to Bougainville 'that in your country you have not distinguished between things with no feeling, no thought, no desire, no will, things which can be left or taken, kept or exchanged without either hurting them or giving them cause for complaint with things which cannot be exchanged, things which cannot be bought, things which have freedom, volition, desires on their own account, which can choose to give themselves or not for a moment, which can choose to give themselves or not for ever, things which complain and suffer from the treatment they receive and which cannot become commodities without ignoring their true character and doing violence to nature.'[5]

All this seems admirable, but as we continue with the *Supplement* we

5   'contraire à la nature parce qu'ils supposent qu'un être pensant, sentant et libre peut être la propriété d'un être semblable à lui . . . Ne vois-tu pas qu'on a confondu dans ton pays la chose qui n'a ni sensibilité ni pensée, ni désir, ni volonté, qu'on quitte, qu'on prend, qu'on garde, qu'on échange, sans qu'elle souffre et sans qu'elle se plaigne avec la chose qui ne s'échange point, qui ne s'acquiert point, qui a liberté, volonté, désir, qui peut se donner ou se refuser pour un moment, se donner ou se refuser pour toujours qui se plaint et qui souffre et qui ne saurait devenir un effet de commerce sans qu'on oublie son caractère et qu'on fasse violence à la nature' (Diderot p. 29, quoted in Duchet (1971) p. 454).

find that while this sexual freedom is the source of a genuinely free existence for the male Tahitians, in the case of women it is functionally instrumental. First, it is a device to reproduce the population effectively, and
Diderot indirectly makes the point that it is not really for women that this
system is good but for the function that they serve, by stressing how barren
women are barred from this freedom and are given black habits as a mark
of shame while their sisters go about joyfully naked. (This is, of course,
also a jibe at the clergy.) Not only do women serve as social procreators,
the continual exchange of women among men serves to bind the island in
one big happy family. This is particularly important because Diderot
argues that it is from this unity that the social responsibility of the
Tahitians comes and hence the virtue and happiness of their society.
Shared women are thus reduced to being the bond that unites the men.

Here again their role is that of instruments for the purpose of society
which is implied to be that of men. In fact the implications of the role
Diderot gives to women in Tahiti totally and precisely contradicts his
general declaration quoted above. Once more, the view that women are
close to nature, especially as sexual objects and mothers, has undermined
the more general liberating dialectic of nature.

It is only in the fourth area of meaning of the notion of 'nature' as 'pre-
contract society' that the situation is less clear. The difference comes in
part from the fact that here the ideas of the *philosophes* of the eighteenth
century link up with the long established and developed tradition of discussing the relationship of natural law and specific legal codes; a discussion
which had had to deal with women. A particular area of this debate which
seems to have concerned many *philosophes* such as Voltaire, Helvétius,
Diderot, d'Holbach and others is its relevance to the legitimacy of divorce.
Basing themselves on the views of Pufendorf they all seem to agree that
marriage is a contract distinct from nature and therefore that it should be
possible to terminate it. This conclusion is, of course, not principally
about women as such but, as for similar debates in other times, the
advocacy of the possibility of divorce, through the fact that it can be
initiated by either party, implies among other things, giving women a
greater control over their destiny. In this area at least, if somewhat indirectly, the rhetoric of nature has some implication for the reform of the
status of women.

## IV

A number of points of different kinds emerge from this brief survey. The
first is the complexity, even the ambiguity, of the notion of nature in most
of the writers mentioned here. This ambiguity is already present in individual writers without our even attempting to synthesize their different
views. However the complexity of the different ideas referred to by the

notion of nature is nothing to the even greater variety of what nature is opposed to. It is not surprising that the uncritical use of these notions, coming as they do from such a troubled source, leads to as many misunderstandings as clarifications. Anthropology is heir to a polemic where the opposition of nature and something else is part of the attempt to understand society and at the same time to criticize it; it is not heir to a set of organized concepts clearly defined. What we find when looking at these notions of eighteenth-century France is the language of challenge. Here we are clearly in the field of ideology in turmoil, where certain notions are challenging others, as is to be expected at such a key period of transformation in the European social formation. It is particularly revealing that the notion of nature versus culture or, rather, society comes to the fore precisely in such a context of opposition to systems of exploitation and of the attempt to undermine the legitimations of such systems by appealing to a pre-existing source of justification. When therefore we see other cultures in terms of the notions of these concepts of nature, as inevitably we must, we should perhaps look more for the ideological polemic which uses this type of notion rather than make the sterile attempt to match our categories to theirs as is implicitly done in much anthropological work. This we believe is the original intention of Lévi-Strauss's use of the notion, since he uses it to reveal the dialectic of cultural transformations, but this has unfortunately been changed in the work of others, who have been trying to match the opposition of nature and culture which they believe was discovered in the eighteenth century as a fundamental matrix of human thought. In the first place no such clear binary opposition can be found from the work of the Enlightenment writers as a whole or in the work of Rousseau in particular. Secondly, there is no reason why an opposition such as this, even if it had existed, should be found in the same substantial form in other places and at other times. Indeed, assuming that the complexity and variety of ideological representations that are found in Africa or Papua New Guinea can be adequately organized around such an opposition only obscures the specificity of the different cases and hinders the task of ethnography. Having said this, however, it would also be wrong to deny that there are not tempting similarities. We would suggest that similarities arise from the fact that such examples as discussed by Ardener, Ortner, Strathern, and many of the contributors to this volume, are cases of ideological discourses concerned with competing ultimate legitimacies for justifying and, in some cases, challenging domination. In such discourse the legitimacy of the realm of nature is likely to recur in an unlimited variety of versions and emphases. What we have inherited from the eighteenth century is an insight into the mechanisms and development of ideology.

When we turn to the problem of women in the schemes of such writers as Rousseau, the interest of these ideas as ethnographic examples becomes even more revealing. What is striking at first sight is the extent to which the eighteenth-century representation of women, as being in certain fundamental ways more bound by nature or closer to nature, is once again reminiscent of that reported from many other parts of the world and underlined by Ortner. One might almost say that the eighteenth-century philosophers had a New Guinean view of woman as dangerous because of her uncontrolled power and as potentially polluting and disruptive. Particularly interesting here is how these types of notions about women and their disharmony with reformed ideas about nature set up modifications, contradictions and interactions between concepts. This enables us to understand further the nature of the dialectic involved in such ideological process generally, especially in critical periods of change. It suggests how 'sleeping' parts of ideology might reassert themselves and lead to an undermining of new conceptualizations, as the 'sleeping' notions about women undermined the *philosophes'* schemes. It also suggests complicated relations between society and ideology. The notions about women in the ideology we have considered matched their social situation well, in the same way as changes in the ideology brought about by the Enlightenment thinkers marked general changes in society, but the two aspects were not then reconciled any more in social organization than in thought and the contradictions we have looked at were certainly not linked simply to the level of ideas. It is therefore rather as an example of ideological processes and perhaps more specially as an example of the significance of gender conceptualization for ideological processes that the ideas of the eighteenth century might in the end be most relevant for anthropology.

## Bibliography

Bloch, J.H. 1974. 'Rousseau's reputation as an authority on childcare and physical education in France before the Revolution', in *Paedagogica historica*, Ghent, Vol. XIV, I.

1979. 'Women and the Reform of the Nation', in *Woman and Society in Eighteenth-Century France*, E. Jacobs, et al., Athlone Press, London.

Buffon, G.L. Leclerc de. 1749–67. *Histoire naturelle*, Paris, esp. vols. II, III, & IV.

Cassirer, E. 1951. *The Philosophy of the Enlightenment*, Princeton University Press, Princeton & London.

Coletti, L. 1972. *From Rousseau to Lenin*, New Left Books, London.

Derathé, R. 1950. *Jean-Jacques Rousseau et la science politique de son temps*, Presses Universitaires de France, Paris.

Diderot, D. 1972. *Supplément au voyage de Bougainville*, Garnier-Flammarion, Paris.

Duchet, M. 1971. *Anthropologie et Histoire au siècle des lumières*, Maspero, Paris.

Helvétius, C.L. 1758. *De l'Esprit*, Paris.
  1773. *De l'Homme*, London.
Hoffmann, P. 1977. *La Femme dans la pensée des Lumières*, Editions Ophrys, Paris.
Holbach, P.H.R.de. 1770. *Système de la Nature*, London.
La Mettrie, J.O. d'. 1966. *L'Homme-machine*, ed. G. Delaloye, Holland.
  1970. *Oeuvres philosophiques*, G. Olms Verlag, Berlin.
Lévi-Strauss, C. 1962. *Le totémisme aujourd'hui*. Presses Universitaires de France, Paris.
Mercier, R. 1961. *L'Enfant dans la société du XVIIIe. siècle*. Daka Macon, Paris.
Ortner, S. 1974. 'Is Female to Male as Nature is to Culture?' in M.Z. Rosaldo and L. Lamphere, *Woman, Culture and Society*, Stanford University Press.
Rousseau, J.J. 1964 & 1969. *Oeuvres complètes*, Bibliothèque de la Pléiade, Gallimard, Paris, Vol. III, Ecrits politiques, Vol. IV, *Emile*.
Roussel, P. 1784. *Système physique et moral de la femme*, Paris.
Stahl, G.E. 1863–4. *Oeuvres médico-philosophiques et pratiques*, transl. Th. Blondin, J.B. Baillière, Paris.

# 3  Natural facts: a historical perspective on science and sexuality

L.J. JORDANOVA

## Introduction

The distinction between women as natural and men as cultural appeals to a set of ideas about the biological foundations of womanhood. Understanding the historical dimensions of these two inter-related pairs of dichotomies in European thought entails revealing the connections between science and sexuality. Sex roles were constituted in a scientific and medical language, and, conversely, the natural sciences and medicine were suffused with sexual imagery. This paper explores the links between nature/culture, woman/man through a historical study of the biomedical sciences and the metaphors and symbols they employed. I draw my examples principally from eighteenth- and nineteenth-century France and Britain.

Since the eighteenth century the polarities seem to have hardened, yet the lived experience to which they supposedly relate was extremely complex. Recent feminist history has shown the diversity of women's social and occupational roles despite the inflexibility of contemporary ideas about them.[1] The lack of fit between ideas and experience clearly points to the ideological function of the nature/culture dichotomy as applied to gender. This ideological message was increasingly conveyed in the language of medicine.

As there seems no easy way to reconcile material conditions with ideas

An earlier version of this paper was read to the Women in Society Research Seminar, University of Cambridge in January 1979. I am grateful to the participants for their comments, and especially to Marthe Bruton Macintyre to whom the paper is dedicated.

Many people have provided specific information and advice. It is a pleasure to thank Renate Burgess, Linda Deer, Elizabeth Haigh, Phyllis Jordanova, Anne Marcovich, Steven Smith, Charles Webster and Paul Weindling for their generous assistance. Catherine Crawford, Karl Figlio, and Robert J. Young read through the chapter, made detailed comments and criticisms, and offered extensive help. Although I have not been able to incorporate all their suggestions, I wish to record my appreciation of their intellectual and personal support.

1  See for example, Hufton (1971: 1975—6).

of sex roles, some feminist scholars have been tempted to turn for help to
another dichotomy, that of oppressor/oppressed. Dichotomies such as
man/woman illustrate the simplistic model of oppression which is useful
because it seems to imply a clear power relationship:

| nature | : | culture |
|--------|---|---------|
| woman | : | man |
| oppressed | : | oppressor |
| (because powerless) | | (because powerful) |

This approach takes a simple social relationship and finds a natural basis
for it, so that, for example, women become the bearers of ignorance and
men of knowledge. We then construct this as a form of oppression. But in
doing so, we abstract from the dichotomy only one of its dimensions. Historically, the notion of women as natural contained not just women as
superstitious but also women as the carriers of a new morality through
which the artificiality of civilization could be transcended. In the same
way, men as culture implied not just the progressive light of reason but
also the corruption and exploitation of civil society. Next to what is presented as the desirable domination of superstition by reason, and women
by men, in Mozart's opera *The Magic Flute*, one must put repugnance for
the exploitation and inequality generated by masculine domination
expressed in the eighteenth-century French novel *Paul et Virginie*. And
in the end, it is not the possibility of finding texts with these extreme
views clearly expressed which is most interesting, but rather the extent to
which they were inseparably intertwined, as, for example, in the popular
books on women published in the mid nineteenth century by the French
historian Jules Michelet.

In our attempts to understand the deployment of symbols and metaphors, we must recognize the fact that one of the most powerful ways of
using them in our culture has been in the form of these dichotomies, where
the two opposed terms mutually define each other. It is not just male and
female, masculine and feminine, or nature and culture, but also town and
country, matter and spirit, body and mind, capitalist and worker — our
entire philosophical set describes natural and social phenomena in terms of
oppositional characteristics. Each polarity has its own history, but it also
develops related meanings to other dichotomies. For instance, the pairs
church and state, town and country also contain allusions to gender differences, and to nature and culture. Transformations between sets of
dichotomies are performed all the time. Thus, man/woman is only one
couple in a common matrix, and this reinforces the point that it cannot be
seen as isolated or autonomous.

The power of dichotomies such as man/woman, nature/culture, city/
country does not just consist in the apparent clarity of definition by contrast. More important is the possibility of a dialectical relationship between

the members of each pair which is an essential part of their social value. The fact that there are a number of related pairs, and that the terms of each one have a complex relationship to one another further reinforces the point that we are not speaking here of simple linear hierarchies. Debates about sex and sex roles, especially during the nineteenth century, hinged precisely on the ways in which sexual boundaries might become blurred. It is as if the social order depended on clarity with respect to certain key distinctions whose symbolic meanings spread far beyond their explicit context. At certain times (perhaps times of perceived rapid change), physicians were deeply concerned about the feminization of men, for which homosexuality could be adduced as evidence, and the masculinization of women, which they believed could result from excessive physical or mental work. Raymond Williams has suggested that oppositional pairs provided a way to explore the parameters of change without upsetting the social order. He takes a case which is analogous and closely related to the one this book addresses − the long established Western dichotomy between the city and the country:

On the country has gathered the idea of a natural way of life: of peace, innocence, and simple virtue. On the city has gathered the idea of an achieved centre: of learning, communication, light. Powerful hostile associations have also developed: on the city as a place of noise, worldliness and ambition; on the country as a place of backwardness, ignorance, limitation [Williams 1975:9].

This quotation illustrates the point that more complexity can be held within dichotomies than at first sight appears. It also suggests that the city/ country opposition has a sexual dimension. The innocence and simple virtues of country people were typically expressed through the unworldly sentiment of women. The negative image of the country, pervasive in Enlightenment writings, portrayed the superstitious and credulous behaviour of peasant women. The 'light' and civilization of city culture were symbols of male capacity for abstract thought and intellectual genius. The negative side of urban life was best expressed in exploitative domination and economic competition, clear metaphors of masculinity. Despite the superficial clarity of the city/country polarity, Williams stresses that it is the relationship between the two which has posed fundamental questions. Cities arise out of the countryside, urban and rural life are inescapably linked, while between cities and the country lie a whole host of intermediate forms of human settlements: villages, towns, suburbs, garden cities. The dichotomy seems to deny historical reality, which suggests that there must be a reason for the persistence of these archetypes; possibly it lies in the way they provide coherence in the face of threatened social disorganization.

The oppositions between women as nature and men as culture were expressed concretely through distinctions commonly made such as that between women's work and men's work. The ideological dimension to these oppositions is discernable in the dichotomy constructed by the elite of the medical profession between male strength and female vulnerability. Social and conceptual changes take place slowly and in piecemeal and fragmented ways. Our project is not to search for neat consistent ideological structures, but through the contradictions, tensions and paradoxes to find patterns we can understand.

There are strong reasons for beginning with the Enlightenment. In this period the shifts in meaning and usage of words such as culture, civil, civilize, nature and life, provide indicators of deep changes in the way human society and its relations with the natural world were conceived. Ultimately, the Enlightenment is no easier to define than notions of nature and culture are, but, in the term itself, we can see an appeal to light as a symbol of a certain form of knowledge which had the potential for improving human existence. Rational knowledge based on empirical information derived from the senses was deemed the best foundation for secure knowledge. Starting with a sensualist epistemology, and a number of assumptions about the potential social application of an understanding of natural laws, many Enlightenment writers critically examined forms of social organization. In so doing, they employed a language fraught with sexual metaphor, and systematically examined the natural facts of sexuality.

Science and medicine were fundamental to this endeavour in three different ways. First, natural philosophers and medical writers addressed themselves to phenomena in the natural world such as reproduction and generation, sexual behaviour, and sex-related diseases. Second, science and medicine held a privileged position because their methods appeared to be the only ones which would lead away from religious orthodoxy and towards a secular, empirically based knowledge of the natural and social worlds. Finally, as I hope to show, science and medicine as activities were associated with sexual metaphors which were clearly expressed in designating nature as a woman to be unveiled, unclothed and penetrated by masculine science. The relationship between women and nature, and men and culture must therefore be examined through the mediations of science and medicine.

## Enlightened environmentalism

In the self-conscious scientism of the Enlightenment, the capacity of the human mind to delve into the secrets of nature was celebrated. Increasingly this capacity for scientific prowess was conceptualized as a male gift, just as nature was the fertile woman, and sometimes the archetypal mother (Kolodny 1975). People had explored their capacity to master and manipulate nature for many centuries (Glacken 1967), but the powerful analytical tools of the natural sciences and the techniques of engineering and technology enormously enhanced their confidence that human power over the environment was boundless. As Bacon expressed it in the early seventeenth century, 'My only earthly wish is . . . to stretch the deplorably narrow limits of man's dominion over the universe to their promised bounds' (Farrington 1964:62). And the process by which Bacon thought this would be achieved was a casting off of 'the darkness of antiquity' in favour of the detailed study of nature (Farrington 1964:69). 'I am come in very truth leading to you Nature with all her children to bind her to your service and make her your slave' (Farrington 1964:62).

In discussions of human domination over nature, the concept of environment comes to hold an important, and complex, place from the late eighteenth century onwards (Jordanova 1979). Above all, the environment was that cluster of variables which acted upon organisms and were responsible for many of their characteristics. An understanding of human beings in sickness and in health was to be based on a large number of powerful environmental factors; climate, diet, housing, work, family situation, geography and atmosphere. This notion of environment could be split into two. First, there were variables such as custom and government which were human creations and were, at least in principle, amenable to change. Second, there were parameters such as climate, meteorology in general, geographical features such as rivers and mountains, which were in the province of immutable natural laws and proved more challenging to human power. In the first case environment denoted culture, in the second, nature.

Taking environment in the sense of culture, it was clear to people at the end of the eighteenth century that living things and their environment were continually interacting and changing each other in the process. This was also true of sexuality, for, although sex roles were seen as being in some sense 'in nature' because of their relationship to physical characteristics, it was also acknowledged that they were mutable, just as physiology and anatomy in general were taken to be. The customs and habits of day-to-day life such as diet, exercise and occupation, and more general social forces such as modes of government were taken to have profound effects on all aspects of people's lives; their sexuality was no exception. The foundation for these beliefs was a complex conceptual framework which spoke naturalistically about the physiological, mental and social aspects of human beings. An understanding of this framework is therefore an essential background for any account of the relations between nature, culture and gender in the period.

In the bio-medical sciences of the late eighteenth century, mind and body were not seen as incommensurable, absolutely distinct categories. Mental events, such as anger, fear or grief, were known to have physical effects, while illnesses such as fevers produced emotional and intellectual changes. I would argue that at the end of the eighteenth century a model of health and illness became dominant in which lifestyle and social roles were closely related to health. This model was applied to both men and women, but with different implications. A tight linkage was assumed between jobs performed in the social arena (for women, the production, suckling and care of children, the creation of a natural morality through family life) and health and disease. Women thus became a distinct class of persons, not by virtue of their reproductive organs, but through their social lives. The total physiology of women could, it was argued, only be understood in terms of lifestyle and the social roles they ought to fulfil, if they were not doing so already.

I want to stress that the model applied to both sexes. For example, people who lived in certain climates, such as men who worked in mines or factories, were known to be susceptible to particular diseases. Physicians therefore advocated that they take precautions to preserve their health: appropriate diet, exercise, housing, clothing, behaviour, regimen. The same argument applied to women, and in fact each way of life held its own particular dangers for the health of men and women which could be held at bay by the appropriate preventive measures. In the case of women, permissible occupation was tightly defined according to putatively natural criteria. There was thus a reflexive relationship between physiology and lifestyle; each affected the other. Through habit and custom, physiological changes took place which had been socially induced.

The emphasis on occupation and lifestyle as determinants of health, which led to a radical boundary being drawn between the sexes, had as its explicit theoretical basis a physiology which recognized few basic boundaries. It conflated moral and physical, mind and body; it created a language capable of containing biological, psychological and social considerations. This is clearly revealed in the use of bridging concepts such as 'temperament', 'habit', 'constitution' and 'sensibility' as technical terms in medicine. These concepts alluded to aspects of human physiology which were not just physical or mental, but contained something of both while being also closely bound to social change. As a result, the temperament and constitution of an individual were seen as products of biological, psychological and social interactions.

Because health was determined to a large extent by variables outside the human body, each person had a distinct physiological make-up which corresponded to his or her unique experience. Groups of people living under the same environmental conditions displayed similar biological and social characteristics. The systematic understanding of these conditions, on which appropriate therapy could be based, was derived from the analysis of a number of distinct variables. The factors affecting groups and individuals had to be clearly delineated. Yet although it was seldom made explicit, there were considered to be limits to the extent to which people could be changed. It was widely acknowledged that there was much vari-

ation among women which derived from different climates, patterns of
work and so on, but that, nevertheless, all women had in common certain
physiological features, not directly a matter of their reproductive organs.
For it was a basic premise of physicians in late-eighteenth-century France
that women were quite distinct from men by virtue of their whole anatomy
and physiology. As Cabanis put it at the end of the eighteenth century:
'Nature has not simply distinguished the sexes by a single set of organs, the
direct instruments of reproduction: between men and women there exist
other differences of structure which relate more to the role which has been
assigned to them' (1956, I:275). The teleological argument was made more
explicit by his contemporary, Roussel: 'The soft parts which are part of
the female constitution . . . also manifest differences which enable one to
catch a glimpse of the functions to which a woman is called, and of the
passive state to which nature has destined her' (1803:11—12).

The ways in which gender differences were conceptualized can be illus-
trated by referring to the medical notion of sensibility. This was a physiological property which, although present in all parts of the body, was most
clearly expressed through the state of the nervous system (Figlio 1975).
The nervous system was taken by many to be that physiological system
which, because it brought together physical and mental dimensions of
human beings, expressed most precisely the total state of the individual,
especially with respect to the impact of social changes. Thus it was said
that increases in hysterical illnesses in women during the eighteenth century were evidence of the growing use of luxuries such as tea and coffee,
and of other changes (Pomme 1782:578—82). By virtue of their sex,
women had a distinct sensibility which could be further modified during
their lifetimes. Women, it was said, are highly *sensible* (in the sense of
sensitive, or even sensitized) like children, and more passionate than men.
This is because of 'the great mobility of their fibres, especially those in the
uterus; hence their irritability, and suffering from vapours' (Macquart
1799, II:511). The peculiar sensibility of women could also be used to
explain their greater life expectancy in a way which associated lifestyle
with the physical consistency of the constituent fibres of their bodies.
Barthez, a prominent eighteenth-century French physician explained:

Probably women enjoy this increase in their average age because of the softness and flexibility of the tissue of their fibres, and particularly because of
their periodic evacuations which rejuvenate them, so to speak, each month,
renew their blood, and re-establish their usual freshness . . . Another
important cause of women living longer than men is that they are usually
more accustomed to suffering infirmities, or to experiencing miseries in
life. This habit gives their vital sensibility more moderation, and can only
render them less susceptible to illness [1806, II:298].

However, he went on to say that because of their 'delicate and feeble constitution', women feel things more deeply than men. This aptly portrays

the ambivalence which we have already noted in the association of woman and nature. Women are tougher *and* softer, more vulnerable *and* more tenacious of life than men. However, more often than not, the softness of women was returned to again and again, and it was a metaphor that was imaginatively built on to construct a whole image of the dependent nature of woman:

This muscular feebleness inspires in women an instinctive disgust of strenuous exercise; it draws them towards amusements and sedentary occupations. One could add that the separation of their hips makes walk-ing more painful for women . . . This habitual feeling of weakness inspires less confidence . . . and as a woman finds herself less able to exist on her own, the more she needs to attract the attention of others, to strengthen herself using those around her whom she judges most capable of protecting her [Cabanis 1956, I:278].

Eighteenth-century physiology was based upon necessary links between biological, psychological and social phenomena, not on the anatomical organs of reproduction alone. Although the physiological presuppositions on which Cabanis' views were based applied to both sexes, there was an important asymmetry in that women's occupations were taken to be rooted in and a necessary consequence of their reproductive functions, whereas men's jobs were unrestricted. Women's destiny to bear and suckle children was taken to define their whole body and mind, and therefore their psychological capacities and social tasks. Men were thereby potential members of the broadest social and cultural groups, while women's sphere of action, it was constantly insisted, was the private arena of home and family. As a result, women became a central part of contemporary social debates which focussed on the family as the natural, i.e. biological, element in the social fabric, and on women, who through motherhood were the central figures in the family.

The links between women, motherhood, the family and natural morality may help to explain the emphasis on the breast in much medical literature. There is a danger in our seeing the uterus as the constant object of atten-tion in the search for the biological roots of womanhood. It seems likely that different parts of the body were emphasized at different periods, and from different points of view. While the uterus and ovaries interested nineteenth-century gynaecologists, the breast caught the attention of eighteenth-century medical practitioners who were concerned with moral philosophy and ethics. The breast symbolized women's role in the family through its association with the suckling of babies. It appeared to define the occupational status of females in private work in the family, not in public life. The breast was visible — it was the sign of femininity that men recognized. It could thus be said to be a social law that sexual attraction was founded on the breast, and a natural law that women should breast feed their own children. Based on the natural goodness of the breast it was easy to create a moral injunction on women to feed their own children. It was, it was claimed, an undeniable law which, if thwarted, resulted in suffering for the child and in punishment for the rest of the mother's life, including the miscarriage of subsequent children. 'It is thus that one exposes oneself to cries of pain, for having been unfeeling about those of nature' (Macquart 1799, I:77). The breasts of women not only symbolized the most fundamental social bond, that between mother and child, but they were also the means by which families were made since their beauty elicited the desires of the male for the female. An excellent example of this fusion of aesthetic, medical and social arguments is Roussel's book on women, *Système Physique et Moral de la Femme* (A Physical and Moral System of Woman) which was an instant success when it first appeared in 1775 and at once became part of literary culture (Alibert 1803:7). It is significant that in praising Roussel, Alibert employed the metaphor of science unclothing woman: 'I would like to see the author ... portrayed receiving ... homage from the enchanting sex whose organism he has unveiled with so much delicacy and so much insight [pénétration]' (Alibert 1803:7).

There was a strong aesthetic component in medical writings on women in this period. Discussing the beauty of the breast in the same breath as its vital nutritive function was not undisciplined confusion but indicative of the conflation of social and physiological functions. The breast was good, both morally and biologically, hence its attractiveness and the resultant sociability between the sexes. Indeed the family and thus society were predicated on natural sociability, a quality which Roussel characterized as a major universal law. In these ways the physiological, the social and the aesthetic aspects of human existence were brought together.

So far we have noted a number of overlapping sets of dichotomies and the extent to which the two members of each pair were blurred:

| | | |
|---|---|---|
| nature | : | culture |
| woman | : | man |
| physical | : | mental |
| mothering | : | thinking |
| feeling and superstition | : | abstract knowledge and thought |
| country | : | city |
| darkness | : | light |
| nature | : | science and civilization |

I have also stressed that these associations worked in two ways so that the association of women with nature had a positive and a negative side. Their sentiment and simple, pure morality constituted the first side, their ignorance and lack of intellectual powers, the second. It was common in the eighteenth century to emphasize the second, negative aspects of female naturalness in attacks on superstition and credulity. *Philosophes* in the vanguard of the Enlightenment believed that they had to fight against the superstition and ignorance of the mass of the people because these were impediments to social progress, and one of the vehicles for their polemic was a form of sex-role stereotyping. The classic example of the problem was the uneducated woman under the thumb of her priest who fed her a diet of religious dogma, urging her to believe things which served his interests alone. This situation was the antithesis of that the savants were trying to promote, where people, free from the influence of the entrenched powers of the aristocracy and clergy, lived according to simple moral precepts derived from the direct study of nature. Women were seen as a major impediment in this process of enlightenment, because they repeated hearsay and tittle tattle and were more prone than men to religious enthusiasm. It was therefore in the interests of savants to polarize women and men, reaction and progress.

The opposition between superstition and tradition on the one hand, and enlightenment and progress on the other, functioned not just in the passionate anti-clericalism of eighteenth- and nineteenth-century France, but in debates about the care of children and about midwifery. The theme of the irrationality and irresponsibility of women's ways with small children was articulated in Britain by William Cadogan in his *Essay on Nursing*, first published in 1748. He argued that 'the Preservation of Children should become the Care of Men of Sense' because 'this Business has been too long fatally left to the Management of Women' (1753:3). He justified the charge of female irresponsibility by invoking the 'superstitious Practices and Ceremonies' which they had inherited from 'their Great Grandmothers' (1753:4). He recommended a transfer from female to male authority regarding infant care. He was not simply co-opting a new field for male medical practitioners for he also wished fathers to take a more active role: 'I . . . earnestly recommend it to every Father to have his Child nursed under his own Eye, to make use of his own Reason and Sense' (1753:29). Cadogan thought that women perpetuated ancient practices such as swaddling which should be abolished in favour of the forms of care advised by physicians. He never suggested that men should take over the care of children, but that women should perform their alloted tasks under the advice of men, both their husbands and their doctors. So, it was not that female functions had been abolished or co-opted, but that a hierarchy had been established where women acted under the supervision of men. Men such as Cadogan did not argue for a changed division of labour but for an altered division of power.

The same image of female irresponsibility was implied in attitudes to midwives. The relationship between midwives and other medical practitioners was a complex one (Donnison 1977). There was the element of competition for patients and the related issue of fees for services. It was commonly implied that midwives were dangerous and ignorant in comparison with physicians and surgeons. This claim must be seen in the context of the great concern about quacks, i.e. unlicensed practitioners, in the second half of the eighteenth century. Among the most common complaints against them was that they sold specific remedies and tried to keep the recipes secret. According to the medical establishment, such charlatans clearly traded on the ignorance and blind faith of the simple people who bought their potions rather than employing the skilled eye and brain of a better educated practitioner. Midwives appeared especially suspicious to enlightened savants. Their territory was the intimate and tightly knit circle of women, at least in the imagination of their detractors. Midwives being women with children themselves, and being associated with birth, were at the centre of stereotypes about women and their world.

The treatment of midwives in Britain and France provides an excellent example of the ways in which women were subject to social regulation in a manner which suggests that they were feared as polluting, morally and sexually. It is well known that the midwife was frequently the butt of caricatures and bawdy humour and that she was castigated for drunkenness and uncleanliness (Donnison 1977:33—4). This suspicion was made explicit in the proofs of morality which were demanded of them. In eighteenth-century France this often took the form of a letter from their priest attesting to their good character.[2] At this time both males and females were trained to be *accoucheurs*, the former becoming surgeons, the latter midwives. The education of these two groups was done separately; in fact the idea of instructing them together was considered indecent. The young surgeons were apparently not subject to the moral restraints applied to midwives. They were typically much younger than the pupil midwives, the boys were mostly in their early teens while the women were rarely younger than 20 and mostly married. One decisive difference between the two groups might be the greater sexual experience of the women who had, in all probability, borne children themselves. We could argue that young boys were in principle just as potentially 'dangerous' in the childbirth situation as married women were, probably from our perspective more so. Yet there is no evidence that it was seen that way at the time by medical men. The reasons are partly sexual, and partly a question of class, since the midwives were certainly of humbler origins than the surgeons. The delivery of babies was performed by both men and women, although it would be hard to devise simple rules which determined whether a man or a woman delivered any particular mother. Here we have a situation where the actual division between the sexes was blurred in that, in addition to midwifery, women from all social strata practised a whole range of medical techniques. What we can detect is an unease about the demarcation between male and female

2   This account is based on my archival work in Lille using departmental and municipal collections. See also Gélis, 1977 and Morel, 1977.

medical practitioners resulting in recurrent attempts to control and clarify the sexual boundaries.

Unease about midwives in relation to their male competitors for custom was expressed quite explicitly in a poem by the medical practitioner turned parson and poet, George Crabbe.[3] In *The Parish Register* of 1807 he describes the battle between an established midwife and a young doctor newly arrived in the village (Crabbe 1823, I:122–5). 'The young doctor . . . sneered at the midwife as "Nature's slave", who trusted only to luck, and in emergencies to prayer, while he, with his "skill" and "courage", took pleasure in bending Nature to his will' (Donnison 1977:38).

The uncomfortable position of the midwife illustrates one of the ways in which beliefs in women as bearers of tradition and men as bearers of modernity worked. The fact that forceps were used by men may have further reinforced their image of modernity and power through new techniques. The professional struggle hinged on who should have charge of birth, the event which, more than any other, occupied the centre stage of many women's lives and of the symbolic structures associated with women.[4]

It was as mothers that women were archetypally seen, and, in the case of anatomical drawings, actually in the state of pregnancy itself. But of course there were other images too, especially those derived from classical mythology and used in engravings, oil paintings, statues, bas reliefs, and representations for ceremonial or official purposes. The classical traditions, and their eighteenth-century transformations are extremely complex from the point of view of sexual symbolism. One example may however be useful to illustrate the association of a female deity with natural health.

In his *Sermon on Exercise* of 1772, Benjamin Rush contrasted the natural therapy of exercise with the artificiality of specific remedies. To illustrate the superiority of the former approach to illness he constructed a parable. A wondrously beautiful woman appears to a group of chronically sick people who are suffering from the disastrous effects of quack concoctions. She addresses them with the words: 'Ye children of men, listen for a while to the voice of instruction . . . My name is Hygiaea. I preside over the health of mankind. Descard all your medicines, and seek relief from Temperance and Exercise alone' (Rush 1947:371). They heed her advice and their natural vigour is restored.

I have argued that there was a complex language in medical writings in the second half of the eighteenth century which employed the nature/culture dichotomy in relation to gender. The attributes of women ranged from ignorance and superstition to true civilizing wisdom. Some of those

3  For a very brief introductory account of Crabbe see Brett (1968).
4  In fiction, Sterne's *Tristram Shandy*, first published 1759–67 provides an illustration of this point.

attributes were visually represented in explicit models, statues, engravings and anatomical plates.

## Images of woman – nature disrobes before reason

An important eighteenth-century example of images of woman rendered visual is the wax anatomical models of human figures used for making anatomical drawings and for display in popular museums. (Haviland and Parish 1970, Thompson 1925, Deer 1977) (see plate 3.1). These were intended for teaching, both popular and technical, and for decoration. Although male and female anatomical organs, especially the female abdomen, were commonly depicted in anatomy texts from the sixteenth century onwards (Choulant 1962), these models are distinctly different. In the wax series, many of which were made in Florence at the end of the eighteenth century (Azzaroli 1975), the female figures are recumbent, frequently adorned with pearl necklaces. They have long hair, and occasionally they have hair in the pubic area also. These 'Venuses' as they were significantly called lie on velvet or silk cushions, in a passive, almost sexually inviting pose. Comparable male figures are usually upright, and often in a position of motion. The female models can be opened to display the removable viscera, and most often contain a foetus, while the male ones are made in a variety of forms to display the different physiological systems (see plate 3.2).[5] The figures of recumbent women seem to convey, for the first time, the sexual potential of medical anatomy. Until this time it was usual in engravings for the actual genitals to be covered by a cloth but in the waxes, as in some contemporaneous medical illustrations, they are not just present, but drawn to the attention. Not only is the literal naturalness of women portrayed, in their total nakedness and by the presence of a foetus, but their symbolic naturalness is implied in the whole conception of such figures. Female nature had been unclothed by male science, making her understandable under general scrutiny. The image was made explicit in the statue in the Paris medical faculty of a young woman, her breasts bare, her head slightly bowed beneath the veil she is taking off, which bears the inscription 'Nature unveils herself before Science'.

Women's bodies as objects of medical enquiry as well as of sexual desire

5   Here I have alluded briefly to what is in fact a very complex issue. There were many different traditions of anatomical models but little has been written about them. See however Thompson (1925), on early ivory manikins, and on anatomical illustration in general, Wolf-Heidegger and Cetto (1967: especially pp. 434, 438, 504, 505, 546–7). Collections which include these or similar figures are: Wellcome Collections, Science Museum, London; Institut für Geschichte der Medizin der Universität, Vienna; Museo 'La Specola', Florence.

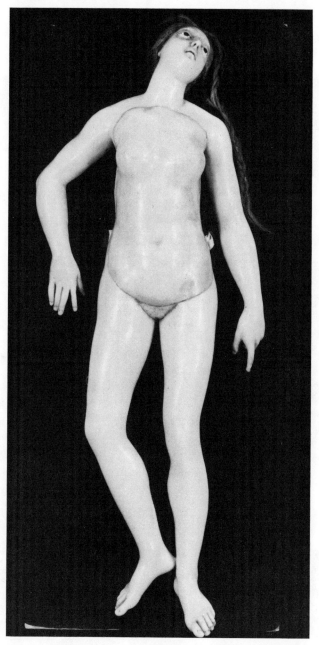

Plate 3.1  French eighteenth-century wax figure. By courtesy of the Wellcome Trustees.

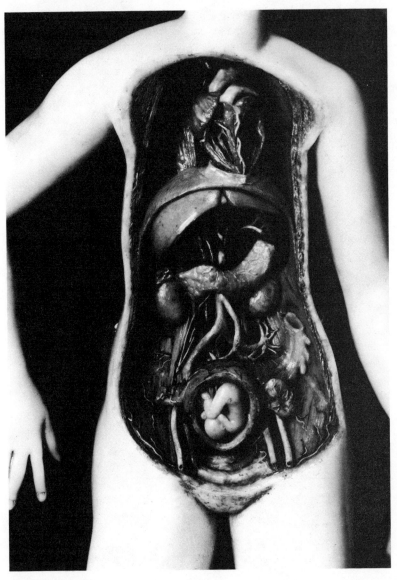

Plate 3.2 French eighteenth-century wax figure with the covering of the trunk removed. By courtesy of the Wellcome Trustees.

became the focus for a physiological literature which expressed a refined aesthetic of women's natural beauty, and found in their bodies an expression of their social condition. To understand women was thus a scientific and medical task which involved revealing the manner of physiological functioning, both normal and pathological, that was peculiar to women. It was for this reason that when Jules Michelet wished to comprehend the condition of women in mid-nineteenth-century France, his first port of call was the dissecting room, and his reading was anatomy texts. In the cadavers of women, Michelet saw their lives revealed and explained before his very eyes. Once again a dual meaning of woman as natural was evoked: she was taken as a creature defined by her biology and as the feminine natural object of masculine science. But perhaps we should add a new third sense. In her pregnant state woman evoked nature yet again through her capacity to reproduce the species, to pass on life. With the definition of life as a new guiding concept at the end of the eighteenth century (Figlio 1976:25ff.), the mechanism whereby life was transmitted took on fresh significance. The capacity to engender life seemed a special elusive force, made concrete through the female reproductive system. This sacred function went hand in hand with female anatomy. One expression of this was the concern among anatomists to discover ideal female beauty. During the eighteenth century medical writers placed great emphasis on the aesthetics of the human body, and on the natural beauty of women which, they argued, should remain undeformed by clothing, and especially by corsets (Choulant 1962:304).

The peak of the sexualized female anatomy was a German painting and lithograph of a beautiful young woman, who had been drowned, being dissected by an anatomist, Professor Lucae, who was interested in the physical basis of female attractiveness. A group of men stand around the table on which a female corpse is lying. She has long hair and well-defined breasts. One of the men has begun the dissection and is working on her thorax. He is holding up a sheet of skin, the part which covers her breast, as if it were a thin article of clothing so delicate and fine is its texture. The corpse is being undressed scientifically, the constituent parts of the body are being displayed for scrutiny and analysis. The powerful sexual image is integral to the whole pictorial effect.[6]

By the 1860s when this engraving was produced, the image it contained might be associated with others which were relatively new to the general public. I am thinking in particular of the fierce public debates about vivisection, which in Britain was opposed, interestingly enough, by a number of women's groups and early feminists (French 1975:239—50). In vivi-

6  The original painting is in the Historisches Museum, Frankfurt, the lithograph is in the Wellcome Institute for the History of Medicine, London. An illustration of the former is in Wolf-Heidegger and Cetto (1967:546).

sectional experiments, pictures of which were prominently displayed in the propaganda put out by critics, there was the same contrast between the utter passivity of the living material used and the active intrusion and manipulation of the experimenters. Despite the long history of anatomical dissections, and the fact that the victim was dead, the anatomizing of the corpse, especially as portrayed in Hasselhorst's picture of Lucae, seems to have similar qualities to the vivisectional experiment. And the exaggerated femininity of the corpse reinforced its passivity. It is almost as if women in their sexually stereotyped roles were made kin to all living objects brought under the penetrating enquiry of male reason.

## The two sides of woman as nature

If in death the female body evoked an image of sexual passivity, it was in the association of women with their capacity to give life that they were seen as active. This activity had a moral nature. As Bernardin de Saint-Pierre said to the female race in 1806, 'You are the flowers of life . . . You civilise the human race . . . You are the Queens of our beliefs and of our moral order' (1966:70—1). Less rhetorically, he explained:

Women lay down the first foundations of natural laws. The first founder of a human society was a mother of a family. They are scattered among men to remind them above all that they are men, and to uphold, despite political laws, the fundamental laws of nature [1966:67]. Not only do women bind men together by the bonds of nature, but also by those of society [1966:68].

These words were written for a new edition of Bernardin de Saint-Pierre's best known work, *Paul et Virginie*, which originally appeared in 1788. It was an immense popular success from the 1790s onwards; its heart-rending story, and in successive editions a series of beautiful plates, made the images of sexuality it contained widely disseminated.

A supposedly true story, it tells of how two young women independently, and for different personal reasons, flee the old world with its social inequalities and consequent inhumanity, to start a new life for themselves and their children in surroundings untainted by human destruction. They meet in the Ile-de-France and bring up their children, Paul and Virginie, together in total harmony with nature. Paul and Virginie knew uncorrupted love, for each other, for their mothers, and for the fertile environment in which they lived. In early adolescence Virginie was called back to France to be educated (and civilized) by a rich old aunt of her mother's. Her mother consented to this since Virginie's awakening sexuality was causing her some anxiety and she wished to avoid an early marriage between Paul and Virginie. Virginie's departure for Europe represents the first rupture of the happy and moral state of nature they had all enjoyed together. Her stay in France was not a success; her aunt wished her to marry against her will and when she refused the offer of a rich husband, she was sent home during the season of storms and hurricanes. Within sight of home the ship went down, and Virginie with it since she refused to take off her clothes and jump into the water with the nude sailor who was urging her to escape. For Bernardin this was a heroic death: 'Virginie, seeing that death was inevitable, put one hand on her clothes, the other on her heart, and lifting up her serene eyes, she seemed like an angel taking wing to heaven' [1966: 159].

*Paul et Virginie* was a moral fable, and one which the 1806 introduction suggests was consciously built on the capacity of women to redeem the ailing civilization of the *ancien régime* and the chaos of revolution.[7] Bernardin idealized women as mothers in his eloquent descriptions of their instinctive, intuitive love for their children. Men, the book implies, are dispensable in the rearing of children. The natural modesty and morality of women manifested in Virginie's death was the foundation on which society would be regenerated. Although Bernardin was politically moderate and held rather conservative religious views, his condemnation of wealth and luxury is obvious enough. But for him there is no political solution to the corruption of a civilization which has lost touch with nature; instead personal morality is appealed to as the means of reform. Bernardin makes no serious allusions to the deployment of power, but argues for the regeneration of pure sentiment.

Mozart's opera *The Magic Flute*, first performed in 1791, stands in marked contrast in conceptualizing the two elements, female/nature and male/culture as locked in a struggle for dominance.[8] Just as *Paul et Virginie* presented clusters of images about women and nature, so did *The Magic Flute*, but the moral judgement went in quite the opposite direction. In the opera there was a battle between good and evil, between light and darkness, which was a struggle between a patriarchal lineage (Sarastro and Tamino) and a matriarchal one (the Queen of the Night) (Mann 1977:591–640). It is well known that the opera contains many allusions to freemasonry, a considerable radical force in late-eighteenth-century Austria (Chailley 1972). This opposition between the enlightenment of free-

7 It should be noted that Bernardin's treatment of women contains certain ambiguities. It was, after all, Virginie's developing sexuality which caused the first disruption of natural harmony of the miniature society. Women as *sexual beings* carry danger; it is really only as *mothers* that they are safe.

8 I have referred to the opera as by Mozart for the sake of simplicity. The words were probably written by a number of people working together, but they were originally attributed to Schikeneder, a Freemason and a friend of the Mozart family (see Chailley 1972 and Mann 1977). For an analysis which employs an anthropological framework, see Hiatt, 1979.

masonry, from which women were, of course, excluded, and the darkness of evil was expressed in sexual terms. Chailley (1972:74–9) argues that the libretto must be seen in the context of contemporary attempts to set up a parallel masonry system for women which were strongly condemned by most (male) masons.

The Queen of the Night was the wife of the Priest of the Sun. She was part of a matrilineal succession but, before his death, her husband had handed to Sarastro, the ruler of the Temple of Wisdom, an emblem of sovereignty to be kept for his male successor. Sarastro kidnapped Pamina, daughter of the Queen, in order to marry her to the new King. One surmises that such a marriage would have served to legitimate the substitution of a patriarchy for a matriarchy. Throughout the opera, play is made on the native ignorance of women needing to be tempered by the reason and wisdom of men. The three ladies of the Queen of the Night represent the state of unenlightenment of the Catholic church. They describe to Tamino, the chosen Prince, how 'a powerful, evil demon' has kidnapped Pamina and the suffering this has caused the 'loving maternal heart' of the Queen (Mozart 1971:42). In the suggestion of the deep suffering of the Queen caused by the cruelty of Sarastro, the Queen and her ladies exploit the nature/culture metaphor to win sympathy for their feminine vulnerability, but the opera firmly places right on the side of male reason. This moral superiority is reinforced by scenes in the Masonic Lodge represented as a temple of wisdom, nature, and reason; these are the places where 'prudence, work and art dwell' (51). Throughout, women are told of their inferior position to men and denigrated: 'women do little but chatter much' (54). Sarastro chides Pamina, 'a man must guide your heart, for without one every woman seeks to exceed her rightful place' (59). He describes her mother, the Queen of the Night, as 'a woman who vaunts herself and hopes to delude the people by trickery and superstition' (62). However, the symbolism is by no means unequivocally demeaning to women and the treachery in the opera is perpetrated by the moor, Monostatos, who wants Pamina for himself. Chailley claimed that at the end of the opera, the marriage of Pamina and Tamino mitigates the generally violent anti-feminist tone by 'a proclamation of the redemption of Woman and her rise to equality with Man in the Mystery of the Couple' (1972:295). However, I would argue that the ultimate victory is unambiguous; light triumphs over darkness, men over women. As a modern commentator has put it: 'The entire opera legitimizes the principle of patriarchy through its assignment to men of the realm of reason, to women the realm of emotionality; its assignment to men, but not to women, of the realm of power and the right to pass it on, including the right to give the daughter away' (Coser 1978:347).

The richness and inventiveness of the imagery is striking in *The Magic Flute*, and I would suggest that it provides some useful clues as to how the sexes were conceptualized at the end of the eighteenth century. Its late-eighteenth-century audience would certainly have found the political message about the bankruptcy of absolute monarchy and the need for a new secular order quite obvious. Presumably they also took the point that this could be seen as a battle between women and men.

History as well as art provides instances of struggles between men and women. In 1835 the Norman peasant Pierre Rivière created a sensation by killing his pregnant mother. His mother's dominating behaviour towards his father, her ownership of land and her consequent power were so fundamentally objectionable to him that he took her life (and those of a brother and a sister) to vindicate the honour and dignity of his father. What is even more remarkable is the lengthy testimony he wrote explaining in minute detail the history of his family and his motivation for committing the crime (Foucault 1973).

In many different ways the dichotomy between women as nature and men as culture was conceptualized as a struggle between the forces of tradition and those of change. This is particularly clear in the anti-clericalism of men like Michelet (Cabanis 1978) who believed that giving women the vote would result in a move towards a more conservative, church-based government, since women were particularly vulnerable to the machinations of the Catholic church, and of Jesuits in particular. Ironically, it was the very qualities which made women the mainstay of society in the family — their delicate feelings — which also made them vulnerable to political exploitation and so becoming a dangerous force if given political rights. Private virtues could easily become public vices.

The ideology of progress which was so deeply entrenched in Enlightenment thought meant that the growth of a humane, rational, and civilized society could also be seen as a struggle between the sexes, with men imposing their value systems on women in order to facilitate social progress. The nature/culture dichotomy thus has a historical dimension. Human history, the growth of culture through the domination of nature, was the increasing assertion of masculine ways over irrational, backward-looking women.

A brief examination of the concept of culture may throw light on this point. There was a transition in the meaning of culture during the eighteenth century from a noun of process, denoting the tending of something, such as plants and animals, to a more abstract usage, often associated with the state of development of human society. Not only did this concept of culture incorporate a historical dimension, but it also allowed the possibility that each nation, each people and its constituent groups had its own distinctive culture (Williams 1976:76—82). In tying culture specifically to the state of civilization, it was logical for writers to stress those features of civilized life they considered paradigmatic of their own society's achievements. Starting in the eighteenth century, and becoming more marked in the nineteenth, was the trend towards identifying these with science and technology, with the capacity for abstract thought. The relative strength of nations was not just a matter of military or economic prowess, but of the extent to which science was cultivated. This is the background of the 'decline of science' debates of the mid nineteenth century, where considerable fears were expressed in Britain about the ascendency of French and German science (Babbage 1830). This notion of progress was one in which men played the dominant role; women were deemed incapable of contributing because of their lack of analytical modes of thought.

The contrast between the qualities of men and women suggested that there was a deep complementarity between them. This was the position held by Jules Michelet, one which he stated with exceptional clarity. It is of some interest because it reveals the mixture of public and private problems thought to result from the differences between the sexes. His profound anti-clericalism has already been mentioned. His beliefs about the illegitimate power priests had over women were closely related to his views on sexuality and family life. Priests, Michelet claimed, created a schism between husband and wife, whereas he thought the woman's basic commitment should be to her husband, indeed it was in her nature for it to be so. Marriage was thus elevated to an ideal moral state where each partner acted as the moral guardian of the other. Michelet identified two major impediments to a more universal state of happiness on which a more healthy society could be built. These were women who worked outside the home and men who were unwilling to marry. Men, he feared, did not wish to be tied down, and preferred to spend their money on drink. If only they would marry, young men would then be reformed by their wives, and boost France's flagging population in the process. The mechanism of reform was the domestic haven the wife provided, impossible to construct if she were working. It was not suitable for unmarried women to work either, because they were exploited by greedy employers, resulting in illness, poverty and death. 'The population is no longer growing, and it is of diminishing quality. The peasant woman is dying of overwork, the working women in industry of hunger' (Michelet 1860:xviii). The moral for Michelet was that women cannot survive alone, they need an asylum, the home, and a protector, the husband. He saw sexual relationships as ideally didactic with husbands instructing younger wives.

The naturalness of female biological rhythms, especially menstruation, were to be adored by husbands, and Michelet looked to medical science and natural history for further information on the state of womanhood, and on sexuality in nature in general. In this he was the heir of Enlightenment traditions. His emphasis was on the natural morality of women (it is therefore no coincidence that he was an admirer of Bernardin de Saint-Pierre) and on the study of anatomy and physiology. These studies constantly reinforced the intertwining of the physical and the moral dimensions of human beings. The immense popularity of Michelet's books on women is significant. Above all Michelet was a constructor of mythologies, and the special interest of his writings on women is the clear comment they make on contemporary social issues, with an eloquence and a power that gained their author enormous influence. In fact, it might be argued that Michelet's thought as a whole was based on his notion of the fundamental differences but underlying complementarity between the sexes. He employed metaphors of sexuality quite consciously in all the areas on which he wrote.[9] Michelet's concern with contemporary political issues is not after all surprising, for if everything in the universe is sexual, either literally or metaphorically, then maintaining the social order was a problem of the regulation of sexuality. The framework within which Michelet cast his ideas was the naturalness of woman *versus* the rational control of husbands and doctors. Furthermore the avowed basis of this was natural history and the bio-medical sciences.

## Conclusion: gender logic

I have stressed that the nature/culture opposition as applied to gender was based on a study of human beings which combined physiology and anatomy, psychology, sociology and anthropology to produce an analysis of people as integrated units. In particular the descriptive and the moral went together to produce a medical science which showed what ought to be as well as what was. I have also argued that the polarity between nature and culture was conceived of as a struggle between two opposing forces.

In the eighteenth century a struggle was imagined inside each individual: between those elements which were thought to be masculine — reason and intelligence — and those which were thought to be feminine — the passions and the emotions. Typically, men were portrayed as serious and thoughtful, and women as frivolous and emotional. This was not a total division of mental properties between the sexes but a continuum according to the extent to which reason dominated, fully consistent with the physiology based on lifestyle which I discussed earlier. Here I want to stress two points. First, there was a battle envisaged between the two aspects of an individual's psychology, just as there was between male and female elements in society as a whole. Second, this sense of psychological division between the sexes became rigidified during the nineteenth century. Michelet questioned whether women were responsible, from a legal point of view, in the way that men were. Lotze in 1852 claimed, 'analytical reflection is so little natural to women that it may be asserted without risk of being far wrong that words like to the right, to the left, across . . . do not signify any

9  For an account which explores Michelet's use of metaphor see Barthes (1954).

mathematical relationships in women's speech but certain peculiar feelings which one has in following these indications while working' (Ploss et al. 1935, I:129).

Some decades later Durkheim expressed similar views in *Suicide*, first published in 1897. He asserted the greater devotion of women to religious practices and summarized the differences between the sexes thus: 'Woman's sexual needs have less of a mental character because, generally speaking, her mental life is less developed. These needs are more closely related to the needs of the organism, following rather than leading them. Being a more instinctive creature than man, woman has only to follow her instincts to find calmness and peace' (1952:272). The pre-condition for Durkheim's statements was a well-developed biological and medical science which gave meaning to such terms as organism and instinct. By using these same terms Durkheim was able to conjure up a set of biological assumptions which, added to the woman = nature stereotype, conveyed a degree of biological determinism for women which far exceeded that for men. I have argued that there was a well established bio-medical tradition going back to the mid eighteenth century which developed a language for speaking about gender, through which savants attempted to provide naturalistic explanations of all facets of knowledge about women. I further stressed that the conceptual divisions between the sexes seemed to be hardening. It is therefore tempting to refer to contemporary changes in material conditions — proto-industrialization; changing forms of family life such as the demise of the family economy, which affected work patterns; child rearing customs, and possibly also the ways the sexes viewed each other. But there is so much geographical and class variation in these conditions that it is impossible to discern a simple pattern emerging in Europe during the period we are concerned with. There is evidence to suggest that men and women shared in their traditions and religiosity, and that in the peasant world of the eighteenth century sex roles were not as uniformly distinct as is commonly believed.

I want to insist that in these nature, culture, gender associations we are not speaking of an ideology which directly reflected material conditions, but a programme of reform to create a universe which did not yet exist. Nor did it or could it ever exist. The normative intentions and the stereotyped categories bore little relationship to the messiness and pragmatic complexity of lived experience for the majority of the population. The nature/culture ideology expressed the interests of the small but influential elite which generated the literature I have been discussing. These writers were not aristocrats or politicians, but intellectuals and professionals from the middle strata of society who gained influence precisely because of their ideas and 'knowledge'. Their concern was to establish the validity of their vision of the world, and their right to debate social issues. They shared by and large a vision of science and medicine as the motors of social advance.

Women occupied a peculiar position in the march of progress. On the one hand, their traditionalism had to be fought to the death, but, on the other hand, they had a major role to play in putting the family on a secure moral footing which was a necessary step in improving social life.

In speaking about the dichotomies between men and women, nature and culture, I have stressed that there was no obvious relationship between the *ideas* about sexual divisions and the way they functioned in day-to-day life. Between the theories of a small elite and the lives of the majority of the people stood a set of assumptions about sexuality which undoubtedly affected both groups in a profound manner. We might usefully speak about these sets of assumptions as myths. Simone de Beauvoir (1972) was right to emphasize the importance of myths in the ways women are seen. She takes for granted, however, that the polarities they contain are basic to the way the human mind works. Thus, for her, it is inevitable that woman has been taken as other by man, and so seen only in relation to him. In her state of otherness, woman is the repository of the myths and stereotypes that de Beauvoir analysed. She did relate her analysis to specific periods of history in specific cultures, but nevertheless asserted her perspective at a level of generality which seems vague and abstract. In particular she did not draw attention to the historical importance of science, medicine and technology in the promulgation of myths of femininity. Precisely through the study of nature as it was conducted after the 'Scientific Revolution' of the seventeenth century did the stereotypes of the sexes become reified and hardened. These notions were not consistent but were necessarily contradictory. It was in elaborating paradoxical stereotypes about women (and men) that the myths became powerful. The different elements clouded and veiled each other, partly perhaps to disguise a deeper antagonism between the sexes (the antagonism that Pierre Rivière was unable to control), and partly because a simple debasement of women by men would not have commanded assent and would not have begun to convey adequately the complexity of full social relations between the sexes.

The importance of de Beauvoir's emphasis on myths of otherness is that she does not employ an evolutionist perspective to describe the different social positions of men and women. For example, Ortner speaks of women as lower than or subordinate to men, stemming from her belief that 'the secondary status of women is one of the true universals' (1974:67). This way of speaking assumes a model of society where there are unambiguous, rigid hierarchies, and so clear criteria for assigning their rank to any individual. Even if we clearly separate issues of value (bad/good) from those of control (sub/superordinate), there are no simple scales on which men and women can be ranged.[10] Women are deemed both good *and* bad, and both evaluations may be represented as stemming from their naturalness. Simi-

10   I have found Brown (1980) particularly helpful.

larly, they may be subordinate in some areas of life (e.g. legal rights) and superordinate in others (e.g. control of the house), and both descriptions could be based on their putatively natural qualities. This pervasive vocabulary which uses notions of simple hierarchies betrays the lasting influence of nineteenth-century evolutionary theories on how we think about gender. Of course, the evolutionist perspective in all its complexity was crucial to the development of anthropology as a discipline in the late nineteenth and early twentieth centuries. But we must not be uncritical of the historical legacies of our disciplines.

Perhaps returning to the Enlightenment can teach us two lessons. First, our ways of thought have a long history, despite the belief that the social sciences are a relatively new field. A more textured understanding of our historical inheritance helps us to analyse current ideas and problems more adequately. Second, recent notions of nature and culture have taken them to be infinitely more simple, reduced categories than they were in the eighteenth and nineteenth centuries. I have stressed the complexity and ambiguity with which ideas of nature, culture and gender were endowed. But I have also pointed to another layer — that of science itself as a sexual activity in its relationship to nature.

While it is important to realize that nature was endowed with a remarkable range of meanings during the period of the Enlightenment (Lovejoy 1960), there was also one common theme. Nature was taken to be that realm on which mankind acts, not just to intervene in or manipulate directly, but also to understand and render it intelligible. This perception of nature includes people and the societies they construct. Such an interpretation of nature led to two distinct positions: nature could be taken to be that part of the world which human beings have understood, mastered and made their own. Here, through the unravelling of laws of motion for example, the inner recesses of nature were revealed to the human mind. But secondly, nature was also that which has not yet been penetrated (either literally or metaphorically), the wilderness and deserts, unmediated and dangerous nature. To these two positions correspond two senses in which women are nature. According to the first, they, as repositories of natural laws, can be revealed and understood. This was Michelet's point in denying that women are unpredictable. On the contrary, he claimed, they are so clearly subsumed under nature's laws, expressed for example in the menstrual cycle, that their states of mind and body can be read by the trained person. For this reason, a systematic study of the anatomy and physiology of women was of great importance. According to the second position it was woman's emotions and uncontrolled passions which gave her special qualities. Women, being endowed with less reason than men, indeed with less need for reason since their social lives required of them feeling and not thought, were more easily dominated by extreme emotions. Women were therefore conceptualized as dangerous because less amenable to the guiding light of reason. According to this second perspective, moves to contain women's dangerous potential are more appropriate than attempts to subject them to scientific scrutiny. Their potential for disorder can be minimized by drawing and maintaining strong social boundaries around them. To these two positions corresponded these positive and negative moral evaluations of the female sex discussed earlier. Ultimately we might say that nature, culture and gender in the history of our own society were and are concepts which express the desire for clarity in areas of life which appear constantly subject to change. Their historical inter-relatedness does teach us important lessons about the ways in which apparently distinct areas of life are linked through sets of symbols and metaphors. Furthermore, the links between these cognitive structures and the behavioural level of sexuality are immensely complex, and still largely unexplored.

I have stressed the role of science and medicine as mediators of our ideas of nature, culture and gender, and argued for the rootedness of these ways of thought in recent Western history. One of the most powerful aspects of scientific and medical constructions of sexuality is the way in which apparently universal categories were set up which implied the profound similarities of all women, and to a lesser extent, of all men. Perhaps one of the problems with the current promiscuous use of the nature/culture dichotomy in relation to gender is that it has taken the claims of Western science at face value, and so lapsed into a biologism which it is the responsibility of the social sciences, including history and anthropology, to combat.[11]

### Bibliography

Alibert, J.L. 1803. 'Eloge historique de Pierre Roussel', in *Système Physique et Moral de la Femme*, P. Roussel, pp. 1–52. Paris: Crapart, Caille et Ravier.

Azzaroli, M.L. 1975. 'La Specola. The Zoological Museum of Florence University', *Atti del 1º Congresso Internazionale sulla Ceroplastica nella Scienza e Nell'Arte*, pp. 5–31 + 9 plates.

Babbage, C. 1830. *Reflections on the Decline of Science in England, and on some of its causes*. London: B. Fellowes and J. Booth.

Barthes, R. 1954. *Michelet*. Paris: Editions du Seuil.

Barthez, P.J. 1806. *Nouveaux Elémens de la Science de l'Homme*. 2 vols. Paris: Goujor et Brunot.

Bernardin de Saint-Pierre, J.H. 1966. *Paul et Virginie*. Paris: Garnier-Flammarion.

Brett, R.L. 1968. *George Crabbe*, revised edition. London: Longmans.

Brown, P. 1980. 'Women as "nature", men as "culture": an anthropological debate as object lesson', mimeo.

11  Haraway (1979), is a good starting point in this enterprise.

68    L.J. Jordanova

Cabanis, J. 1978. *Michelet, le Prêtre et la Femme.* Paris: Gallimard.
Cabanis, P.J.G. 1956. *Oeuvres Philosophiques,* 2 vols. Paris: Presses Universitaires de France.
Cadogan, W. 1753. *An Essay upon Nursing and the Management of Children from their Birth to Three Years of Age.* 6th edition. London: The Foundling Hospital.
Chailley, J. 1972. *The Magic Flute, Masonic Opera: An Interpretation of the Libretto and the Music.* London: Victor Gollancz.
Choulant, J.L. 1962. *History and Bibliography of Anatomic Illustration.* New York and London: Hafner.
Coser, R.L. 1978. The principle of patriarchy. *Signs. Journal of Women in Culture and Society,* 4, no. 2, pp. 337–48.
Crabbe, G. 1823. *The Works of the Rev. George Crabbe.* 8 vols. London: John Murray.
de Beauvoir, S. 1972. *The Second Sex.* Harmondsworth: Penguin.
Deer, L. 1977. 'Italian anatomical waxes in the Wellcome Collection: the missing link', *Rivista di Storia delle Scienze mediche e naturali,* 20, pp. 281–98.
Donnison, J. 1977. *Midwives and Medical Men. A History of Inter-Professional Rivalries and Women's Rights.* London: Heinemann.
Durkheim, E. 1952. *Suicide. A Study in Sociology.* London: Routledge and Kegan Paul.
Farrington, B. 1964. *The Philosophy of Francis Bacon. An Essay on its Development from 1603 to 1609 with new Translations of Fundamental Texts.* Liverpool: Liverpool University Press.
Figlio, K. 1975. 'Theories of perception and the physiology of mind in the late eighteenth century', *History of Science,* 12, pp. 177–212.
       1976. 'The metaphor of organisation: a historiographical perspective on the bio-medical sciences of the early nineteenth century', *History of Science,* 14, pp. 17–53.
Foucault, M. 1973. *Moi, Pierre Rivière, Ayant Egorgé Ma Mère, Ma Soeur et Mon Frère . . . Un Cas de Parricide au XIX^e Siècle.* Paris: Gallimard/Julliard. (Available in English, 1978. Harmondsworth: Penguin.)
French, R.D. 1975. *Antivivisection and Medical Science in Victorian Society.* Princeton and London: Princeton University Press.
Gélis, J. 1977. 'Sages-femmes et accoucheurs: l'obstétrique populaire aux XVII^e et XVIII^e siècles', *Annales: Économies, Sociétés, Civilisations,* 32, part 5, pp. 927–57.
Glacken, C. 1967. *Traces on the Rhodian Shore. Nature and Culture in Western Thought from ancient times to the end of the eighteenth century.* Berkeley, Los Angeles and London: University of California Press.
Haraway, D. 1979. 'The biological enterprise: sex, mind, and profit from human engineering to sociobiology', *Radical History Review,* no. 20, pp. 206–37.
Haviland, T.N., Parish, L.C. 1970. 'A brief account of the use of wax models in the study of medicine', *Journal of the History of Medicine,* 25, pp. 52–75.

Hiatt, L.R. 1979. 'Queen of the Night, mother-right, and secret male cults', in *Fantasy and Symbol; Studies in Anthropological Interpretation*, ed. R.H. Hook, pp. 247–65. London: Academic Press.

Hufton, O. 1971. 'Women in revolution 1789–1796', *Past and Present*, no. 53, pp. 90–108.

1975–6. 'Women and the family economy in eighteenth-century France', *French Historical Studies*, 9, pp. 1–22.

Jordanova, L.J. 1979. 'Earth science and environmental medicine: the synthesis of the late enlightenment', in *Images of the Earth: Essays in the History of the Environmental Sciences*, ed. L.J. Jordanova and R. Porter, pp. 119–46. Chalfont St Giles: British Society for the History of Science.

Knibiehler, Y. 1976. 'Les médecins et la «nature feminine» au temps du code civil', *Annales: Économies, Sociétés, Civilisations*, 31, part 4, pp. 824–45.

Kolodny, A. 1975. *The Lay of the Land*. Chapel Hill: University of North Carolina Press.

Lovejoy, A.O. 1960. ' "Nature" as an aesthetic norm', in *Essays in the History of Ideas*, pp. 69–77. New York: Putnam's.

Macquart, L.C.H. 1799. *Dictionnaire de la Conservation de l'Homme*, 2 vols. Paris: Bidault.

Mann, W. 1977. *The Operas of Mozart*. London: Cassell.

Michelet, J. 1860. *La Femme*. Paris: Hachette.

Morel, M.-F. 1977. 'Ville et compagne dans le discours medical sur la petite enfance au XVIII$^e$ siècle', *Annales: Économies, Sociétés, Civilisations*, 32, part 5, pp. 1,007–24.

Mozart, W.A. 1971. *Die Zauberflöte*. London: Cassell.

Ortner, S.A. 1974. 'Is female to male as nature is to culture?', in *Woman, Culture and Society*, ed. M.Z. Rosaldo and L. Lamphere, pp. 67–87. Stanford: Stanford University Press.

Ploss, H.H., Bartels, M. and Bartels, P. 1935. *Woman. An Historical Gynaecological and Anthropological Compendium*, 3 vols. London: Heinemann.

Pomme, P. 1782. *Traité des Affections Vaporeuses des Deux Sexes*. Paris: L'Imprimerie Royale.

Roussel, P. 1803. *Système Physique et Moral de la Femme*, 2nd edition. Paris: Crapart, Caille et Ravier.

Rush, B. 1947. *The Selected Writings of Benjamin Rush*. New York: Philosophical Library.

Sterne, L. 1967. *The Life and Opinions of Tristram Shandy Gentleman*. Harmondsworth: Penguin.

Thompson, C.J.S. 1925. 'Anatomical manikins', *Journal of Anatomy*, 59, part 4, pp. 442–5 + 2 plates.

Williams, R. 1975. *The Country and the City*. St Albans: Paladin.

1976. *Keywords. A Vocabulary of Culture and Society*. London: Fontana/Croom Helm.

Wolf-Heidegger, G. and Cetto, A.M. 1967. *Die Anatomische Sektion in Bildlicher Darstellung*. Basle and New York: S. Karger.

# 4 The power of signs: gender, culture and the wild in the Bolivian Andes

## OLIVIA HARRIS

When Simone de Beauvoir wrote her account of the condition of women thirty years ago, she drew on many different insights from biology, literature, philosophy, psychoanalysis, anthropology, history. In statements such as 'In woman are incarnated the disturbing mysteries of nature, and man escapes her hold when he frees himself from nature' (1972:107), she was articulating a view of femininity and masculinity current in western culture and mythology. However, even within our own ideology the very consistency of her portrait calls for reappraisal, and still more care is required in assessing its pretensions to universality.[1]

The development within anthropology of the opposition between nature and culture derives particularly from the opus of Lévi-Strauss, for whom it has provided a unifying theme in much of his writing. While it is not my purpose here to give a further account of his complex use of these concepts, a significant dimension which anthropologists have little commented on is their close relationship with certain aspects of Freudian theory. Various writers have indeed noted the debt that Lévi-Strauss owes to Freud (Leach 1965; Badcock 1975). Conversely, recent psychoanalytic theory has drawn heavily, if eclectically, on Lévi-Strauss. Lacan in particular has reinterpreted Freud in a structuralist theory that places central importance on the role of language in the development of the individual. In his reading, the Oedipus complex is the moment at which the individual enters what he calls the 'symbolic order', that is, a system of signification which positions the individual within a given structure of meaning. Meaning is organized around the recognition of difference, and is based on the presence or absence of the phallus, here understood as a strictly symbolic rather than physiological entity.[2]

Lacan's concept of the symbolic has much in common with Lévi-

---

1  Particular thanks to the editors and Rosalind Coward for their many helpful comments. Ortner's argument (1974) is also explicitly about the claim to universality. Much of my discussion is in response to de Beauvoir's and Ortner's stimulating ideas.
2  See especially 'The signification of the phallus' in Lacan (1977a) and also Coward and Ellis (1977).

Strauss' use of culture.[3] Within the Lacanian tradition the phallus is a key signifier which inscribes certain power relations within discourse such that males, who command discourse, occupy a privileged position in the structure of society. Men enter more completely into the symbolic order than do women who remain, comparatively speaking, in a state of nature.[4] There is a clear connection between systems of representation and the way males and females are brought into the social order as sexual and social beings. As Strathern argues (see chapter 8), the European concept of nature includes in its meaning that which is, or should be, controlled. The ways that power is associated with language and representations of the social, non-social and wild are the principal themes of this paper.

The opposed categories of nature and culture have not been used extensively in Andean ethnography, although at first sight they seem to have clear resonances in Andean symbolism. Especially in spatial terms, the social is contrasted with the wild in an opposition between inhabited and cultivated space on the one hand and rugged terrain on the other. However, many of the resonances attached to these English terms are not applicable to Andean representations, and to use them as a shorthand would preclude a full understanding of what associations are actually being made.

The Laymi Indians of the central Bolivian highlands are an interesting example of the enormous variety of ways that the themes we associate with nature and culture can be represented. Where most of the ethnic groups cited in discussions on nature and culture practice shifting cultivation or hunting and gathering, the Laymis are settled peasants, cultivating a variety of cereals and tubers, and rearing livestock. An Aymara-speaking group numbering approximately 8,000, they inhabit a region of the north of the department of Potosí that has at least since Inka times been an important source of metal — gold, silver, and, more recently, tin.[5]

3 It is founded particularly on Lévi-Strauss' formulations in *The elementary structures of kinship* (1969), but becomes both more elaborated and more restricted in Lacan's work. (See Lacan 1977b: 279; also Macey 1978:116.) Lacan extends Lévi-Strauss' idea of the incest taboo as marking the transition from nature to culture, and the implications of the social laws that regulate marriage ties and kinship for the structures of language. (E.g. Lévi-Strauss: 'The emergence of symbolic thought must have required that women, like words, should be things that were exchanged', (1969:496); and Lacan 1977a: ch. 3.)

4 This equation of the symbolic with culture is already contained in the way Lévi-Strauss' work is used (see note 3 above). The identification of femininity with nature is found explicitly in the work of various feminist writers, e.g. Irigaray (1977), Kristeva (1977), Lipshitz (1978), Montrelay (1978).

5 In accord with current practice in writing native Andean languages, I have preferred Inka to the more familiar Inca.

Today the area is dominated by the huge tin-mining complex of Catavi-Siglo XX, but in spite of having this ready market for their produce and labour, the Laymis have retained a largely subsistence-based economy, and a culture which is firmly distinguished from that of the urban *mestizos* and those of European descent. Both their subsistence practices and their long association with mining and precious metals, as we shall see, are significant for the ways they represent the wild and the forces antithetical to society.

A second reason why the Laymis are interesting in the context of Ortner's thesis is because this is a culture with an emphasis on the unity of wife and husband, and little strongly-marked symbolization of difference between the sexes.[6] In agriculture both sexes, young and old, work together in most tasks. The care of livestock is divided so that women herd sheep and goats, men llamas, and both sexes tend the rest of the household's livestock. In textile production, again, the division of labour assigns comparable and complementary tasks to each sex. The nuclear household is the unit that organizes production and consumption for most of the year, and the sexual division of labour ties husband and wife to each other within this unit, while giving women a freedom of movement unusual in peasant societies of other parts of the world. In order to analyse the ways Laymis represent male and female, it is necessary to appreciate the degree to which husband and wife are linked in primary economic dependence.

*Women, men and the symbolic order*

The Laymis represent the process by which a new-born individual becomes a fully-socialized human being in terms of the child's progressive ability to speak. The different stages of the formative years are defined by the child's relation to language; a baby becomes a boy or girl when it can speak. At this point a ceremony takes place in which its hair is cut for the first time, removing the filthy, matted locks that represent in a very vivid way its imperfect humanity. Similarly, the passage from childhood to young adulthood, with the assumption of many new activities, such as music, dancing, weaving, fighting, is said to occur when the individual can speak and understand fully. This transition is a gradual process, not marked by a specific ritual.

It is also significant that socialization is based primarily on language. Laymi women say that weaning and toilet training are done by talking to their children, and that the process is completed when the child 'understands'. To my knowledge, children are virtually never punished, not even in the mildest of forms. To most Laymis the very idea of punishing a child is shocking, precisely because of the child's limited command of language,

6   See Harris (1978a) for an elaboration of the concept of *chachawarmi*,
    man-and-woman, in Laymi culture.

and thus imperfect understanding of what it had done. This is adhered to even in cases where the misdemeanour of the child is so serious as to bring retribution from the spirits or retaliation through magic.

Laymis make little differentiation between the sexes in the way they perceive individual development up to adolescence, but within adult life there are two important domains in which participation is represented in terms of the ability to speak, and, in both of these, women are said to have a different relation to language from men. Firstly, political activity and decision making are centred on the local assembly, in which all adult men participate. Women are rigorously excluded, and one reason frequently given me for their absence was precisely their inability to speak. Adult women do join in decision making through informal means, but formal speech is commanded by men.[7] The second domain concerns relations with the spirit world. There is a hierarchy of ritual specialists, and while women can and do practice at the lower levels, performing certain cures, or reading coca leaves as diviners, they do not attain the highest rank, that of the spirit medium, who undergoes an apprenticeship that culminates in learning to speak directly to the spirits. This is a frightening experience that demands great psychic strength and the ability to speak well.[8]

In both politics and communication with the spirit world then, women's non-participation in the Laymis' view is derived importantly from their relationship to language. But there are other spheres of symbolic practice in which women are far from muted. In all public rites at least one woman must be present and in some ritual sequences women's active participation is of central importance. In particular, their involvement in the two major forms of artistic production gives them a voice.

Music is an integral part of the ritual cycle, of the definition of time, and is performed by young men and unmarried girls. Music could almost be described as the discourse of courtship. Young men must acquire a wooden pipe and a *charango* (a small mandolin), the instruments respectively for the rainy and the dry seasons, in order to be taken seriously by girls. Indeed the phallic symbolism of these instruments, particularly of the pipe whose mournful tones pervade the whole period of fertility and

7   Community decision making, which is formally in the hands of men, is organized in such a way that women's opinions are heard and taken into account. Any decision requires two separate assemblies; one for the matter to be raised, and a second one some days or even weeks later, when a decision is reached after taking everyone's opinion into account.

8   The general term for a ritual specialist is *yatiri*: 'one who knows'. Those who speak to the spirits are known by Laymis as *wayuri*. Tschopik translates this type of specialist as 'magician' (1951). I heard of the existence of older women who were *wayuri*, but was never able to meet one.

growth, is extremely explicit. Young men going courting or to a fiesta are invariably accompanied by their instruments, and in fiestas where they encounter strangers playing music is an overtly aggressive act.

The contribution of girls is to sing, while the men play. Men can and do sing also, but on public occasions it is the girls who must sing, in high-pitched voices with incredible bravura. In consequence it is the girls who are said to compose new verses for the songs while young men are chiefly responsible for the melodies. In the genesis of a collective art-form it is hard, and probably mistaken, to attach too much significance to author-ship, but still it is quite clear that Laymi women make a contribution as important in the process of musical creation as that of men, and some girls in particular are renowned for their skill as composers. In this case, it is not men but girls who are said to have the greater command over words.

The other field of artistic expression is the weaving for which the north of Potosí is justly renowned. While men knit highly-intricate patterns into their *ch'ulus*, or woollen caps, women are responsible for the vast outpour-ing of motifs, of densely-composed bands of design, particularly on the carrying-cloths, belts and bags woven by them. What must be borne in mind is not only the degree of artistic investment that these weavings represent, but also that they are key elements in the code by which ethnic groups in the Andes differentiate themselves. Thus it is women's symbol-ization, handed from mother to daughter, and shared as a professional skill among all women, that is a major repository of ethnic identity.

How do women interpret their own symbolic expression in weaving? Certainly my attempts to discover a specifically female symbolic language met with failure. In fact it was men who provided me with most infor-mation on the meaning of symbols in weaving. The fine analysis of Andean weaving symbolism made in northern Chile by Veronica Cereceda notes the same phenomenon: women would name the different motifs, whereas men moved from these names into a metalanguage where each weaving could be said to represent the whole society (1978). Thus while women use language metaphorically in weaving, as in the complex symbolism of songs, it seems that more elaborate discursive speech is typically the domain of men.

Overall, in describing the relationship of Laymi women to different forms of symbolic discourse, it is important to stress the significance of the life-cycle. Women experience a major rupture at marriage. While she is unmarried, a girl will sing, dance, get drunk. She will fight against other girls in the ritual fights, *tinku*, that take place at big fiestas. In particular, the presence of unmarried girls is essential for the success of the group of male warriors who go together to the *tinku*. This same group of warriors and unmarried girls, known as *wayli*, has an important ritual function for the community, since it is they who intercede with the sun-god for protection and for pardon, especially if epidemic or disaster strikes (see plate 4.1).[9]

However, at the moment that a girl goes to live with a man she partially retires from many areas of symbolic discourse. She must stop her singing and dancing, at least for a while, and will join in ritual only very shyly and passively. She will hide herself away, sometimes for many years, dressed in an all-encompassing black dress that replaces the gaudy and picturesque clothes she wore as a girl. Only weaving is an unbroken activity, a major feature of household production.

While Lévi-Strauss asserts that 'words do not speak while women do' (1972:61), we should not assume that men and women stand in identical relation to the language by which they communicate. In the examples given here, the women's apparently lesser command over formal language has direct material consequences in their total or partial exclusion from moments when power is being asserted, either by the individual spirit medium who attempts to manipulate the spirits, or collectively by the corporate assembly of adult males who make decisions on behalf of the community. On the other hand it would also be mistaken to privilege this language to the exclusion of other forms of symbolic production. It is principally through weaving, song and music that Indian culture in general symbolizes its separation from the outsiders that dominate it, and that Laymi culture distinguishes itself from other similar ethnic groups. In these forms of expression the men's contribution is more than matched by that of the women.

The Laymis then have a clear idea that language is the instrument which forms the human being, starting from the initial act of naming, and continuing until the person attains full understanding at adolescence, and in a sense throughout life, since capacity to speak improves with age. But is there any sense in which this process is seen by them as a transition from nature to culture? In many ways it is, since if a baby dies before it is ritually named, it cannot be buried in the cemetery, but must be interred in a specific place far from habitation to be 'eaten' by the mountain spirits who are especially identified with the wild. In this belief there is a direct association of the pre-social individual with a wild that is spatially located. This is reiterated in the significance attached to the first hair-cutting, when the baby has learnt to speak. The matted locks (*quli*) it retains until this point are the same as those of the mythical figure − known as Quli Uma − who embodies anti-social behaviour; and the mourning made for a child

---

9  *Wayli*: cf. Spanish *baile* = dance. The activities of this group are highly ritualized in every respect. The girls have the place of standard-bearers in the troop, carrying flags and sacred images; they must also help the 'major' maintain discipline in the ranks.

Plate 4.1 *Wayli* marching to battle. The girl flag bearer is essential for the success of this sacred group of fighters.

who dies after the hair-cutting ceremony is of a different order from that for a baby.

However, notably absent in Laymi representation is the punitive element in the concept of repression that we use to express the process by which a baby is socialized. In Laymi thought the transition from the pre-social to the social is marked and made discontinuous by the two simple rituals of naming and hair-cutting, but there is no suggestion of 'crisis', with the associated notion of society imposing a particular identity on the individual.

## *Sexuality and representation*

In the theories of writers within the Lacanian tradition, female sexuality is seen as 'perverse', 'narcissistic', not fully repressed and hence in a state of nature.[10] In anthropological accounts, on the other hand, we often find emphasis on the polluting, dirty, dangerous and thus anti-social character of women's sexuality. The combination of menstruation and childbirth is given as justification for treating women as less than fully cultural by Ortner.

None of these characterizations are apparent in the way that Laymis represent female sexuality. Children grow up in an atmosphere in which there is constant reference to sexuality, and joking about sexual activity. Sexual experience comes with the assumption of adolescent status. There is no value attached to virginity and most people have a variety of experiences before they eventually get married. The initiation of sexual relations takes place when a girl is out herding; a young man who desires her and has some basis for believing his feelings are reciprocated will go out 'herding' too, often without even the pretence of taking any animals, dressed in his finest clothes and carrying his pipe or charango. Knowing looks are exchanged as he struts through the hamlet.

The act of seduction itself is a chase. The girl runs away and will not allow herself to be caught without a struggle. There is no exchange of gifts. Young people will try to steal articles of clothing from each other, a belt or coca-bag, or maybe even a hat or carrying cloth. To steal clothing is to show desire, and where there is reciprocal stealing there is an established relationship. There are no gifts from the man to the girl in return for sexual services, neither is stigma attached to a girl who gets pregnant. There is thus little of the asymmetry familiar from peasant societies in so many parts of the world, where ideologies of masculine virility are matched by the high value attached to passivity, chastity and modesty in women. In Laymi sexual encounters, the male is the 'aggressor' while the female runs away, but her flight is an active participation, and girls who are passive or immobile are thought foolish.

10   See the references in note 4 (above).

Cohabitation is based on a mutual decision of both parties. The girl elopes with her lover to his parents' home without warning any of her kin. Only when the liaison is a *fait accompli* will the new couple go to ask formal permission of the girl's parents with offerings of coca and alcohol. If their compatibility is established, they will complete the rituals of marriage about three years later. If not they will separate, again without any long-term stigma. After marriage, the union is for life.

While after marriage the restrictions on a woman's activity are far greater than those on her husband, this is not accompanied by a negative valuation of her sexuality. Menstruation, for example, far from being thought of as polluting or destructive, is said to be the moment at which she is most fertile. When a woman gives birth, she does so in her own house, and there is no ritual that marks either separation, cleansing or reintegration. This is not a strongly pro-natalist culture, and the measures taken by women to limit family size, far from being seen as threatening and destructive, are considered entirely proper. Neither women's sexuality, then, nor their procreative powers directly produce an ideology which categorizes them as closer to nature than men, or even as anti-social.

However, a clear opposition *is* made between the sexual activity of the unmarried, and that of a couple that is married, or at least established in cohabitation. The proper place for sexual activity between those not recognized as a couple is on the hillside, or down by a stream or river, all places classified as the wild. Conversely, the sexual activity of a couple takes place inside a house-building. Thus it is not *female* sexuality that is identified with the wild but sexual activity that is free and uncommitted. This is contrasted with sexuality which has been integrated into the complex series of social and economic ties that make of man and woman a household.[11]

In practical terms Laymi organization of sexuality gives little support to any classification of women as outside culture. Neither does it provide a clear-cut case of the exchange of women which for Lévi-Strauss is the moment at which culture is brought into being (1969). The active role of women argues against such an interpretation. And when Laymis give their own version of the institution of the incest taboo which inaugurated culture as they know it, they do not speak of men exchanging their sisters but of *all* people ending liaisons with their kin in favour of marrying out.

On the other hand, some writers have argued that the exchange of women should be understood at a more metaphorical level referring to

11    A similar identification between the sexual activity of the unmarried and the wild is found in Isbell (1978), and also in Albó (1973) and Carter (1977). However, in other respects their accounts are significantly different from mine.

symbolic aspects of gender relations.[12] If we accept this then perhaps at some level of analysis Laymi women are exchanged. In this virilocal society, women are to some extent under the control of their husbands and husbands' kin. Thus a woman who goes to live with her husband and his kin should be obedient to their wishes, particularly towards the husband and his mother. Although within the nuclear household the relationship between spouses is one of complementarity, and women have a major voice in all decisions, nonetheless it is the husband who represents the household in the community as a whole. A woman's access to land in this system of agnatic inheritance is normally through either her male kin or her husband. The most overt expression of men's control over women is the physical violence which most men from time to time use towards their wives.

The affinal relationship is typified as that between brothers-in-law.[13] Marriage or cohabitation is embarked on by mutual consent of the couple concerned, but the term used in Aymara speaks of the man 'stealing' the woman from her home (*warmi suwaña*). This imagery is confirmed in the outrage that must be displayed by the girl's male kin against the 'robber' who has taken away their sister/daughter. The paradoxical nature of this representation, given that the girl herself is party to the 'crime', would seem to mediate the contradiction between the close relations of lifelong warmth and cooperation that Laymis see as especially proper between a sister and brother, and the need for exogamy. A man is bound to avenge his sister for the supposed outrage upon her, and will sometimes attack his brother-in-law during the marriage ritual itself. Certainly in later years he must repay any ill-treatment of his sister by her husband by fighting the man.

Seen in this light, then, women may be 'signs' in the kinship system. While they are not objects of exchange, they are the mediating links in a structure of power that is fought out between men. However, if this is the mythical starting-point of 'culture', as Lévi-Strauss argues, then the Laymis certainly attach different value to the term. In their myths, the time before the incest taboo was one of plenty, in which all their favourite food grew ready-prepared around them, and clothing was produced miraculously from the earth, a veritable golden age in which work was unnecessary.

For those working within the Lacanian tradition, Lévi-Strauss' theory of the exchange of women has been used not only at a social level, but also symbolically to interpret the way the individual child enters into culture.[14] In this reading, culture is phallocentric by definition, and while

12 See Rubin (1975:176). This is clearly the way in which Lacan has read Lévi-Strauss' theory of kinship (see above, note 3).
13 See Harris (1978b) for an account of the relationship between brothers-in-law.
14 Apart from references already cited, Mitchell (1974) and Cowie

biological essentialism in any form is rejected, men's domination of the symbolic order is said to be more complete than that of women. In Laymi representation, for all the egalitarian sexual ideology, with its complementary division of labour, for all the organization of sexuality around a principle of balanced reciprocity, there are also phallocentric elements.

In particular these coalesce around the imagery of power and strength. A person who has performed some action out of the ordinary is said to have a big penis (Aym: *jach'a alluni*), and on a few occasions I heard this term used of women. In general to call somebody a 'real man' (Aym: *suma chacha*) is a term of approbation; conversely to call somebody a woman in a certain tone of voice is an insult. In fact, the standard insult hurled by men at each other when fighting is 'woman' or 'whore' (Aym: *q'incha warmi*). Women employ these terms as well as men, and even though women are far from sparing in their disparaging comments about men in general and their husbands in particular, it is simply not possible to insult somebody by calling him or her a man.

## Spirits and the wild

Laymi society is bounded by the mountain peaks known locally as *kumprira* (cf. Sp. *cumbre* = peak), which dominate not only the landscape but also guard over and influence their lives. They are the source of weather, of hail, thunder and rain. They are sacred and powerful places and also the source of life. They are simultaneously guardians and malevolent beings, bringers of fertility and health but equally disaster and illness. They protect the flocks who graze on the mountainsides, but the fox and mountain cat and the rapacious condor who all prey on the flocks are also their creatures.

Each unit of landholding has its tutelary deity known as *sänku*, located in a spot where lightning is reported to have killed an animal from the flock, or, more rarely, a human being. As such they are closely connected with the *kumprira* who send the lightning, and are often high on the mountainside above the level of cultivation. *Sänku* must be ritually 'made good' every three years with offerings similar to those given in many rituals to the *kumpriras*. The *sänku* are frequently the cause of illness.

Not all *sänku* are owned or associated with particular land-holdings: in fact those which have not been made good by ritual offerings and thereby incorporated into the social order, known as *muru sänku*, are the ones that most commonly cause illness and bad luck. The word *muru* signifies something maimed or defective (Bertonio 1612) and it is also used of a baby that dies before it is ritually named with salt and water. The *muru sänku*

(1978) have useful discussions on the relationship of Lacan's thought to Lévi-Strauss.

are thus non-socialized, unresponsive to human manipulation; they are hungry and threatening in an apparently random way.

Along with a host of other tutelary beings with greater or lesser degrees of individuation is a general category of *saxranaka*, evil ones also known by the Spanish-derived term *yawlu* (Sp. *diablo* = devil), who pervade the world outside cultivated and inhabited space. These evil ones are the direct agents of the illness and misfortune sent by the *kumprira* or the *sänku*, and it is to them that the ritual specialists speak when they perform a curing ritual. They inhabit particularly wild places, gullies, rocks, waterfalls, which human beings avoid where possible.

The *condenados*, the spirits of those who have committed some form of incest, are associated with the evil ones in the threat they pose to human society. They bring illness, eat babies, and, both in their habitat, the open mountainside, and in the stones and cactus that are tied to their feet, they are clearly identified with the wild. The bodies of *muru wawa*, babies who die before being named, belong to the *kumprira* themselves. If these are not buried outside the cemetery for the mountains to eat, hail will ruin the crops.

Associated with these beings are the spirits of the dead, known as ghosts (*amaya*). It is significant that the Aymara term for grandfather/ ancestor (*achachila*) is used also for the mountain deities. Ghosts and ancestors are welcomed back into society at the feast of sowing in November, and remain until harvest when they are ritually dispatched at the feast of Carnival (Feb.–March). They are seen as a source of fertility, and fertility in Laymi ritual is often represented as the wild. In ritual libations and in the harvest festival at Carnival, fertility is represented by wild flowers (see plate 4.2). In the songs accompanying marriage rituals, it is especially trees, again uncultivated, that are brought to represent the fertility of the new couple (Harris, 1978b). At Carnival, the ancestors are impersonated by men and women who dress up in black goatskins, and carry huge bundles of wild flowers and plants in bundles on their backs, dancing drunkenly round the village. The spirits of the dead can be a threat as well as a source of increase. Anybody who walks alone at Carnival is liable to be carried off by them, and they are known as evil ones (*saxra*), and devils (*yawlus*), in a way that clearly identifies them with the beings described above. In Laymi terms all these 'supernatural' beings belong to the 'evil sphere' (*saxra parti*) which is defined in contrast to 'our sphere' (*jiwas parti*).[15]

When people die, they have to cross the *sirqa*, the water that surrounds the world, in order to reach the land of the dead. The same word, *sirqa*, is used to designate those animals that are not domesticated, that do not

---

15  As Tschopik emphasizes, not all 'evil ones' are positively malevolent, for example the spirit-guardians of the house are not (1951:189).

Plate 4.2  A sponsor of Carnival, bedecked with wild flowers, blowing a horn to the mountain spirits in celebration of harvest.

belong within human space. Whether *sirqa* is represented as the non-domesticated, or as water surrounding the earth, it is a concept that unites death with that which is non-domesticated, outside of human society.

Evil ones are not only associated with fertility but also with musical creation. In certain gullies, or by waterfalls, are places known as *sirina*. These places give their tunes to those who leave their musical instruments there at night with offerings to the *sirina*, and the tune is communicated either in a dream to the owner of the instrument, or directly through the instrument which plays in a new way. Since it is men who own the instruments it is they who are the main recipients of this wild source of creativity.

Indeed the spirit world poses a threat to women. They should never walk alone in the night, for this time belongs to the evil ones. A woman should not sleep alone either, for the devils, and particularly a newly-dead ghost, will come to her in the night and make her pregnant. When an evil one impregnates a woman, the baby that is born is only half, the left half, and has feet like a dog. Again, a woman cannot remain in the cemetery while a corpse is buried, since she is particularly vulnerable to being carried off to the land of the dead. It is because of this vulnerability also that after a curing ritual has taken place, it is always men who must take out to the mountainside the ritual items that have been used to cleanse and protect the patient, so that the devils may eat these items instead of 'eating' the ill person. For the same reason it is in general only men who are strong enough to become *wayuri*, the spirit medium who is able to speak to the evil ones, the mountain deities and all the other beings of the night.

It is important to note that the restrictions placed upon Laymi women, for example that they cannot walk alone at night, are expressed in terms of their vulnerability to these spirits of the wild who are 'evil' and, especially, will make them pregnant. I never heard of women's much more practical vulnerability to molestation by human men mentioned as the reason for their restricted mobility. At the same time it *is* their physiological specialization as reproducers that is seen as the source of their weakness. Thus, living in a space surrounded by threatening forces, which can bring illness, death, or disaster to anyone, man and woman alike, but which are also the source of fertility and creativity, Laymis see women as afraid of these forces. Thence men, who are more able to confront them, command the few points of power within the social structure. I heard it said on several occasions that the reason for the complete absence of women from the formal decision-making process was because there were certain community tasks, particularly that of messenger, that they could not perform since they could not travel by night.[16]

16  While this view seems at first sight incompatible with my earlier assertion that women's exclusion from full political participation is due to their inability to speak, in fact this point refers to a different

Various commentators have noted an opposition between the 'civilized' village at a moderate altitude, and the 'savage' highlands dominated by the powerful mountain-spirits (Fioravanti-Molinié 1975; Isbell 1978; Platt 1978). The former two report the association of high pastures and mountain peaks with incest, both the act itself and as the dwelling-place of those who have committed incest. Fioravanti-Molinié indeed explicitly contrasts the civilized lower inhabited world with the savage highlands in terms of culture and nature (pp. 55–6). Few Laymis speak Spanish and thus would not use terms such as *civilizado* or *salvaje* (wild) which are commonplace amongst Spanish speakers both rural and urban. Nonetheless the spirit of Laymi cosmology has undoubtedly been affected by Christian concepts of 'civilization'.

There is a myth concerning two brothers, Rawanitu and Kristianu: the former died while the latter survived and 'that is why we are all Christians today while the devils went underground'. Rawanitu appears to derive from the Spanish word *rabano* (a radish, i.e. a bitter-tasting root); Kristianu is the Aymara form of Christian. Laymis, then, contrast themselves as Christians with the telluric devils, but also recognize their kinship with these beings. The task of reconstructing the cataclysmic moment in which the European order subjugated that of the Andes obviously requires an understanding of the clash of cosmologies.[17] However, Laymi religion suggests not only that Christian domination produced a major rupture with local deities who were metaphorically, and in many cases literally, pushed underground, but that possibly also the imposition of Inka state religion with compulsory worship of the sun-god Inti may itself have produced a comparable rupture in indigenous cosmology.[18] Inti is today the highest deity worshipped by the Laymis, identified both with the sun itself, known as 'our father', with the Host in the Catholic mass, and with the Monstrance used in benediction.

Inti is also God (*Tyusa* from the Spanish *Dios*: god) and is a more abstract deity than the spirits described above. He is the source of life and vigour, he watches over humans and punishes misdemeanours, but as the symbol of moral order, not with the all-too-human attributes of the devils. The moon is the wife of the sun and together with the saints and the 'miracles' they belong to 'god's sphere' (*Tyusa parti*) which is contrasted with the 'evil sphere' and with 'our sphere' mentioned already. 'God's sphere' is worshipped by day and offered masses and incense, while the

aspect of political participation: to mobility rather than to the assembly.
17  See Wachtel (1977), and Duviols (1971).
18  Tschopik (1951) describes the sun as a remote deity, although it is in principle the head of the Aymara pantheon, and implies that it has been brought in from outside. Garcilaso de la Vega (1960) gives many accounts of the Inka imposition of sun-worship.

'evil sphere' is worshipped by night with offerings of dried animal fetuses and an aromatic plant named *q'uwa*, which is burnt to accompany all invocations to devils.

However, in spite of the apparent clarity of these categories, there are many ambiguities which argue caution in assigning classifications of nature and culture. For example, the moon is said to be wife of the sun-god but her time is the night which is also the time of the 'devils'. She is associated with silver and thence money, which in libations are called 'like the moon' (*p"axsi'ma*); but silver comes from the ground, and mines are the domain of another devil (*tiu*) who is associated with mountain spirits.

We thus have seen a series of identifications made in Laymi symbolic thought:

| | | |
|---|---|---|
| human : wild | :: | day : night |
| day : night | :: | sun : moon |
| sun : moon | :: | male : female |

On the other hand, while syllogistic thought might proceed to deduce that the wild is therefore identified as female, I found no indication that Laymis themselves made this step. To apply 'logical' procedures in this case is to forget that what are being compared are complex concepts, and that in each identification it is different and specific characteristics of these phenomena that are selected for comparison.

The mountains also have their female counterpart, the earth mother or *Pachamama* who is the incarnation of space and time.[19] *Pachamama*, wife of the mountain peaks, shares the night-time offerings made to them, and she too is invoked by the spirit medium. But she also is ambiguous for she is cultivated land and thus mediates between inhabited space and the wild mountain-tops. A ritual indication of this ambivalent status is that *Pachamama* can also receive daylight offerings of incense during the agricultural cycle, and yet as I noted these are characteristic of 'god's sphere'.

Viewed in this way it might be argued that Laymi cosmology presents us with two opposed categories of supernatural being, in both of which the male term incarnates the contrasted properties in their most specific form, while the female term is a mediator. In the case of 'god's sphere' the moon is wife to the sun-god, but is also identified with the night and the silver-mines that are the domain of devils. In the case of the 'evil sphere' the *Pachamama* is both associated with the mountain peaks and the wild and yet is cultivated and worshipped in the way proper to 'god's sphere'. Nevertheless, it would again be inaccurate to deduce that the male

19  Cf. Bertonio (1612) for the significance of the word *pacha* in Aymara. However male/female bifurcation occurs also within the class of male mountains, such that some are seen as 'marked' and superior (the Aymara term is *mallku*), and others as lesser and female (Aym: *t'alya*). See Martinez (1976:12), also Platt (1978:1093).

|       | evil sphere | god's sphere |
| ----- | ----------- | ------------ |
| night | *kumprira*  | moon         |
| day   | *Pachamama* | Sun          |

terms are more clear-cut and bounded, the female terms more ambiguous, in any absolute sense. Even the mountain peaks which are identified categorically with the wild have their 'domesticated' aspect, in that they are the guardians of the flocks, and thus through their own creatures provide meat, wool, milk, and beasts of burden, to humankind.

From another perspective there are further ambiguities. In Laymi categories there is a clear-cut distinction between people (*jaqi*), and outsiders (*q'ara*). 'People' includes all who share Indian culture, which is identified particularly in terms of clothing and music, and also of food and language. The term *q'ara*, which includes not only whites and *mestizos* but also those born as people who have rejected Indian culture in favour of urban ways of life, means literally naked. Thus while the Laymis contrast themselves as Christians with the world of devils, they also subtly but continuously relegate those who are the source of Christianity to the status of undressed and thus not fully cultural.[20] This attribution goes together with many dark rumours about how the *q'aras* are witches, commit incest, or eat donkey and dog flesh (non-food).

Lévi-Strauss comments on the close relationship between the natural and the supernatural (1977:320). Nature is a way for humans to approach the supernatural, but conversely the supernatural is a way in which natural forces are humanized, so that they are named and brought into a chain of signification, and become part of a communication system by which human beings can manipulate the unpredictable desires and moods of the wild. To acknowledge this is not to assign a fixed meaning or value to nature and the wild. Both these concepts, and the manifestations that the ethnographer can identify with them, are polysemic. Nonetheless as personifications, as representations, of the wild, they are to a large extent discontinuous and discrete in their meanings.

On the other hand, human society is built from given raw materials. For the Laymis, what stands for and embodies their being-within-culture is primarily their distinctive clothing, their music, food, ritual and the ordered space within which they live, that is to say the unique way that they order their environment. In the sense that clothing is made from raw wool, and food is cooked, the cultural is a transitive, rather than a discontinuous and discrete category. It has frequently been pointed out that women are seen

20  Isbell (1978:60−1) notes a similar representation. Cf. also Ardener's discussion of the 'fortuitous overlap of the old wild and the urban jungle' (1975:13).

as primary agents of the creation of culture in this sense, through the multifarious transformation activities by which raw materials become the symbols of culture. Laymi women too cook, weave, socialize and care for young children, but Laymis do not therefore think of women as being closer to the wild or to anything we mean by the term 'nature'. In explaining the absence of such representation it is important to bear in mind that in the production of food and clothing the 'nature' thus transformed is in fact highly domesticated. The very fields cultivated today were almost certainly under cultivation before the Spanish conquest,[21] and the domestication of the major cultigens and animals precedes that by millennia. This is in contrast to societies based on shifting cultivation and the direct appropriation of undomesticated products, from which the greater part of the anthropological literature on nature and culture has stemmed. Laymi secular domestication and transformation of nature through agriculture is the basis for the cosmological ambiguity of the *Pachamama*, the earth mother. Also of significance is the belief that the ancestors watch over the agricultural cycle. They too are a transitive category, having crossed the water surrounding the known world and entered into the sphere of the devils and thus the wild.

## The union of female and male

The very organization of the household and its importance within Laymi representation is a further reason why Laymis do not make great symbolic use of women's transformational activities nor of their reproductive capacity to classify them as closer to nature than men. Human beings are in one sense brought into culture through the ritual of naming with salt and water that takes place soon after birth. In another sense they can be said to acquire culture only as they learn to speak. In still another sense they become fully cultural only when they marry. There is no absolute criterion for distinguishing the pre-social from the social. Again, while all spirits of the dead are creatures of the night, associated with the devils and thus in a sense with nature, there are differences of degree. The ghosts of those who committed incest, for example, are entirely antithetical to human society. But there is also a distinction made between those who die unmarried and those who are married. The former are interred with a symbolic companion for the after-life, a hen for a man and a cock for a woman. They have a hard journey to the land of the dead, since the road they must travel is over the thorn bushes by night, while the souls of married people are said to travel by day on cleared pathways. Roads and paths are an illustrative case of social intrusion into the wild, since they must pass over the mountains and across the rivers in order

21   Archivo Nacional de Bolivia, Sucre; Tierras e Indios 149 (1592).

to provide the communicating link between different areas of inhabited space.

Within this representation, married souls are seen as more social beings than the unmarried. Marriage is the basis of the nuclear household which is the unit of production and consumption in many aspects of Laymi economy. Marriage is the domestication of sexuality, the bringing of sexual activity into the inhabited community. It is the union of two pre-viously unrelated persons, the joining of what was discrete. The new household is in a very real sense a unit, a unity. The joining of male property and female property, and the cooperation between wife and husband that is structured by the sexual division of labour give it a certain independence vis-à-vis other similar units.

Many writers, Ortner included, have argued that women's primary identification with the household is antithetical to the interests of the wider society. While one can substantiate this claim to some degree in the Laymi case, it is not correct to claim in pursuit of this argument that the household, and the individual woman within it, is an anti-social force against a solidary group of males who embody society or culture. On the contrary, Laymi representation identifies the individual household, and the married couple that forms its core, with the whole ethnic group con-ceived spatially. Thus the tuber-producing highlands and the more temper-ate valleys where maize is grown are respectively female and male, and are also seen as the kitchen and the storehouse of which each Laymi house-hold is made up.[22]

## The power of signs

I noted at the outset that writers such as de Beauvoir and Ortner make use of a wide variety of material in constructing their image of the female, and my description of Laymi gender organization too has drawn on hetero-geneous elements to construct a necessarily impressionistic account. How-ever, while I have included the sexual division of labour, household struc-ture, the social organization of marriage and sexuality in my discussion I have been above all concerned with representations: with how the attrib-utes of masculinity and femininity, the proper behaviour of men and women, are constructed within Laymi culture. Though I have not con-sidered the substance of gender relations systematically, it is impossible to separate a discussion of male and female as symbols from the material practices in which men and women relate to each other.

It is on the issue of the categories of female and male, nature and cul-ture as existing within particular systems of representation, that Ortner's argument seems at its weakest. While she is careful to say at the beginning

22   This section is a summary of the argument of Harris (1978a).

of her essay that she is dealing with conceptual categories, she then slides into unargued assumptions about the universal implications of certain physiological and physiology-related characteristics. That is, she moves from empirical observations to assertions concerning their universal meaning, and the admission that these meanings may be unconscious (1974:75) does little to clarify her argument.

The issue revolves around whether, or to what degree, one is to treat systems of representation as composed of signs which are arbitrary in themselves; whether the relationship between signifier and signified, to use Saussure's classic distinction, is conventional or motivated. For de Saussure the arbitrary, conventional nature of the sign was a fundamental principle, in that meaning was constructed not by the relationship of each signifier to a signified, but by the positioning of each sign within an entire signifying system. The structuralist tradition, which owes so much to his ideas, is in principle committed to the conventional basis of representation. In Lévi-Strauss' work a classic, and in this context apposite, example of this commitment relates to the exchange of women. For him, the elementary structures of kinship are a kind of language (1972:61) in which women operate as the 'words'. True to his analogy he asserts that women's place as signs exchanged by men does not imply anything about their material position in society, and even suggests that there is no theoretical reason why it should not be women that exchange men rather than vice versa (stating, however, that this is empirically never the case).

A similar commitment is found in Lacan's assertion of the neutrality of the phallus as signifier;[23] and also in Ardener's protestation that his use of terms such as culture and the wild have no value-laden connotations.[24] But one is left with the feeling that some elaborate conjuring trick has been played. Within linguistics itself a recognition of the arbitrary *phonetic* basis to words has been complemented by the establishment of other levels of meaning, in which the operations of condensation and displacement, of metaphor and metonymy, are far from arbitrary.[25] Thus meaning is rarely, if ever, an innocent process of denotation, but depends on a whole series of other meanings, connotations and structures of a given social order. If this is true of language itself, then it is *a fortiori* true of other systems of meaning whose constituent units are not arbitrary phonemes. Myths, for example, are not merely systems of communication; they are also charters, to use Malinowski's term, which fix individuals and groups in particular social positions.

Ortner, on the other hand, errs in the opposite direction. For her the

23  Cf. Burniston, Mort and Weedon (1978:116–17).
24  In his reply to the criticisms of Mathieu, Ardener states: 'for many of us, a position "in the wild" . . . still has no negative connotations. I am quite prepared to be defined as "nature" by Mathieu' (1975:25).
25  See particularly Jakobson (1962).

representation of nature and culture appear to be anything but arbitrary, and in her portrayal of women she assigns a series of essential character- istics which have a single value, a fixed meaning. Her argument continually asserts a necessary and univocal relationship between signifier and signified, when clearly the relationship is more complicated. Woman and man, nature and culture are neither entirely arbitrary and neutral as signs, nor are they fixed and universal in their meaning. While, as Ardener suggests, nature is a category which gives the illusion of being 'walkable into' and is thus endowed with a spurious air of objectivity, this objectivity in fact derives from the way that such concepts are 'naturalized' within our own signifying practice, as other contributions to this volume have dis- cussed.

In a previous article I argued that a dominant focus of Laymi represen- tations of male and female was the married couple as complementary unity (Harris 1978a). Here I have suggested that the married couple is the embodiment of society itself, and is contrasted to unmarried people who in certain respects are relegated to the wild. Given that in these represen- tations it is the opposition unmarried:married that is assimilated to that between the wild and the fully cultural, Ortner's thesis is clearly not supported by the Laymi case at this level of representation.

However, to restrict oneself to the analysis of the ways that male and female *as symbols* are brought into relationship with the categories that most closely approximate to Ortner's use of nature and culture is to miss out some of the most interesting questions. In practice most writers on this subject are also concerned with the ways that women and men as *social beings* stand in relationship to these categories. In the case of the Laymis this aspect is important since there is relatively little symbolic elaboration of different characteristics assigned to each sex. In particular I have suggested ways in which women and men might be said to have a different relationship to the symbolic as such, and in doing so I have drawn on the work of writers using Lacan's theories.

Starting from very different premises, Ardener put forward a suggestively similar hypothesis, that the conceptual models used by women of their social world are not bounded in the same ways as those of men and that since male structures prevail, women are muted and inarticulate relative to men (1972; 1975).

Laymi culture uses command over language to define social being, and in certain key respects Laymis perceive women as standing outside language in that they cannot participate directly in the discourse of power, whether over other men, other communities, or over the spirit world. In the case of weaving symbolism men seem to have a more ready command over meta- language than do women. In linguistic usage too there are some indications of an explicit phallocentrism. All these observations provide some support for the Lacanian position; however, to move from this to equate culture as such with *certain forms* of language and thus to locate women as outside culture is not justified.

In weaving, women's production of symbolism is primarily plastic; however, in song it is precisely symbolic *language* that women create. Song and dance are necessary accompaniments to all ritual occasions, but remain separate from ritual action itself. While the language of native Andean song has been little analysed, central themes involve the celebration of sexuality and fertility, and sexual joking. There is little direct invocation of the spirit world, to which ritual action is addressed. In both cases women typically have a different relationship with the symbolic from that of men but it is not adequate to characterize women's relationship as an absence, as less complete than men's.

And what of the spirit world itself? Certain ambiguities become clear in representations of non-human forces. These representations are shared by all, by both men and women, and at least one woman must participate in all ritual sequences, usually as one of the married couple that sponsors the ritual. There is no system of sex-specific rituals or ritual secrets. However it is also true that men's participation in ritual and in the pouring of libations is far greater than that of women. Men's presence is expected and necessary, and while the participation of large numbers of women is not excluded, neither is it actively encouraged.[26]

If we consider the spirits of the wild themselves, it becomes apparent that they are primarily represented as male, even though it is a principle of Andean cosmology that all supernatural beings have a counterpart, a spouse of the opposite sex. The mountain peaks are male, even though within this male category there are subdivisions of male and female *kumpriras*. The *sänku*, the tutelary spirits that inhabit the spots where lightning has struck, are also primarily male. They too have a female counterpart, vague in definition, of which there are far fewer than the male *sänku*. The female counterpart is known as *llant'u*, which means literally shadow, and while the *llant'u* too has spatial location it is rarely clear exactly where it is. General opinion among Laymis whom I questioned was that the *llant'u* originates merely in order that the male *sänku* should have a spouse.

In the case of ghosts and ancestors, there are clearly females as well as males but, nonetheless, in a system where land is transmitted agnatically, male forebears are remembered and identified more than female. The general category of devils and evil ones again is in principle composed of both male and female, and a few devils are explicitly female. The great majority, however, are implicitly male in conceptualization, and this obviously accords with the threat they pose to (human) women.

---

26  While this is the case for ritual activity and especially ritual drinking, feasting is a moment in ritual when the whole community's presence is enjoined, including women and children.

Women and men as social actors do then stand in different relations to the wild, women as more vulnerable to it, men more in the position of communicators, of mediators with the wild, though of course both sexes are vulnerable to the devils as bringers of illness. In practice it is men too who mediate more than women with the outside world, with the urban world of *q'aras* whom Laymis also classify as behaving in non-social ways. However to deduce from this that men are closer to the wild than are women, or that the wild is conceived as male in any simple sense would be to ignore the fact that the supreme representative of the moral order, the sun, is also seen as male. The impossibility of classifying male and female in terms of nature and culture is highlighted by the central position of domesticated plants and animals, of *Pachamama*, the earth that is cultivated, in Laymi ritual and cosmology. The themes of fertility and abundance, of growth and reproduction, have a central place in ritual. The 'wild' mountain tops are the spouse of the cultivated earth and the guardians of domesticated as well as wild animals, and the 'domesticated' sexuality of the married couple that plays a central part in ritual represents the increase on which Laymi economy depends.

I have used a variety of terms and images in order to elucidate the complexity of how society is constructed by the Laymis, and it is clear that to reduce language, the wild, inhabited and cultivated space, the married and the unmarried, music and spirits, to a single tabular form of manifestations of a nature:culture opposition would be to do violence to 'oral complexity' in the interests of 'graphic simplicity' (cf. Goody 1977:70). It is also important to note that what I have said here about the different relationships of Laymi men and women to the symbolic is not to be confused with an essentialist position by which the attributes of women and men are seen as determined by physiology. There are women who do travel alone at night. In the case of ritual specialists who talk to the devils, Laymis were most insistent that it was possible for women too to hold this position (although I never met one who did), and of course most men are afraid of the devils as well. Again it is important to reiterate the significance of the life-cycle. Women and men are not pre-given, eternal categories but change their relationship to the symbolic in the course of their lives.

Nonetheless, to take into account the changing definitions of the male and the female is also to recognize that the harnessing of women's sexuality within marriage is also the point at which their lives become most restricted, while for men it is the point at which as householders they become fully integrated into the structures of community decision making. I argued earlier that the language of power is one to which men have privileged access, and it is this aspect which can perhaps most easily be selected as a universal feature of gender relations. But as, for example, MacCormack argues (chapters 1 and 5), this putative universality is by no means self-evident, and, even in the Laymi case, to identify certain structures of masculine dominance cannot of itself lead to the conclusion that culture in its entirety is the domain of men. This would be to make the mistake in Bourdieu's words, of privileging 'the *structure* of signs, that is, the relations between them, at the expense of their *practical functions*, which are never reducible, as structuralism tacitly assumes, to functions of communication or knowledge' (1977:24). Jordanova (chapter 3) emphasizes the need to distinguish clearly issues of value (good/bad) from those of control (sub/superordination). In Laymi life, today at any rate, the structures of male power are very limited. They are cross-cut by a household organization that separates men and unites each with his wife, and the region that has been dominated for centuries by external state structures so that it would be misleading not to take into account the forms of political control that are outside any control of the Laymis themselves. Just as the 'dominant code' in Ardener's terms 'universalizes' its own vision of the world and is thus unable to hear a muted code, so it is all too easy for anthropologists using the dominant discourse of European culture to universalize our own categories of male and female, nature and culture, and thus render ourselves deaf to alternative ways of structuring the world.

## References cited

Albó, Xavier, 1973. *Esposos, suegros y padrinos entre los aymaras*, Cuadernos de Investigación CIPCA, no. 1, La Paz.

Ardener, E., 1972. 'Belief and the problem of women', *The Interpretation of Ritual*, ed. J. La Fontaine, London: Tavistock.

1975. 'The problem revisited', *Perceiving Women*, ed. S. Ardener, London: Dent.

Badcock, C.R., 1975. *Lévi-Strauss. Structuralism and sociological theory.* London: Hutchinson.

Bertonio, Ludovico, 1612. *Vocabulario de la lengua aymara*, reprinted La Paz, 1956.

Bourdieu, P., 1977. *Outline of a theory of practice*, Cambridge studies in social anthropology 16, Cambridge: Univ. Press.

Burniston, S., Mort, F. & Weedon, C., 1978. 'Psychoanalysis and the cultural acquisition of sexuality and subjectivity', *Women take issue. Aspects of women's subordination.* Women's studies group, Centre for Contemporary Cultural Studies. London: Hutchinson.

Carter, W., 1977. 'Trial marriage in the Andes?', *Andean kinship and marriage*, ed. R. Bolton & E. Mayer, American Anthropological Association special publication 7, Washington.

Cereceda, V., 1978. 'Sémiologie des tissus andins: les *talegas* de Isluga', *Annales: Economies Sociétés Civilisations*, 33e année, no. 5–7, 1017–35.

Coward, R., & Ellis, J., 1977. *Language and Materialism.* London: Routledge and Kegan Paul.

Cowie, E., 1978. 'Woman as sign', *m/f* 1, 49–63.

de Beauvoir, S., 1972 [1949]. *The Second Sex*. London: Penguin.

Duviols, P., 1971. *La lutte contre les religions autochthones*, Trav. Inst. Fr. des Etudes Andines, 13, Lima.

Fioravanti-Molinié, A., 1975. 'Contribution a l'étude des sociétés étagées des Andes: la vallée de Yucay', *Etudes Rurales*, 57, 35–9.

Garcilaso de la Vega, Inca, 1960 (1609). *Primera parte de los Comentarios Reales*, Biblioteca de Autores Españoles, vol. 133, Madrid.

Goody, J., 1977. *The domestication of the savage mind*. Cambridge: Univ. Press.

Harris, O., 1978a. 'Complementarity and conflict: An Andean view of women and men', *Sex and age as principles of social differentiation*, ed. J. La Fontaine, ASA 17, London: Academic Press.

　　1978b. 'De l'asymétrie au triangle. Transformations symboliques au nord de Potosí', *Annales. Economies Sociétés Civilisations*, 33e année, no. 5–6, 1108–25.

Irigaray, L., 1977. 'Women's exile', *Ideology and Consciousness*, 1, 62–76.

Isbell, B.J., 1978. *To defend ourselves: Ecology and ritual in an Andean village*, Austin: University of Texas Press.

Jacobson, R., 1962. *Selected Writings*. The Hague: Mouton.

Kristeva, J., 1977. *About Chinese women*. London: M. Boyars.

Lacan, J., 1977a. *Ecrits*. London: Tavistock.

　　1977b. *The four fundamental concepts of psycho-analysis*. Harmondsworth: Penguin.

Leach, E., 1965. 'C. Lévi-Strauss — anthropologist and philosopher', *New Left Review*, 34, 12–27.

Lévi-Strauss, C., 1969. *The elementary structures of kinship*. London: Eyre & Spottiswoode.

　　1972. *Structural Anthropology*. London: Penguin.

　　1977. *Structural Anthropology II*. London: Allen Lane.

Lipshitz, S. (ed.), 1978. *Tearing the Veil. Essays on Femininity*. London: Routledge and Kegan Paul.

Macey, D., 1978. 'Review article: Jacques Lacan', *Ideology & Consciousness*, 4, 113–28.

Martinez, G., 1976. *El sistema de los uywiris en Isluga*. Centro Isluga de invest. andinas, Publ. 1, Isluga.

Mitchell, J., 1974. *Psychoanalysis and Feminism*. London: Allen Lane.

Montrelay, M., 1978. 'Inquiry into femininity', *m/f*, 1, 83–101.

Ortner, S., 1974. 'Is female to male as nature is to culture?', *Woman, culture, and society*, ed. M. Rosaldo & L. Lamphere, Stanford University Press.

Platt, T., 1978. 'Symétries en miroir. Le concept de *yanantin* chez les Macha de Bolivia', *Annales. Economies Sociétés Civilisations*, 33e année, no. 5–6, 1–81–1107.

Rubin, G., 1975. 'The traffic in women: notes on the "political economy" of sex', *Toward an anthropology of women*, ed. R. Reiter, New York & London: Monthly Review.

Tschopik, H., 1951. *The Aymara of Chucuito, Peru*, Anthropological Papers of the American Museum of Natural History, vol. 44, pt. 2, New York.

Wachtel, N., 1977. *The vision of the vanquished*. Sussex: Harvester.

# 5    Proto-social to adult: a Sherbro transformation

CAROL P. MacCORMACK

People who live along the Sherbro coast of Sierra Leone share assumptions which are similar to structuralist assumptions about nature and culture. They talk a great deal about children who do not have 'sense' and who need 'training'. The animal-like greed and wilfulness of children must be curbed as they are guided away from a proto-social to a fully social state. In initiation ritual adult society dramatically displays symbols which manifest concepts of rule-bound human behaviour. Humanness is specifically contrasted with animalness, rule-bound cooperativeness (whiteness) contrasted with wilfulness (blackness). That is not to say all individualism is suppressed. The personality shines forth in an adult's style of dancing, dressing, and even in one's flair for cutting rice in the fields. But in broad view, thought in this Sherbro area of West Africa stands in clear contrast to the Mount Hagen area of Papua New Guinea. In the latter, children are not seen as needing training into adulthood from a pre-social state, and society is not conceived of as enforcing a set of controls over and against the individual (see chapter 8).

If nature and culture are useful categories with which to think in the Sherbro country, so are male and female. But here their folk model clearly parts company with structuralist assumptions. There is a sexual division of labour in procreation and in productive tasks. Adolescent males, during their liminal period in initiation rites, demonstrate masculine farming skills and other male skills such as weaving cloth. Adolescent females demonstrate mastery of feminine farming skills and spin cotton. Female spinning and male weaving aptly symbolize gender interdependence in the division of labour. Both men and women, after initiation, are designated 'those who may procreate', and are publically recognized as having a minimal level of 'adeptness' in adult roles. Like the Laymis of Bolivia (see chapter 4), the fully cultural is the unity of adult male and female in a domestic unit capable of producing goods and services and physically reproducing cognatic descent groups. The Sherbro folk model presents the analogy that nature is to culture as children are to initiated and married adults. It stresses gender interdependency rather than male domination.

The domestic—political opposition has been assumed by some to be universally associated with nature, culture and gender (Rosaldo 1974):

nature     :     culture
female     :     male
domestic   :     political

But Sherbro perceptions and actual practices deny the validity of this metaphoric set. Both men and women work within the domestic compound where women, for example, spin cotton, daub mud house walls, and train children. Complementarily, men weave, thatch house roofs and train children. Outside the domestic compound both men and women farm, market produce, exchange goods and services to build social networks, and mature to be respected elders in control of communal land and political offices (MacCormack 1972; 1974; 1978; 1979). Men and women alike become revered ancestors of cognatic descent groups. They are 'fed' and named in ancestral ceremonies and are asked to confer health and fertility on the people and on the land. There is social ranking, but not on a male—female axis. The more salient contrasts are junior—elder, and commoner—aristocrat. Some cognatic descent groups originated with pioneering or conquering individuals who, historically, have been females as well as males. Sherbro descent groups bear the name of their founder, those beginning with Ya (mother) originating with a woman, those beginning with Ba (father) originating with a man. Descendants of founders have rights to land and high office that descendants of clients and slaves do not have (MacCormack 1977).

## Geographical and political setting

Kagboro and Timdel Chiefdoms cover an area of about 40 miles along the Sherbro coast of southern Sierra Leone, and extend inland about 40 miles. The low-lying topography seldom exceeds 50 feet in elevation, is frequently cut by broad tidal rivers, and has vast areas of swamp. Population density is less than 100 people per square mile. Malaria and a broad range of other tropical diseases are endemic. On average, women at the end of their reproductive span have lost more than half of the children they have borne.

The economy is based on shallow water fishing and hoe cultivation of rice and other crops. The soil along the coast is sandy and leached of nutrients by 180 inches annual rainfall. In slightly elevated areas the earth is a fragile tropical lateritic soil. In both types of soil, only one rice crop can be harvested before the soil must be left fallow for from 6 to 15 years. That amount of time is necessary for the land to recover enough fertility to yield another single upland rice crop. People are now shifting to the cultivation of watery black organic mud in the swamps, but it is difficult, unpleasant work, with risk of schistosomiasis in freshwater swamps, the annoyance of leaches, and the danger of snakes and even crocodiles. The fertility of people and the land is a constant practical consideration and is explicitly reflected in Sherbro ritual.

Pre-colonially, the area was a loosely-organized system of polities headed by the notable persons, often descendants of a founding or conquering historical personage. Heads of chiefdoms, heads of towns, and even heads of residential compounds attempted then and now to build up the number of their dependants and followers by marrying them, begetting them, attracting them through clientage, and, in the past, capturing or buying them (MacCormack 1977). In the colonial period chiefdom maps were drawn and a limited set of ruling descent groups, the producers of chiefs, were named. Today, those chiefdoms are articulated within the system of national government.

## Gender contrast and cultural unity

Thoma[1] is a Sherbro sodality 'owning' secret knowledge. It is equivalent in its function to Poro, an organization of men's congregations, and Sande, an organization of women's congregations[2] (Little 1965; 1966; and Mac-Cormack 1979). Where Poro initiates only boys into life-long responsibility of social manhood, and Sande initiates only girls into womanly responsibility, Thoma initiates both sexes. A family with three children might initiate the boy in Poro, the girl in Sande, and the third child in Thoma. The membership of the three sodalities is mutually exclusive, and a boy initiated into Thoma could not later be initiated into Poro, for example.

With Poro and Sande, the contrastive gender categories are split apart and the uniqueness of each gender is emphasized, but always with the final view that the complementarity of the two constitute human society, the full cultural unity. Thoma is a microcosm of the whole. Its local congregations or chapters are headed by a man and a woman, co-equal leaders who are 'husband and wife' in a ritual context but are not married in mundane life.

Sherbros hold a strong cultural assumption that society must be perpetuated. Adult husband and wife farm, rear children, and have other explicit responsibilities for maintaining healthy, orderly, rule-bound society. The cooperation of adult men and women in these activities which perpetuate society are conceived as metaphors for the cooperation of man and woman in procreative sexuality. Within Thoma the unity of male and

1  The name is pronounced with an aspirated T, followed by a long O, not a theta as in thumb. Research has been funded intermittently over the past 10 years principally by the National Science Foundation, the American Philosophical Society, and the (British) Social Science Research Council.
2  This women's sodality is known as Sande in the Mande group of languages, and Bundu or Bondo in the West Atlantic group of languages. Bondo is the Sherbro word, but I shall use Sande, the term which is more common in the literature.

female in reproduction of human society is raised above the uniqueness of each gender category. This theme of gender complementarity within cultural unity is restated in a different modality in Sherbro ideology of cognatic descent.

## Description of Thoma

Although it functions as an initiation society, Thoma members constitute a congregation for the rest of their mundane lives, and throughout ancestral time. Members stress that the Thoma society's primary function is to 'wash the bush'. In a literal sense, this means that forest leaves are crushed in water, in a wooden bowl, to make 'medicine'. That 'medicine' is sprinkled by officials of the Thoma society on the farming land and bush fallow at the entrance to a village, to cleanse the land and the village from evil and restore its fertility and well-being. Officials of the Thoma society also walk through some villages, going from residential compound to compound, 'washing' the household, and receiving money, food or alcoholic spirits from the head of the compound in return.

'Medicine' is any preparation which links people to extraordinary, or non-mundane, power. The leaves are chosen because their particular qualities call forth, by analogy, the desired state to be achieved by the 'medicine'. Water, as the medium for cleansing, has a particularly rich symbolic meaning which will be discussed later.

The Thoma society is regarded by Sherbros as unique to their ethnic area. It does not have the very deep antiquity that Poro and Sande have in the Sherbro country. I was told that Paramount Chief Thomas Stephen Caulker, who reigned from 1831 to 1871, sent to the north for Thoma, requesting that the 'medicine' be brought to 'wash the bush' because there had been bloodshed. The deep, watery earth is the abode of ancestors and blood shed upon the earth is an offence to them. When they are offended they withdraw their blessings, and the land and its people lose their health and fertility.

There is agreement among Sherbros that Thoma came from the north, from the area which is now Guinea. I was told that Thoma (tōma) in the Kissi language means old, and is also the name for Kissi initiation ceremonies. The cognatic descent group founded by Madam Ya Bom are said to be the 'owners' of the Thoma society. Madam Ya Bom brought the secret knowledge, 'medicines', ritual, masks and other material accoutrements to Thumba, in Kagboro Chiefdom, and was the first co-leader of the Thoma society in the Sherbro country. Therefore, Sherbros should defer to members of the Ya Bom descent group in all Thoma matters. This, of course, is a statement about etiquette and not necessarily a statement of empirical fact. To this day, the Thoma society in Kagboro Chiefdom is still located in Thumba, its ritual grove being the burial place of Ya Bom and other notables who are now potent ancestors/ancestresses.

Membership in the Thoma society is not restricted to the descendants of Ya Bom, nor to any particular descent groups, but is open to all Sherbros. The recently deceased co-leader of the Thoma society at Thumba, for example, had some of his children and grandchildren initiated in Thoma, some in Poro, and some in Sande. If only one parent of a child is Sherbro, the child may be initiated providing both parents are in agreement.

The village of Thumba is near the coast, about half a mile from the end of a motorable dirt track. The village is nucleated, as Sherbro villages are, with cleanly-swept open space in the centre of the village. It is in the protective shadow of two groves of virgin forest, each containing several towering cotton trees. One is the sacred grove of the Thoma society, the other is the sacred grove of the Poro society. The two sodalities do not exist in conflict, but in a relationship of respect for each other. When one holds its initiation season the other constitutes part of the respectful audience.

The swept space of the village ends abruptly at the edge of the forest. During an initiation season this margin is marked by a screen of palm fronds, and a portal through which the candidates for initiation, and members of the society, pass. The sacred grove functions as burial ground, as a site for communication with ancestral spirits, and as sacred space for rites of passage and other congregations. The cotton trees act as a focus for communication with extraordinary powers. They form a vertical axis, between the sky of an ultimate creator, and the deep earth/ground water of ancestral abode.

## Masks

There are four Thoma society masks. They are helmet-type, completely covering the head, or sitting on top of the head, of the wearer. All are painted black, white and red (pink). From the bottom of the mask descends a fibre cape in two tiers. The upper tier descends from the mask to below the fingers, overlapping the second tier which descends to the ground. When the masked figures dance, the cape sways and swirls outward. The masks are manifestations of spirits (*min*), but every adult knows that there is a completely hidden person inside. The wearers of the masks can be any members of the Thoma society who have a flair for such things, and are usually young, tall, and athletic. The masks of the Thoma society at Thumba were carved by a local man who is not a member of Thoma, but of Poro. Men also carve Sande masks and need not have any ritual qualification to be carvers.

The masks appear in two pairs, an animal pair and a humanoid pair. Collectively they are called *mbekebu*, manifestations of spirits. They are

potent, and appear only when initiates are nearing the end of their
seclusion in the forest. Although uninitiated persons may see these masked
spirits, they must keep a respectful distance from them. They are complemented by a third pair of spirit manifestations which are heard but never
seen by the uninitiated. They are the most potent and must not be
approached by the uninitiated on pain of death. One, Laben, is female.
She is accompanied by her 'husband' Gboka.

The first pair of masked spirits to appear in initiation ritual are animal-
like, representing the dwarf duiker, a grey antelope about 14 inches high
(*Philantomba*), and the dwarf hippopotamus (*Choeropsis liberiensis*) (see
plates 5.1–3).[3] The duiker is a forest mammal, relatively benign in contrast to the 'cannibalistic' leopard, very quick and intelligent. It is a common character in animal stories told for entertainment, and for the instruction of children at home and in secret society initiations. The stories often
end in a moral which clearly enunciates honourable behaviour. Sometimes
the stories end in a dilemma, and the listeners are encouraged to debate
alternative endings, thereby exploring conflicts between self-interest and
the common good. The duiker (male or female) is a well-mannered trickster
who mediates forces in nature and human society to get a spouse, children,
food and other valuables. Duiker's forethought and restraint is contrasted
in stories with spider's greedy excess; spider's schemes usually ending with
his being flung out of the village, desocialized and dehumanized (Cosentino
1976:390–4). The duiker is thought to be active by day and by night,
mediating a further contrast between well-mannered restraint (white) and
greed (black).

The dwarf hippopotamus is also relatively benign in contrast to the
'cannibalistic' crocodile, grazing on waterside plants by day and night. It
stands in contrast to the duiker by being a water rather than a land animal.

The duiker and hippopotamus masked figures travel with members of
the Thoma society to villages which are being 'washed' during the initiation
season. The masked figures dramatically display themselves within a circle
of fire light or lamp light during all-night dancing before the village is
'washed' on the following morning. They are the first pair of masks to
appear in initiation rituals. They symbolize that 'wild', unsocialized children are being transformed into cultured adults, but will retain the fertile
vigour of the animal world.

The two humanoid masks (*rɔŋ*) are ancestral spirits, one male and the
other female (see plate 5.4). They appear at the climax of initiation ritual,

3   The hippopotamus or 'water cow' mask has rudimentary horns. If
    Thoma originated in a northern savanna environment, this mask may
    have been cow, and the opposition was duiker=forest vs. cow=domestic.
    Whatever the original symbolic form, the mask is now adapted to the
    swampy Sherbro physical environment and the 'watery' cultural
    cosmos.

when the ancestors have been well 'fed' with libations and offerings of cooked food, and the initiates are about to be re-born in their new social status. These ancestral manifestations appear only after a long period of ritual preparation, when people and places have been 'washed' clean from secret malice and all the infractions of ancestral law which have been committed. Only after careful ritual preparation will ancestral blessings be made manifest.

## Death and rebirth

*Min* is the Sherbro word for spirit, including forest spirits, water spirits and

Plate 5.1  Duiker mask.

ancestral shades. The latter two are *min menei*, literally spirits below. Ancestral spirits are also known as *min si a bɛn*, spirits of a foreparent; old. *Min* is also the verb to eat. At about five year intervals a great forest spirit residing in the sacred grove of the Thoma society awakes and hungrily begins to 'eat' initiates. The members of the Thoma society in Thumba rush into action and within hours build a mud house in the grove in which 'medicines', masks, and other ritual accoutrements will be stored. It is also the place where initiates sleep at night. At the end of the initiation season this house is left to fall into disrepair again.

Plate 5.2 Hippopotamus mask.

Plate 5.3  Duiker and hippopotamus masked figures, dancing.

Fig. 5.4 Humanoid masked figures; female Janus-faced figure in foreground, male figure behind.

The initiates pass through the portal dividing the village and its mundane domestic preoccupations from the dangerous, potent, sacred forest. Initiates are carried straight into the maw of the great forest *min*, die as distinct social persons, and will be born from the vagina of the *min* after three or four months of liminality. This forest spirit symbolizes the potency of gender unity, and has both scrotum and womb/vagina.

The initiation season which I observed in 1970 began in early January, in the dry season after the rice harvest was in. After the harvest, food is plentiful and no demanding agricultural labour is needed until near the end of the dry season, in three or four months' time. The rites culminate in early April, just as the first thunderstorms, harbingers of the rainy season, begin.

About 20 children were initiated, ranging in maturity from pubescence to early childhood. Children enter the initiation grove at different times over the four months. The ones who enter first become most experienced, acquire most wisdom, and act as 'headmen/headwomen' over the other co-initiates. The initiates undergo ordeals and pleasures, learning the rules and skills of social responsibility in a concentrated, highly dramatic context. They are preparing for only the first grade of adult wisdom, and may later, by asking questions and demonstrating adeptness, rise to higher grades within Thoma (see MacCormack 1979).

Inside the grove, the initiates are stripped of their clothes, as a foetus has no clothes. An official pounds white clay and leaves, making 'medicine' which initiates apply to their lower legs each day.

When the initiation season begins, libations of palm wine or imported spirits, called 'cold water', are poured onto the ground of the sacred grove, calling the shades of past officials of the Thoma society and other notables who abide in the ancestral underworld. Their blessings are sought for the Sherbro country and the children going through a second birth.[4]

These individuals will undergo another ritual 'rebirth' when, as old men and women, they die and join the company of ancestors. In all the 'births' into infancy, adulthood, and ancestorhood, individuals are without clothes or any remnant of the old status which is being transcended. Thoma society members, at the end of mundane life, are laid naked in the ground, on forest leaves, covered with more leaves, then with earth.

4  The following is an example of communication (not in an initiation context) with ancestors following the offering of 'cold water' and food: 'This is the food we present to you. Eat it with contented minds. We ask you to send us good health and good fortune. Lengthen our days. Let whoever hates us die. Your grandson [name] is a fisherman. He goes out fishing and catches no fish. We ask you to send him fish. Let all those who are assembled here in your honour receive good luck from this house [compound, ancestral place, descent group]. We finish. You hear.'

In Thoma society initiation ritual, when the spirit has 'eaten', and the ancestors are 'fed', not only the grove, but all the village of Thumba and the farm land immediately around it become sacred space. The ancestors of the deep watery earth have been 'fed' and 'called'. The great forest *min* had also awakened and been 'fed' with the initiates. The surface of the earth is the scrotum of the great forest *min*. Therefore, no one may wear shoes or sandals, nor run in proximity to the entire village of Thumba at this time.

No one on the outside of the screen marking off forest from village speaks of the children, nor sees them. Their marginalization is as death. As their period of instruction to new social roles nears its conclusion, the members of Thoma beat on the 'belly' of the forest spirit (beat on buttress roots of the cotton tree or an up-turned canoe), announcing its labour has begun. Young trees in the grove are shaken, and people on the outside 'hear' the pains, and 'see' the *min* thrashing about in labour. The sounds of the long double-headed Thoma drum and women's chanting voices are also heard. The chant ends in a drawn out 'uh wheeeee' of labour pain, followed by silence. Then, the drumming, chanting, and terminal 'uh wheeeee' are repeated, in the rhythm of labour contraction followed by rest.

*Inside ritual*

In the terminal rituals of the initiation, a group of Thoma men, the *Ndeŋ-kema*, in ritual dress, move in a weaving, running, dancing line between the sacred grove and the village, mediating between the sacred and the mundane (see plate 5.5). Their dancing line, each dancer following the one before him, rushes through the town and back into the grove while the long double-headed drum is beaten and Thoma women sing Thoma songs. The dancers, the *Ndeŋkema*, are called 'locusts' because they seize things in the town and are voracious 'eaters'. When the forest spirit begins to 'labour', they seize a final pair of young children in the town, passing them from man to man, through the portal, and into the maw of the *min* to stop up its mouth. Now it cannot vomit up the initiates, but must bear them as all mammals bear live beings.

The *Ndeŋkema* correspond to a similar corps of young males in Poro. In both secret societies they are chosen because they are considered to be beautiful. In Thoma, they are complemented by a chorus of beautiful young women, who come and go through the screen, singing and dancing. The *Ndeŋkema* wear a head cover with a rattan and raffia superstructure representing long locks and 'streamers' of hair. Sherbros are not able to grow long hair, but admire it as a sign of health and beauty. In Sande initiations, women comb black cotton wool into their hair to make it look fuller. Hair arrangements are one of the most important stylistic elements carved into Sande society masks, and are also a feature of the male human-

Plate 5.5 The *Ndeŋkema*, male dancers who mediate between the initiation grove beyond the palm frond boundary marker, and the village in the foreground. Gbana Bom, the mediator who 'translates' messages from unseen spirits in the initiation grove, stands at the left.

oid Thoma mask. In ritual context, hair is a metaphor for forest trees which grow thick and tall, manifesting the fertility of the land (Boone 1978).

Some *Ndeŋkema* wear a skirt wrapped around their hips, others pull the 'skirt' up into the loincloth men wear while working. Their faces, lower arms and lower legs may be covered with white clay, but in the ritual I observed they were not. Each dancer grasps a four foot wooden staff with both hands. They do their running dance, bent forward at the waist, swinging the sticks in a motion similar to paddling a canoe, digging the earth, or 'lifting filth'.

Inside the grove the initiates have no hair at all, having had their heads shaved bald, as a foetus has no hair. Once the mouth of the *min* has been stopped up with the last boy—girl pair of initiates, all the initiates are washed in water containing an infusion of leaves from the cotton tree. This 'medicine' leaves their bodies covered with a slimy coating, analogous to the slime of parturition. Relatives, the sponsors of each initiate, then lift the children up by their feet, draping them over their shoulder, the candidates' heads hanging down as though they were helpless and newborn. The candidates go into a final period of seclusion. On emerging from that, they move in a body along a path, analogous to the birth canal, to greet the elder co-heads of the Thoma society. These two elders, *soko nɔ* (those who are most adept), are known by the titles Beko for the man, and Kose for the woman.

Obstructions, such as heavy stones and logs, have been placed on the path leading to the *soko nɔ*. The ground is strewn with excrement and dirty sweepings. The initiates must 'labour' in lifting or rolling the heavy stones and logs away. As they approach the two elders, they must have their bodies bent forward at the waist, with the palms of their hands upward, to scoop up, and clean away all the filth. If anyone shirks, or even turns his/her palms downward, symbolizing unwillingness to clean away filth, he/she will be flogged. When they at last reach the two elders, the initiates make formal obeisance, bending their backs and knees, lowering their hands, palms upward, to the ground before them. They sing 'My *soko nɔ*, I am coming to leave a hand.' When they have made the final obeisance, one of the co-heads touches their shoulder with a broom, giving a blessing.[5] The hand broom is carried by adepts of the Thoma society as a symbol of their rank. The broom also symbolizes 'cleanliness' in contrast to 'filth'.

The inside ritual ends when the initiates eat white rice, and swear never to reveal to an uninitiated person the secret knowledge they have learned. Libations are poured to the ancestors, and they are 'fed' with offerings of cooked food, placed at the foot of a cotton tree. If a white cock comes to eat the food, all know that the ancestors have heard their 'children' and are pleased with the sacrifice, giving their blessing. Then there is general feasting

---

5   This is formalized ritual for begging and forgiveness/assent.

in the sacred grove. The initiates are washed, dressed in new clothes, and the scene is set for the ritual of aggregation. The sacred and the mundane are merged for the moment in which the initiates reenter human society in their new status.

## Outside ritual

While the above is happening, a 'master of ceremonies', the Gbana Bom (see fig. 5.5), stands in the swept clearing of the village. He is a Thoma man, dressed in a woman's wrap-around skirt and head tie. This role reversal in dress symbolizes that normal historical time has stopped and sacred time is reversed, with pubescents becoming foetuses (see Leach 1961:136). He holds the hand broom in one hand and an iron bell, with a finger-ring external clapper, in the other hand.

Gbana Bom is a title, designating the role of headman/headwoman and mediator. The first boy and first girl to enter the Thoma initiation grove are Gbana Bom to the rest. The Thoma official standing in the centre of the village is Gbana Bom, speaking for the sodality and interpreting it to the uninitiated. The spirit world also has its Gbana Bom, often recently-deceased officials of the secret society who mediate with the ancestors embedded in 'deep' ancestral time. The male humanoid mask in Thoma initiation ritual is also called Gbana Bom.

The Thoma official designated Gbana Bom stands in the village clearing, ringing his bell, and announces the appearance of the dancing line of *Ndeŋkema*. The first time they appear they return to the grove with the last 'mouth stopping' initiates. The fourth time they appear, they bring out the reborn initiates.

In their second appearance, the *Ndeŋkema* bring out the two animal-like masked spirits, *Nɔnkɔ bɛ* and *Mɔkɛlɛ*, representing the potency of nature. These masked figures dance and display themselves to the town. Then the unseen spirits are heard, Laben, the female flute 'crying' in the forest, and the gruff 'strong' male voice of Gboka warning people to be 'clean'. Gbana Bom interprets their voices to the village.[6]

When the *Ndeŋkema* dance/run forth into the village the third time, they bring the two humanoid masked spirits *(Rɔŋ)*, and the two living co-heads of Thoma (Beko and Kose) (see plate 5.6). The *Rɔŋ* appear after the ancestors have been 'fed' with libations and cooked food in the sacred grove. The female masked spirit is referred to as 'Mammy Queen', and the

6  When a person dies, part of the mortuary ritual includes a post-mortem examination of internal organs to look for signs of witchcraft. Detection of witchcraft will explain bad harvests, infertile women, death of children, and other misfortune. The female spirit Laben is present at the examinations, and her 'husband' Gboka makes the announcement that the individual did or did not have a 'clean belly'.

male as Gbana Bom. Thus, a living Gbana Bom (headman/mediator) and a spirit Gbana Bom, for this ritual moment, are on stage at the same time, uniting the following metaphoric set:

|            |   |                      |
|------------|---|----------------------|
| inside     | : | outside              |
| forest     | : | village              |
| potent/fecund | : | cooperative/domestic |
| spirit     | : | mundane              |
| liminal    | : | historical           |

The two domains have been bridged through the energizing prelude of drumming and dancing, formal 'calling' to the ancestors/ancestresses, pouring 'cold water' onto the ground, and placing cooked food, especially white rice, at the foot of a cotton tree for them. After this preparation, the masked ancestral figures appear.

Plate 5.6  The co-leaders of Thoma with the male masked figure.

Historical time

Surface of the earth 'scrotum' of the min

Gbana Bom and the earthly living

Gbana Bom and the deep ancestors

Ancestral immortality

Liminality — Cotton tree, drumming, dancing, singing, and libations mediate between the two planes

## Aggregation

The *Ndeŋkema* appear the fourth time, followed by the initiates, shielded under a canopy of local woven white cotton cloth. The younger children are brought out on the shoulders of their sponsors. They are dressed in a wrap-around skirt and a head tie. Their shaven heads are 'soft', as the heads of the newborn are.

It may happen that children die during initiation ordeals in the forest. As the forest *min* begins to 'labour', the sound of its pain in the forest is matched in the village by the crying of women. They fear that their son or daughter will not be reborn, but had died in the 'belly' of the *min*. When the children are brought into the village, the canopy of cloth is removed, and they stand in a line. If any has died, at that moment the Thoma sponsor of the dead child steps forward, removes a clay pot with black and white spots from the concealment of his skirt, and smashes it on the ground before the dead child's mother. None died the year I observed the rituals, but if there had been death that was not transformed into rebirth, the lament of mothers would have been mixed in bitter-sweet chorus with the rejoicing of the rest of the village.

The initiates were re-absorbed back into their families. The four masked spirits and the co-heads of the Thoma society assembled on a cloth covered platform. The *Ndeŋkema* danced forward, in pairs, to honour them. The paddling, digging, lifting-of-filth motion of the dancers was transformed into the phallic lifting and thrusting of healthy fertility, signalling the return of potency to the sea, the land, and the people following this long period of ritual cleansing and seeking of ancestral blessing.

The pair of animal masked spirits returned to the forest after the first pass of the *Ndeŋkema*. The humanoid masked spirits retired to the forest after the second pass of the *Ndeŋkema*. On the third pass, the *Ndeŋkema* honoured the co-heads of Thoma. On their fourth approach to the co-heads of the Thoma society, the people at the margin of the ritual space began dancing where they stood, then fell in behind the line of dancing/running *Ndeŋkema*, followed by general village dancing and rejoicing in the fading light and throughout the night.

## Colour

Sherbro moral precepts and cosmological ideas are encoded in the masks and body paint. The masks are painted white, black and red (pink). The living co-heads of the Thoma society wear white and red (pink) body paint on black skin. White and black constitute opposed categories. Animals used in ancestral sacrifice should be white. The animal a person presents to another person in tribute or as a token of amity should be without blotches of black fur or feathers. Pure whiteness symbolizes that the giver's 'belly'

is 'clean', without the hidden darkness of envy, malice, or witchcraft.
Black is night, when witchcraft causes bad luck, disease, barren wombs,
and death. Darkness is selfishness and strong passions such as hate. It is
also 'dirt' of refuse and excrement on the path or in the village, the dirt
under the foreskin of the penis, or around the clitoris. If a boy has not
been circumcised before Thoma initiation, he will be made 'clean' while in
the grove. Girls will become 'clean' through clitoridectomy in the initiation
grove (see MacCormack 1979).

Blackness is contrasted with the pure sacrifice of a white animal, given
not for selfish reasons but out of generosity, concern, and moral duty.
Whiteness is open and clean, not hidden and dark. It is the observation of
cultural rules to sweep the compound free from filth, to prepare food
properly, keep wells clean, and wash with water.

Water itself is whiteness. Semen is referred to as 'water'. Water/white-
ness is also breast milk, procreation and nurturing. Water is the lower part
of the cosmos, the abode of ancestors. Initiates in the sacred grove of the
Sande society are 'under water'. Unfortunately, I do not know if Thoma
uses the same idiom of expression. The lower part of Thoma initiates' legs,
the part of them in contact with ancestral earth, are covered in white clay
every morning. Libations of 'cold water' mediate between the living and
the dead. Living things germinate in water. In the initiation grove ancestral
information is imparted which allows fertility to root and grow, not to be
blighted by the blackness of selfishness and witchcraft. During the sacred
time of Thoma initiation the entire chiefdom renounces past sin and is
'washed'.

Red is such a 'strong' colour that a weaver may put only a single red
thread in an entire blanket-sized cloth. In the past, men wore locally-woven
shirts dyed red (red-brown) when hunting or engaging in war. Red is the
strength to kill in warfare or hunting, and the strength to bear children. It
is activity, power and vitality, but it is dangerous. Power can be used
selfishly (black), or in a way controlled by rules of social responsibility
(white). It is the deep obligation of Thoma society officials, especially the
co-heads, to see that the initiates learn to turn toward whiteness, away
from blackness.

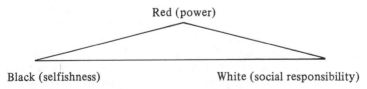

Red (power)

Black (selfishness)                    White (social responsibility)

After the initiates have made their way along the path/birth canal,
removing obstacles and lifting away 'filth', they face the co-heads of
Thoma. They look upon those two elders, each with one eye circled in

white. The choice is clear: social responsibility and adult status or childish selfishness and destructiveness.

These ritual colours encode the most basic human social relationships as Sherbro understand them.[7] White, as semen, is the conjugal relationship between husband and wife. The co-heads of Thoma, 'husband and wife' in the ritual context, are dressed entirely in white, except for red and white body paint. White is also breast milk signifying the relationship between mother and child. Red is the pain of birth, black is death which comes before rebirth into adulthood, or into ancestorhood.

The masks of the dwarf duiker and the dwarf hippopotamus are painted white, black and red. These animals are both diurnal (white) and nocturnal (black); fecund and strong (red). The duiker is a benign forest animal, contrasted with the leopard which eats humans to destroy them. The great forest *min* also eats humans, the initiates, but eats so that they might be reborn with enhanced humanity. The hippopotamus is a benign water animal, contrasted with the crocodile which eats humans to destroy them. The crocodile and the leopard nourish their own power from the human flesh they eat, as witches and cannibals do.

The duiker and the hippopotamus are solitary, do not live in social groups, and do not observe rules about eating, defecating, fornicating and giving birth. They neither fish nor farm. These animal spirits appear first in the ritual, but are superseded by the humanoid *rɔŋ*. The second pair are manifestations of ancestors (male and female), the source of human wisdom encoded in cultural rules. They guarantee strength and fecundity to those who follow ancestral laws.

## Cosmology and time

The masks of both humanoid spirits are topped with bird feathers. The masked figures represent the vertical axis from sky, the place of the ultimate creator, to the watery underworld of ancestral consciousness. Birds mediate between sky and earth. The masked *min* dance to the rhythm of the Thoma drum and the chorus of Thoma songs. This energy penetrates to the ancestors who hear and are pleased. Thus, the masked figures, by their dancing, mediate between the earth and the ancestral underworld.

The mask of the female, 'Mammy Queen', has the neck rings carved into all Sande society masks, symbolizing a fertile woman who is so healthy and full-bodied that her neck creases with plump fatness (MacCormack 1979; 1981). The female mask is also Janus-faced, as the fertility of women looks back to the ancestral past, and forward to those not yet born (see plate 5.7). The Janus-faced mask encodes the ritual process itself in which mundane historical time is ritually interrupted, but will resume again

7  See Turner 1967:59—92.

following the period of sacredness. The mask appears at the ritual threshold, after the initiates have been 'eaten' in a rite of separation from normal village life, but before they have been 'reborn' and reunited, through a rite of aggregation, with normal village life. Time is reversed. Pubescents become foetuses, then become adults at the conclusion of the rites.

Elements in the rite of aggregation are similar to, but the reverse of, elements in the rite of separation: ancestral sacrifices are made to begin the initiation season, then made to conclude it. Children's clothing was taken off on entering the grove, and put on before leaving it. Restrictions on activities and foods were imposed, then lifted. Their hair was shaved, then allowed to grow again. They were washed in 'medicine' to protect them while in the 'belly of the *min*', and washed to remove the last traces of parturition. The children left the world of mundane work when the rains and farming season had ended; they reentered the world of mundane work as the rains of the next farming season began.

Plate 5.7  Kose, the woman co-leader of Thoma, wearing a pangolin skin. There is a Janus-faced female mask in the background.

Sherbros are using art and ritual to symbolize the conceptual categories into which they divide the universe and make it orderly. They make a categorical distinction between 'wild' animals and 'social' human beings, giving contrastive attributes to each. Animals are further divided into those of the earth and those of the water. Human beings are also divided into the living on the earth, and ancestors in a watery domain.

Human beings live by moral laws, and occasionally recapture wisdom from ancestral time by going 'under water'. The secret wisdom, the most valuable property of the Thoma society, has been revealed to the living in experiences 'under water'. A person may be bathing in a stream, or feel an irresistible urge to go into water. There he/she is seized and carried down under the water. Below, the seeker encounters a strange village with strange people, who teach the seeker to make and use 'medicine', teach rules of conduct which constitute Thoma law, and even give special skills, such as those of a dancer or carver.

Human beings must abide by ancestral rules of conduct if they are to be healthy and fertile. Indeed, they wish to be as healthy as strong forest, as fecund as animals which give birth in litters. Only by becoming fully 'cultural', vowing to live by ancestral laws, may they hope to avoid illness and barrenness. Paradoxically, although animals observe no social rules, not even the incest taboo, they are suffused with vitality and fecundity. This paradox is symbolically mediated by the pangolin, or scaly anteater (*Maxis tricuspis*), unifying all the conceptual categories into a unified system. Kose, the woman co-head of the Thoma society, wears the skin of the pangolin on her head (see fig. 5.7). The pangolin is highly anomalous in terms of Sherbro thought categories, and is therefore a powerful symbol of mediation between the categories. It has the scaly body and tail of a fish, but it is a forest animal with legs, which climbs trees. Thus, it mediates the three cosmological tiers, from deep ancestral water to the sky which trees penetrate.

Because of its scales, the pangolin is associated with water/whiteness (semen, milk, ancestral blessing), and because it is a forest animal it is associated with the 'redness' of animal vitality and fecundity. Furthermore, it speaks to the paradox that animals, which do not constrain their behaviour in accord with ancestral laws, are more fecund than socially responsible humans. For the pangolin, though an animal, is thought not to give birth in litters, but to single young, as humans do, and the paradox is further mediated (see Douglas 1957:50).

The pangolin symbolically links humans, animals and ancestors into a single interrelated system. The 'blackness' of anti-social volition in one domain will affect the other domains, causing the ancestors to withdraw their blessing, the crops to wither, and people to be sickly and barren. During Thoma initiations the ancestors are 'fed' with 'white' sacrifices and respond by blessing the land and humans, giving them the 'red' vitality of giant trees and strong animals.

## Conclusion

People in the Sherbro coast of Sierra Leone encode folk wisdom into sets of oppositions, symbolically expressing them and their mediation in ritual. Children are considered proto-social, egoistically greedy and wilful. They are analogous to spider who, in folk tales, has human appetites untempered by rule-bound decency. Spider's mishaps always plunge him back into the domain of nature. Children, however, are carefully trained by their parents, and intensively educated during their liminal status in initiation ritual. With the image of the dwarf duiker before them, they concentrate on keen intelligence and graceful acts. Duiker and hippopotamus are benign, positive mediators between 'natural' egoism and 'cultural' restraint. But as the ritual builds toward the climax of transformation those mediators retire, giving the stage to unequivocal human adult representations.

Although Sherbros have categories I wish to label as nature and culture, female and male do not constitute a metaphoric transformation of nature and culture. Woman is not spider, plunged back into 'nature' when appetite overcomes training.[8] Sherbro women take their vital place in the division of labour and are no less social and adult than men.

Meanings subsumed under the terms nature and culture are not universal for all societies making such distinctions, nor are they uniform within a single society. In European thought, for example, nature is not commonly associated with selfish witchcraft and cannibalism. But at a specific period in history or by a minority of people it may have been. Nor would all Sherbros agree with the folk model I have constructed. Most would indeed say that witches and cannibals as a category are opposed to Thoma elders who uphold the commonwealth by their adherance to moral rules. Other Sherbros would say 'how do you think those officials got their power?', implying that they resorted to anti-social acts. The same ambiguity that Jordanova identifies in European thought (see chapter 3) is in Sherbro minds as well. Douglas (1967:66) is correct in insisting that before we can discern the elements of structure we must know the culture well, in all its variation and ambiguity.

8  In the mythology of the neighbouring Mende people, duiker is either masculine or feminine but spider is always masculine (Cosentino 1976: 391).

118    *Carol P. MacCormack*

## Bibliography

Boone, Sylvia. 1978. Personal communication. Department of Art, Yale University.

Cosentino, Donald J. 1976. *Patterns in Domiesia: The Dialectics of Mende Narrative performance*. PhD dissertation, University of Wisconsin.

Douglas, Mary. 1957. 'Animals in Lele Religious Symbolism', *Africa*, 27, 46–57.

    1967. 'The Meaning of Myth, with Special Reference to "La Geste d'Asdiwal" ', in *The Structural Study of Myth and Totemism*, ed. by E.R. Leach, pp. 49–70. London: Tavistock.

Leach, E.R. 1961. *Rethinking Anthropology*. London: Athlone Press.

Little, Kenneth. 1965 and 1966. 'The Political Function of the Poro', Parts I and II, *Africa*, 35, 349–65 and 36, 62–71.

MacCormack, Carol P. (Carol P. Hoffer). 1972. 'Mende and Sherbro Women in High Office', *Canadian Journal of African Studies*, 6, 151–64.

    1974. 'Madam Yoko: Ruler of the Kpa Mende Confederacy', in *Woman, Culture and Society*, ed. by M.Z. Rosaldo and L. Lamphere, pp. 173–88. Stanford: Stanford University Press.

    1977. 'Wono: Institutionalized Dependency in Sherbro Descent Groups', in *African Slavery: Historical and Anthropological Perspectives*, ed. by S. Miers and I. Kopytoff, pp. 181–204. Madison: University of Wisconsin Press.

    1978. 'The Cultural Ecology of Production: Sherbro Coast and Hinterland', in *Social Organization and Settlement*, ed. by D. Green, et al. pp. 197–212. Oxford: British Archaeological Reports.

    1979. 'Sande: The Public Face of a Secret Society' in *The New Religions of Africa*, ed. by B. Jules-Rosette, pp. 27–37. Norwood, New Jersey: Ablex Press.

    1981. 'Health, Fertility and Childbirth in Southern Sierra Leone', in *Ethnography of Fertility and Birth*, ed. by C.P. MacCormack, London: Academic Press.

Rosaldo, M.Z. 1974. 'Woman, Culture and Society: A Theoretical Overview', in *Woman, Culture and Society*, ed. by M.Z. Rosaldo and L. Lamphere, pp. 17–42. Stanford: Stanford University Press.

Turner, Victor. 1967. *The Forest of Symbols*. Ithaca: Cornell University Press.

# 6 Gender, sexuality and marriage: a Kaulong model of nature and culture

JANE C. GOODALE

## Introduction

Almost from the very first day of our fieldwork among the Kaulong and Sengseng peoples of southwest New Britain, my colleague Ann Chowning and I realized that our host's assumptions concerning gender, sexuality and marriage were salient features of their culture.[1] In both our communities men feared, and regularly postponed, marriage until late in life (sometimes forever), sexual intercourse was considered a statement of marriage for both men and women (and rarely occurred outside of marriage traditionally), and contamination from women was believed to lead to certain chronic illness and eventually to early death for men. Finally, there was little separation of men and women in public or private spheres of life, which contrasted with a noticeable separation between individuals who were married and those who were not; a separation both physical and symbolic. Describing these related assumptions and behavioural manifestations

1 The fieldwork on which this paper is based was carried out during four periods totalling thirty months between 1962 and 1974. Grateful acknowledgement of funding is extended to the National Institute of Mental Health (1962), the National Science Foundation (1963–4, 1967–8), and to the American Council of Learned Societies and Bryn Mawr College (1974). During the first two field periods, the research was coordinated with that of Ann Chowning among the neighbouring Sengseng peoples. I am particularly grateful for access to Chowning's data and to numerous discussions with her in the field and elsewhere of many of the points raised in this paper. An earlier version of a portion of the discussion was written in direct collaboration (Chowning and Goodale 1971). Finally, portions of the argument have been presented and discussed in a number of symposia held during annual meetings of the Association of Social Anthropology in Oceania between 1973 and 1978. Feedback and comparative points raised in symposia discussion have been invaluable in formulating the argument presented here. I acknowledge the help of participants at these symposia collectively in gratitude. I also wish to thank Judith Shapiro, Ann Chowning, and the editors for helpful comments on the present draft.

has been a long involved process of seeking and exploring various explicit and implicit Kaulong explanations of the order of their physical and social world for explanation and comparative understanding.[2] In this chapter I present a folk model of world order which, I believe, informs Kaulong relationships with both the physical and social aspects of their personal environment. Like other contributors to this volume, I have been challenged by a number of studies in which the usefulness of the nature/culture opposition to our understanding of related cultural distinctions has been argued.[3]

Of primary influence to my developing argument has been Ortner's 1974 paper. She takes as a self-evident and universal concept the idea that because culture works to transform nature, nature is considered lower in value than culture. Where culture is creative, nature is innate. Ortner argues that although women are not equated in their entirety with nature, they are closer to nature than men, being naturally creative. Men create through cultural means. Although women are not *in* nature, they are in a medial position in the hierarchy represented by nature and culture and thus can be said to also mediate between these two oppositions. It is because they are closer to nature, Ortner argues, that they are universally placed in an inferior position to men in social and cultural orders (1974:84).

The hierarchical order of culture over nature, of men over women, is of course familiar to all who share Judaeo-Christian concepts and beliefs, but considerable empirical evidence is now available to demonstrate that this model is not a universal valid folk model. Just as Ortner's discussion of the relationship of the nature/culture opposition does not, for example, help explain Kaulong concepts of gender, neither does a related discussion focussed specifically on Melanesia by Forge (1972). He considers that the oppositions of male/female and nature/culture are better seen as complementary to each other rather than on a single scale of superiority and inferiority. He apparently agrees with Ortner that Melanesian women's powers of reproduction are considered innate and natural while men express creativity through ceremony, magic and other 'cultural' means. But more importantly he sees men and women in these cultures as interdependent, and adds that women may in fact be a source of inequality among men, as they complement to a greater or lesser degree the productive and political activities of the men. To summarize the two discussions: where Ortner sees culture and nature as polar unequal positions, with women mediating between the inferior and superior positions, Forge considers culture to be different from nature in such a way that equality or superiority is not a pertinent question. In both discussions there is an implicit assumption that as people in all societies make a fundamental dis-

2  See bibliography for papers relating to this topic which were presented in symposia. Manuscript copies are available from author.
3  For example see Huntsman (1975), Shore (1978) and Weiner (1979).

tinction between natural and cultural orders so they also make a related distinction in gender categories. Furthermore, gender distinction is a 'key symbol' (Ortner 1973) summarizing many common social and cultural concepts which underlie significant behavioural aspects of human life. I contend that these assumptions will not help us understand Kaulong attitudes toward gender distinction, the characteristic relationship between genders, nor how these attitudes relate to concepts of what is natural and what is cultural.

Ortner presents yet another image of nature/culture when she writes: we may envision culture in this case as a small clearing within the forest of the larger natural system. From this point of view that which is intermediate between culture and nature is located on the continuous periphery of culture's clearing; and though it may appear to stand both above and below (and beside) culture, it is simply outside and around it (1974:85). Ortner places women on this periphery and considers that 'women's intermediate position may have the implication of greater symbolic ambiguity' (ibid.).

This spatial–horizontal view of nature/culture is remarkably close to the folk-model I have deduced for the Kaulong world view of their social and moral order with, however, one major distinction: the Kaulong do not place women on the periphery; rather they have placed married persons of either gender in this medial, marginal and ambiguous position. In the Kaulong model:

|  |  |  |
|---|---|---|
| culture | : | nature |
| clearing | : | forest |
| unmarried | : | married |

In this chapter I discuss these formulations and show in what ways the Kaulong consider the married/unmarried distinction to be of greater saliency than the distinction they make between male and female, and how their concepts concerning sexuality relate to their view that it is the married person, not the female of the species, who is marginal, intermediate and ambiguous.

## The forest and the clearing

The Austronesian speaking Kaulong of Papua New Guinea inhabit a region north and inland from the administrative centre at Kandrian, located on the southwest coast of New Britain.[4] The area between the coast and the

4   Fieldwork was conducted in two separate locations among the Kaulong; first in the foothills of the Whiteman Mountains, and secondly in the region between the foothills and the coast. Chowning's data is also drawn from two Sengseng locations. While regional variability is to be found in the patterns and concepts (and where pertinent is noted in the paper), the data presented here are derived from all these regions.

foothills of the Whiteman Mountains is sparsely settled. Kaulong number about 2,000 persons and are linguistically related to the Sengseng, Miu and Karore who together make up a population with a density of approximately two or three per square kilometre. Heavy forest is rooted rather uneasily in shallow soil over a sharply undulating limestone base. Yawning potholes and numerous streams, subject to rapid flooding during the heaviest periods of the 250-inch annual rainfall, are both hazards to life.

Scattered throughout the forest and separated from each other by two or more kilometres are small clearings. These clearings average 2–3 hectares, and contain at least one house, called a *mang*, and perhaps one or two smaller lean-to type shelters, called *mok*. Surrounding the clearing are permanently planted trees such as areca palm, coconut palm, Tahitian chestnut, *ficus* and breadfruit, as well as others. Such a clearing is considered to represent a place of orientation for all cognatic descendants of the original clearer of the ground and is referred to by suffixing the appropriate possessive pronoun to the word *bi-* (place) as in *bidanu*, 'our place'. I shall gloss *bi-* as place, hamlet or central clearing in this discussion.[5]

Not all of these cognatic descendants of the original founder/clearer of the ground alive at any period of time will live at or be affiliated to a particular place or *bi-*. Rarely will there be more than twelve or fifteen residential affiliates at any given time. Non-resident descendants may choose to maintain their ties and keep their residential options open, through periodic visits and exchanges of valuables and goods with their kin who reside at and maintain the clearing and its resources. While a son should preferably reside at the *bi-* of his father (his natal place), and a married woman with her husband, much variability is found and it is quite common for both unmarried males and females as well as married couples to change their residential affiliation a number of times throughout their lifetime. Residential affiliates who die are buried inside the main structure, the *mang*, and, finally, all who so maintain their rights of affiliation also share equally in the ownership of the place and the resources. A *bi-*, place of orientation and affiliation, is the only geographical space which is owned on a permanent basis. The cognatic group sharing in the ownership also share an identity as *poididuan* (glossed as 'all related' or in Melanesian Pidgin as either *barata* 'brother' or *bisnis* 'business').

All activities associated with each place are managed by the *midan*, (big man, or leader) who is the founder or represents, by replacement, the original founder. A manager directs activities which concern the clearing

5    Larger aggregates of houses and individuals, termed 'villages', were artificial social units established while the region was under the control of Europeans. Data from my 1974 trip, on the eve of Independence, showed almost complete return to the hamlet pattern of residence and activity on a permanent basis, and the related abandonment of larger residential aggregations.

itself; the harvesting and distribution of shared resources, and the ritual and public activities concerning these resources. Major ceremonial activity at a place always involves the sacrifice of one or more domestic pigs belonging to affiliates, allowing the pig's blood to soak the ground and the bones of deceased affiliates buried there, while the flesh (uncooked pork) is distributed for consumption to visitors who are not of the place.[6] Activities occurring in the context of *lut a yu* (singing displays and pig meat, distributions) are key activities in which one's social identity is formed, displayed and developed.

Surrounding the permanent clearing is the forest where all the major subsistence and productive activity of the Kaulong take place. Here gardens are made by temporarily clearing the tree cover in order to plant taro, the basic staple, and other tubers, greens, bananas, as well as tobacco and sugar cane. While the garden takes up considerable production time, it provides only a portion of the subsistence and surplus products for trade. The forest and streams are extensively exploited for protein (small game, insects, fish, shellfish and birds) as well as carbohydrates (wild tubers, nuts, seeds, and greens). In the foothills of the mountains where soil is shallow and terrain steep and gardens typically scattered and small, I estimate that 60% of subsistence products come from forest activities, while in the gently undulating area closer to the coast 40% of subsistence is from the forest. Patterns of activities relating to these complementary aspects of the diet are inversely proportional to the time and energy expended in producing them. Both forest and garden are essential for the maintenance of life and for the production of surplus for trade and transaction. Men and women, as well as children of either gender, are all equally 'at home' in these productive environments.

Single unmarried male affiliates of a *bi-* usually clear and maintain gardens closest to the *bi-*, and return to it at night to sleep in the main structure, the *mang*. Married affiliates and their young children maintain gardens deeper into the forest on the further perimeter. They are separated from each other, from the gardens of the single men, and from the *bi-* by greater distances. In these outer gardens, a couple and their young children usually sleep in a small lean-to, sometimes in an available cave or other natural shelter. Only when involved in garden activities or when a major ceremony is scheduled do a married couple and children return to a central *bi-* for a few days, or go visiting and trading to other established places.

Domestic pigs spend the day in the forest searching for food and shelter from the sun, returning to the *bi-*, or sometimes a hut near an abandoned

6  In both myth and explicit explanation Kaulong contrast human consumption of pork with demon consumption of human flesh, considering this dietary preference as a key symbol defining the distinction:

human   :   demon

garden, to receive additional food and human attention from their appointed caretaker necessary to their continued domestication. Male pigs are castrated; thus sows leave the *bi-* to become impregnated in the forest by wild boar. Pregnant sows return to the clearing of their caretaker and the young piglets are raised there. As we shall see, there is a parallel between this pattern of pig production and that of human reproduction, where sisters of a place leave to become impregnated by outside males since their close brothers at home may not impregnate them. Children belong to their mother's natal place as well as to the place of her impregnator.[7]

There is some division of labour in productive activities, but the division is not necessarily based upon gender. Some men make entire gardens and raise pigs alone without the aid of women's labour, and some women carry out nearly all the necessary tasks relating to garden production save the clearing of heavy timber and fence building, although they may also help males in these tasks. Both men and women own the taro stalks they plant and maintain through successive replanting and regeneration. They own the bananas and other food plants and trees which they individually plant and care for and they may transact with any surplus fruit, nut or shoot which they produce. Men and women alike own and plant tobacco for consumption and for trade. Pigs are owned by both men and women and may be cared for by either, although more frequently they are cared for by women.

While there is no distinction in ownership of resources by quality, there is in relation to quantity. Men will control through productive activities more of these resources than will women, enabling them to a greater degree to transact in surplus products on their own behalf and thereby increase their political influence. Some women do achieve considerable notice through production and trade of surplus garden and other domestic products, but not equal to the upper limits men may reach.

Certainly it is cooperation in production which results in increased resources, and ambitious men and women work to achieve the economic (labour) support of both male and female kin, single and married. What is not necessary, however, is that the cooperating individuals be married to each other, as I shall discuss below.

To summarize: in the cultural division of geographical space, a basic contrast is made between the forest and the clearing, with gardens occupying a medial position. Men, women and pigs are to be found equally in these three areas; however, the activities associated with each area are dis-

7   Sibling terms are extended to all degrees of parallel and cross cousins; however, incest restrictions only apply to 'siblings' who share a parent. While marriage is common and to a limited extent preferred between cross cousins, parallel cousin marriage does occur rarely (see Goodale 1980 for further discussion of sibling and spouse relationships).

tinctive. Activities involving maintaining and developing personal, social and kinship identity are primarily associated with the clearing, while production and biological reproduction are associated with garden and forest.[8] It is the activities of production and reproduction which spatially separate the married from the unmarried, with the married closest to the periphery (furthest from the centre). In contrast to the unmarried, the married are involved in sexual reproduction of themselves, and in this they are close to the animals in the forest (cf. chapter 4). The forest is not only the place where wild animals engage in sexual intercourse and where humans and pigs retreat to do the same, it is also the place of non-human spirits and demons of varying characteristics and whose relation to man is capricious at best and dangerous at worst.[9] Let us add to our model as follows:

| *Clearing* | *Garden* | *Forest* |
|---|---|---|
| unmarried human | married human | spirit/demon; non-human |
| 'work' ritual and transaction | garden production | sexual reproduction |
| non-subsistence activities, male/female | subsistence activities, male/female | |

## Person, male and female

Kaulong assumptions regarding the necessary characteristics for being considered 'human' as opposed to 'non-human' or demon, along with the defining characteristics of gender categories, involve relationships of *placement* and identity, as well as additional concepts relating to definition of self, mind, and growth, and finally concepts concerning sexuality.

As discussed above, an individual may affiliate with any place *bi-* with which he or she can trace a linkage through either parent and ascending links of either sex to a founder, the clearer of the ground and establisher of the place. At the minimum, each child maintains rights to affiliate with his father's and mother's natal place. While these rights are usually considered

8  I use production here to refer specifically to subsistence items of prime cultural significance (e.g. taro). Certainly the nut and fruit trees of the hamlet are 'productive', but in no way are they considered essential as 'food' items.

9  Chowning comments that the Sengseng equate unrestrained and public display of sexuality more with dogs (than pigs) who, because they are not castrated, are obvious examples to contrast with 'human' behaviour. My data indicate that among the Kaulong 'tame' male dogs to be used in hunting wild pigs are usually castrated as puppies. The only reference to humans as dogs was by a Kaulong male characterizing his wife's promiscuous behaviour as 'like a dog, and typical of her Sengseng origin!'. Obviously more data are needed from both regions.

to carry equal weight, a child has, in some situations, greater rights in his father's place than do children of his father's sister, and in these same situations fewer rights in his mother's place than do children of his mother's brother. These weighted situations manifest Kaulong belief that, sometimes, complementarity between descendants of men of the group (*da mulu*, of the barkcloth) and the descendants of the women of the group (*da songon*, of the skirt) is more significant than is the usually stressed *solidarity* and *similarity* of all descendants of a place (and its founder).

Children of men of a place and children of women of a place are otherwise equally entitled to share in the activities and resources of the *bi-*. They are equally obliged to maintain the continuity of the cleared place and its resources over time. Ambitious and energetic individuals will continue to maintain active ties with a number of *bi-* in addition to the one to which they are residentially affiliated. While they will not reside at all these places over their lifetime, they keep their options to do so open by making visits and transacting in important affairs with resident kin of the place. In this way they maintain their social identity and build social networks throughout the region (see Goodale 1978 for further discussion of transaction).

People's identity is shaped by their activities in their place of residence. These activities are a matter of considerable importance to them. While discussing kinship a person travels the social landscape in a chronicle of contemporary and historic placement of ancestral identity. Through travel to places and by engaging in transactions while there, one creates one's own place in a group of co-relates. To be without a place is to be without relatives, to be a social non-person. Placement thus gives an individual identity in a group of related persons, and recognition of legitimacy as being born of properly placed human parents.

Affiliates of a place and their active non-residential relatives are responsible for maintaining the clearing, the structures in which deceased affiliates are buried and where the living congregate. They are also responsible for the continuity of the productive trees, and for the people of the place. Continuity of the line of productive trees is assured by the replanting of a shoot, sprout, seed or nut in the same general place as its parent, when the original tree dies. The young plant is considered as the direct replacement of the elder, and genealogies of plants and the planters are correlated items of knowledge maintained by affiliates of the place.

Affiliates of a place are buried in the ground of the *bi-*, in the floor of the main structure. In the past, it was normal for a child of the affiliate to bury the parent, and to replace that parent in the *bi-*, thus maintaining the parent's place in the locale. Traditionally a wife was strangled and buried with a deceased husband. The wife's identity however, was primarily located in *her* natal place and concern for her replacement, for continuity, arose when she left her natal place on marriage, not on her death. Thus, normally, complementary lines of descendants will be produced in each generation who share the responsibility of maintaining the continuity of all plant and human resources defining a place through a process of one-to-one replacement of identity. Plant replacement is, of course, without regard to gender. Human replacement tends to follow gender lines, but this is not considered essential: a daughter can carry on a father's identity and a son that of his mother.

If people have no children to maintain their identity, that identity is considered to have been lost. Some individuals can lose their placement through outrageous behaviour and exile from all places to which claim could be made. Permanent loss of control over one's mind, or one's soul or self, may also cause displacement. Such displacement rapidly leads to social classification as non-human, perhaps demon of the forest or stream.[10]

The Kaulong consider the human body (*wo*), composed of skin, flesh, bone and blood and various organs, to be a container for both the self (*enu*) and the mind (*mi*). When the body, self and mind are all intact one can refer to the person as *potunus* (literally plural pronoun + good, or alive). These elements are inter-related yet independent of each other and together affect the well-being of the total person. While the self may detach itself from the body, and frequently does so during sleep and at other times during an individual's life, the mind never leaves. The mind controls the self and the body, directing each to put into action the thoughts, desires and intentions of the person.

The self is that part of the body in which all experience and knowledge is internalized and, as experience and knowledge accumulate, the self grows in volume independent of the natural growth of the container, the body. A rapidly growing self causes the skin to be tight and shine, and is itself reflected through the eyes. A body which grows more rapidly than the self, or without a self, or with a diminishing self is wrinkled, dull and without vitality. A self detaches itself during sleep and, if under normal control, will return; however, temporary or permanent loss of self may occur through sudden awakening, fright, accident, illness or loss of control through sorcery. The variable size, health and effectiveness of individuals is directly related to the health and quantity of self. It is believed that in causing things to come into being, whether object or event, some partial displacement of self occurs and becomes part of the created object or event. Continual displacement of self requires continual replacement in order that the person can maintain or increase their effective activity. A big person (*pomidan* (male); *polamit* (female)) is one who is able to continu-

10  A particularly well remembered big man responsible for many deaths, unusual exploitation of others as well as other asocial actions, is now considered (in death) to have become a demon (*marsalai*) and to dwell permanently in a stream rather than in the mountain region where human spirits are to be found after death.

ally maintain or increase the knowledge and effective power contained within their self. An individual who loses control of self, or who expends without replenishment becomes ineffectual, unable to accomplish anything constructive; if the loss is permanent the individual becomes a social non-person.[11]

There is no evidence that this notion of personhood (being of sound and controlled mind, body and self) is in any way different according to whether the body is male or female. The differential qualities are in size of self, the differential ability of the mind to control and put into action its desires, and the health of the body so that it may physically carry out the activities necessary for achieving desired social and personal goals. Because of what Kaulong consider to be periodic bodily illness (menstruation and childbirth) females are less able to work continually to increase the size of self. Some females, however, do achieve considerable differential social status, measured on the same quantity scale of self as males (see Goodale 1976; 1977 for further discussion).

The key activities necessary for social achievement are those concerned with production and display through transaction of those objects and events containing self. Both men and women work to produce taro and pork in order to exchange them for other symbolic valuables, especially gold-lip pearl shells. Demonstration of self achievement is not in accumulation of goods, but rather in the display of one's whole person in visible good health and bursting vitality and in continual productive and transactional success. More men than women display bigger, stronger persons, but development of self and its display is not gender specific.

The most important display of self takes place at pork exchanges made between residential hamlets. The transactions are preceded by competitive singing throughout the night, by a contest between hosts and visiting place-affiliates. These events traditionally included spear fights between men of the two or three groups involved, courting attacks initiated by young girls against young men, as well as the all important transactions in pork and shell valuables. They were and are rituals of considerable cultural and social significance, quite the most important event to be carried out in the *bi-*. A man said:

In the beginning women carried spears and shields and went to the 'sing-sings' and fought, while men slept in the bush with their sickness. Then the women asked the men to carry their shields and spears and in return the men gave the women their sickness. Now men go to the 'singsings' while women sleep in the bush with their sickness.

11   Panoff (1968) reports a case among the Maenge where an unfortunate individual was not buried at death for he was known to have lost his soul prior to bodily death. Burial of the body was therefore considered unnecessary, as the self was no longer there and the person of no consequence.

Gender in Kaulong is a given for all occupants of a 'place'. Human beings, pigs and dogs are linguistically differentiated *at birth* into discrete male and female categories (*wala* – female; *masang* – male), but animals of the forest do not appear to be initially so differentiated. While categorical distinction is also made in reference and address terminology relating to kin categories, little distinction in socialization is noticed, nor in the gender of the social-izers throughout the early development period of life. Fathers as well as mothers, and other close affiliates of the *bi-* of all ages and either gender share in the rearing of children of the *bi-*. This joint responsibility is par-ticularly noticeable when a child is exceptionally robust and vital – a child seen to be of great potential for self development. Such a child is truly a 'child of the place' with all adults concerned in his/her care and develop-ment.

There is regional variability in the assumption of gender specific genital coverings (barkcloth, now cotton, for males; vegetable fibres for women). Generally by the age of ten individuals have regularly assumed such dis-tinctive clothing. Activities of children are as undifferentiated by gender as are those of their elders. In patterns of approved aggression, however, there is a noticeable gender distinction, and socialization for aggression begins very early in life. Young toddling males are encouraged to play roughly with other boys, are given sticks to return an attack and to persist and defend themselves and not run. Boys are also taught to avoid such behav-iour with girls. Young toddling girls, on the other hand, are encouraged to act aggressively toward young boys, usually striking blows with sticks. Since the boys may not return a girl's attack he can only run to escape, and the girls are encouraged to keep up the attack by pursuing the escaping victim. Hand fighting is considered appropriate between girls. The differ-ential training in cross-sex aggression is an all-important pattern for court-ship leading to marriage, as we shall see below. But it is first necessary to examine more closely beliefs concerning the major distinction to be found between men and women, the menstrual/childbirth 'sickness' and its power to contaminate and cause illness.

From some time before puberty to after menopause, females are con-sidered capable of polluting. The ability, or power, is a continuous one, with periods of increased intensity during the menstrual blood flow and during childbirth. While in these two intensely polluting conditions a woman must remove herself from the *bi-*, stay clear of all gardens and dwelling places located there and all drinking water supplies and sources. She may not touch anything with which a man may come in contact. During these times the polluting effect spreads outward, laterally, in all directions from the woman. Periodic total isolation of the woman is the most efficient means of control.

Contrasting with the concept of periodic lateral contamination, mature women are also considered at all times to be capable of polluting anything they pass over or rest upon, the pollution spreading vertically and directly downwards, and permanently affecting anything below.

Female pollution is dangerous only to males. They become contaminated and made ill by ingesting anything so polluted, or through consumption of anything which itself has been in contact with a polluted object, or by placing their own body directly underneath a contaminated object or polluting woman. There is some indication that males only gradually become susceptible to such contamination. If it so happens that a mother resumes menstruation while still nursing a young child, the child will normally accompany his/her mother into isolation. Even if weaned, sons are frequent visitors to their mother in her menstrual isolation. Young lads are frequently sent into contaminating areas by older males, to retrieve objects of value before the objects become seriously affected. The respiratory illness which results from prolonged and cumulative female pollution leads to an early death.

The concept of vertical pollution gives rise to certain habits being adopted in forest travel and to particular architectural features found in garden huts and major dwellings. While on the trail, men must take care not to pass under any fallen tree or natural or constructed bridge, for one must always assume that a woman has walked on the tree or crossed over the bridge. Women need not exercise such care as they are not subject to their own pollution.

In the *bi-* and in the garden all houses were traditionally built on the ground. The raised houses which recent Australian administration advocated as being healthier were very unpopular precisely because of the health problems they caused for males. If a contaminating woman has once been inside such a raised house, no male may shelter underneath, nor may he retrieve or use any object which fell through the floor boards. A male could eat no food which had been cooked underneath the house and the raised floor made inside cooking difficult and dangerous. Wood stored under the house could not be used for cooking. In the traditional houses there are usually two or more bed/benches made of loose poles supported with fires built between the beds. Cooking is restricted to one particular fire or to one particular region of the larger *bi-* structures. Food is stored above or away from the bed/benches where women sit and firewood for cooking is kept in between roof beams, and water containers hung from the side walls. In the main *bi-* structure, single men commonly cook their own food and some married men prefer to cook there for themselves as well, considering the possibility that food cooked by women has been prepared carelessly in the wrong fire. While some men expressed fear that some women may be deliberately feeding them contaminated food, most merely considered women generally to be careless and unconcerned about this contaminating matter. From my own observations, I rarely saw women show concern for their own pollution effect on others, with the exception of mothers who regularly protested when their young sons were sent to retrieve objects dropped by men through the floor of my raised house.[12]

Female pollution is conceptually well defined. The continual or daily polluting effect is transmitted in a restricted downward vertical direction to anyone or anything below. Avoidance of such vertical contamination is fairly easy and does not necessitate lateral separation of the sexes. In the main structure of the *bi-*, women as well as men freely enter and involve themselves in discussions and activities occurring there during the day. At night the structure is usually restricted to males for sleeping, a restriction relating to incest and marriage rules more than to pollution. Close bodily contact is permitted between primary kin of opposite sex from infancy throughout adulthood; siblings of opposite sex maintain the closest of all primary kin ties in adulthood with the possible exception of mother and son. Such dyads are often found grooming each other's heads for lice, sleeping in the same house and generally caring for each other's welfare with affection and concern, but also with due respect to avoidance of pollution from sister to brother. These dyads are also the most cooperative in economic ventures (Goodale 1980).

Periods of intensified pollution during menstruation and childbirth when the pollution spreads laterally from the women are the only times which necessitate the lateral separation of the woman from the physical domain of all men, including the house, garden and mutually used possessions. Menstrual huts are built at the periphery of the central clearing (*bi-*), or outside the garden fence just beyond the cleared areas. Childbirth may take place in a rock shelter or artificially constructed hut deeper in the forest if possible, but certainly within the 'forest' outside any clearing. The isolated menstruating woman is able to collect her own food from forest and stream, but drinking water and garden produce must be provided for her, left nearby for her to collect if the supplier is male. She wears special disposable leaf skirts, uses disposable leaf water and lime containers. Other women may freely visit the isolated woman, tending a new mother and infant. Males may approach only within a distance of approximately ten to fifteen metres.

My data show that before European contact the Kaulong did not ritually mark the onset of menstruation. Nearer the coast, however, a menstrual ritual is being introduced into the interior region by inmarrying women from the Arawe speakers of the coast. This ritual involves shaving the young girl's head, presenting her ritually with special skirt fibres and materials, symbols of production (e.g. taro stalk, coconut, yam, etc.) as well as firewood which transforms taro into food. She is verbally instructed

12 Chowning reminds me that some pigs are also thought to get ill if they pass under a bed on which a woman has slept. My data confirm this for both male and female pigs, but only those considered to have exceptional potential for growth.

in the names of the objects and skirt fibres as well as that of menstrual blood. She is also instructed concerning pollution and restrictions. Parents, married males and females and unmarried females observe the ritual. Observers are necessary for making the woman's new polluting power public knowledge. The vulnerable categories of people have then been warned to protect themselves from the woman's expected lack of concern and probable carelessness.

There are other initiatory rituals that are traditionally carried out with male initiates, although occasionally fathers have been known to arrange such affairs for their daughters. They involve application of a black mineral (manganese oxide?) to the teeth of the young initiate in his/her late teens or early twenties. It is said that should the initiate have sexual intercourse prior to this application, the blackening will not harden on the tooth enamel. While the mineral is in contact with the tooth enamel, the initiate is kept in the main *bi-* structure, for four or five days. He is allowed to eat nothing and may only swallow water avoiding contact with his teeth. Through this initial period, affiliates and visiting kin sing nightly. After this period the initiate leaves the clearing and gardens, and lives in the forest, hunting and exploiting streams for food which, however, he may not eat but must give to others. Until the mineral is fixed and hard, the initiate may not chew or consume any hot food. Although I have no direct data concerning the relationship of toothblackening and pollution of women, a male initiate should not be seen or attacked by courting girls during this period.[13]

In spite of the rather restricted nature of female pollution, Kaulong males showed an extraordinary amount of fear and anxiety concerning it. Their concern was verbalized almost daily by male informants and was particularly emphasized when marriage was suggested to any single male. The equation of sexual intercourse with marriage and contamination, and male fear and avoidance of all three was an impressive and distinctive feature of Kaulong life.

## Marriage

One of the most significant aspects of cultural and social change which has come through contact with European legal and moral codes is marriage and sexual behaviour.[14] What I describe here are the pre-contact beliefs,

13  Panoff (1968) reports that the Maenge, who also blacken their teeth with this mineral, consider it as a prophylaxis against contamination occurring in the sexual act.

14  German contact, beginning in the late nineteenth century, only penetrated the area immediately inland from the coast, as did the early Australian contact which followed the First World War. Patrols into the more remote foothill region were as late as the 1950s and

many of which inform contemporary behaviour, though significant changes affecting the underlying thesis of this chapter will be noted.

Kaulong equate sexual intercourse in thought or in fact with marriage. There is one word, *nangin*, by which to refer to 'sleeping' in the same house with an eligible partner, an act implying 'sexual intercourse'. It also means that a formally acknowledged 'marriage' has taken place. It is quite impossible to speak of sexual intercourse without implying marriage as well. Should intercourse occur between ineligible persons then death to both was the sanctioned outcome. Sexual intercourse/marriage between siblings with a common parent was punished by death. Parent and own child incest was also taboo. Women who were already married were considered ineligible to both married and unmarried males. The offender (male), and in a number of cases the adulterous woman as well, were killed in pre-colonial times.

Should the sexually involved, but eligible, pair decline to consider themselves married with all its consequences (see below), the sanction was death or exile. From a number of cases, it is apparent that in such situations the couple were eventually persuaded to recognize their marriage as a fact. Today, the death sanction underlying the taboos and persuasions is no longer enforceable: the national legal system forbids violent 'self help' and would not recognize the grounds for such action. As a result sexual affairs without acknowledged marriage are occurring with increasing regularity, as is marriage of women to successive men, a rare and exceptional occurrence in the past. Prior to European contact, Kaulong bride and groom were expected to be virgins when they married. Sexual intercourse was sometimes delayed for a number of days or weeks after a 'marriage'

Men are quite literally scared to death of marriage (and sex). Young men often repeated the phrase 'I am too young to get married and die.' Or they said, 'When I am old and ready to die, I will get married and find a replacement for myself who will bury me.' I was told by one man that the youngest of a set of brothers should remain single throughout his life so that as his older brothers died (from marital contamination), and their

have never been intensive. Both Roman Catholic and Church of England missions have been established on the coast since the early 1930s. The former have extended their influence into the interior while the latter concentrate their efforts on the coast among the Arawe speakers. Neither group has acknowledged any great success with the interior peoples. However, both legal and church codes run counter to much that was traditional concerning marriage and sexuality. For example, with girls acting aggressively in courtship, it was hard for the Kaulong to convince the European that if sexual relations followed it was to be considered as rape, and either death or marriage must follow!

wife or wives were strangled and buried with them, the younger brother would remain alive to look after the orphaned children.

Sexual intercourse is not only considered intensely polluting for the male; it is also considered 'animal-like' and should take place away from *bi-* and garden in the forest. Neither gender should show overt interest in copulation. Married couples who spend long periods of time together and away from the public area of the *bi-* may be suspected of 'inhuman' pre-occupation with marital sex. A woman who becomes pregnant before a previous child can walk independently is considered over-indulgent; the resulting child may be killed at birth.

I do not know whether the Kaulong consider the foetus to be formed through complementary contributions occurring in sexual intercourse, as is reported in many Melanesian societies. Kaulong men and women are extraordinarily reluctant and painfully embarrassed when asked to discuss such issues. There is little doubt that Kaulong do consider the act of sexual intercourse to result in the formation of a child and that both parents are replicated in the foetus and therefore are responsible for its form and substance. But I also believe that the exegesis of this concept is not an essential part of their social/cultural philosophy. I believe Kaulong equate human reproduction more with the replacement pattern common to much of their tropical world, and in particular with the plants which spontaneously reproduce themselves through cloning, creating replications of themselves without the bisexual activity required of animals (Goodale 1980).

That Kaulong men and women marry to reproduce themselves is the central meaning given to both marriage and sexual activity. Both men and women desire replacements and those who are in a sexual relationship and do *not* produce children are considered as an anomaly. Genealogies indicate that suicide was an accepted resolution for the unproductive partnership. Husband and wife who were too old to procreate were known to resort to suicide when their child or children died before them. Not having replacements and being incapable of producing them made their sexual activity (and marriage) without meaning and caused them shame (*mangin*).

For a woman, marriage with a single sexual partner was contracted for life. When her husband died she was strangled by her close primary male kin and buried with her husband. Colonial policy forbade such practices and today a new social category of widow has emerged. Many of these widows remain unmarried, particularly if they are beyond childbearing age and/or when their own children are full grown. Frequently a widow attaches herself to a son's establishment, helping him in his productive endeavours. Others remarry and may produce children with their new sexual partner. Some men marry more than one wife, requiring the previous wife's acceptance. There are a number of cases in my data where a husband strangled himself upon the prior death of a wife. Before the colonial period, Kaulong considered that any sexual partnership was for life (and death). There was no 'divorce' to terminate a marriage. Together, a couple produced children who replaced them in the world. With immortality achieved, death could follow for both.

With men afraid and reluctant to commit themselves to marriage, it is the women who assume the dominant role in courtship. Although there is some regional difference in courtship, the pattern may include all or some of the following activities: girls may offer cooked food or tobacco to a man, or they may initiate *'tokplei'* (Melanesian pidgin for play talk) or physically attack the man using supple long switches or knives. The attacked male must either flee, if he can or so desires, or he may withstand the attack without countermeasures until an agreement is reached, the attacking girl accepting offers of goods, valuables or money from him. Women use magical substances inserted into the offered food or tobacco to cause men to lose the desire, or even the ability, to flee. Such magic acts to control the mind (*mi*) of the man. Men wishing to be courted by girls will also use magic substances and formulae as well as sweet fragrances, leaves, flowers, oils and colourful bodily decorations to attract the attention of eligible single women.

As mentioned above, from infancy girls are encouraged to behave aggressively towards males, and men are taught to submit to such attacks without retaliation, or run. Should a male initiate an act of courtship toward a woman it is considered rape, and in the past marriage or death was the expected result. Women are allowed almost complete choice in the eventual selection of the man they wish to marry. Close kinsmen of either sex are consulted by the girl and they (particularly her brothers) will usually aid her in the persuasion of the often reluctant groom. This persuasion may involve deception, luring, and capture. The groom may be forceably restrained in the same house with the bride who has chosen him for as long as it may take him to accept his fate and pay off the guards with shells so they can leave. While a woman may postpone making her choice until she reaches her twentieth year or later, most eventually do marry. Rarely, however, is a woman forced into a marriage not to her liking and then only under exceptional circumstances.[15]

With sexual intercourse considered a definition of marriage, a potentially lethal act (for both men and women), and to be animal-like rather than human behaviour, it is not surprising that there is some social distinction between those who participate in sexual activity, the married, and those who remain celibate, the unmarried. What is surprising is the

15  Big men may force an unwelcome marriage on a woman. In the several cases I recorded, the wife resorted to suicide within a relatively short time.

degree of spatial, behavioural and symbolic separation between these two categories of persons.

I have already discussed the spatial separation found in the usual residential arrangement of married and single affiliates of a place (*bi-*). The main *bi-* structure is usually utilized on a regular basis by single males only, and these individuals also utilize garden sites closest to the *bi-*. Married couples make their gardens at some distance from the *bi-*, and regularly sleep in huts they construct there. Since the married are in the outer perimeter they are not only separated from the unmarried males, but from other married couples as well. Sexual jealousy runs high among married couples in spite of the fact that death was the traditional punishment for adultery. But I believe that sexual shame and embarrassment is also a cause for the isolation of the sexually active couple.

Changing from unmarried to married status requires an abrupt modification of behaviour. Immediately after a marriage is publicly recognized the bride and groom cease all activity but that which is most essential to maintain physical life. They stop nearly all social interaction aside from that with their own closest primary kin and with each other. The cessation of all physical activity is considered essential, I was told, because 'they are weak'. They can do no household tasks, nor may they work in the garden. They will be given small amounts of cooked food to eat, and they may bathe in a stream, but, generally, I was told and observed, 'they sleep'.

This weakness may last a week or more, but gradually the pair regain their strength; however, a complex series of taboos, affecting both bride and groom similarly, severely restrict and restructure their interaction with all the cognatic kin of their spouse, whether alive or dead, resident or non-resident.[16]

A married person may not use the name of any affine (other than their spouse), nor may they use the word from which the name was derived or resembles. The result of this rule is a major change in each married person's vocabulary as they substitute alternative words for those now taboo to them. Kaulong call this form of speech the speech of the married as though it were a single vocabulary set used by all married individuals, but this is not the case, as the choice of alternative word and the peculiar set of affines (ancestral and contemporary) give every married person an individual distinction in his or her speech. It takes rather a long period of time before married persons are set in their new lexicon, and when newly

---

16  This period of weakness resembles the liminal period often found in transition rites between young and adult. The 'rebirth' imagery explicitly symbolized here emphasizes the completeness of the status/role changes which marriage forces on both the bride and groom. The subsequent reestablishment of social identity processually reflects an infant's developmental stages of growth and socialization.

married and unsure of the extent and nature of the name/word taboos they tend to remain remarkably quiet and verbally hesitant.

Married persons may not eat or drink in front of any affine, nor may they act aggressively in front of or to an affine. While these, and the name/speech taboos, are permanent, other temporary behavioural restrictions related to them are imposed upon the newly-wed individuals. Neither may eat any food carried on an affine's head, or over an affine's body (alive or dead). Neither may they walk over an affine's body, nor raise any part of their own body above that of an affine. With these taboos, neither bride nor groom may visit each other's natal *bi-*, or any *bi-* where affines are buried, nor may they eat any food from an affine unless specially carried and prepared to meet the restrictions. And, finally, neither bride nor groom may go behind any affine, nor act in any way aggressively toward them. Initially this rule includes directing any speech to an affine, although this restriction as well as others mentioned above will be modified over time.

The modification of affinal restrictions are at the wish and timing of the affine and accomplished by the payment of a gold-lip pearl shell to each affine for each modification. Gradually bride and groom present shells to their individual affines allowing them to become affiliated with/or visit each other's *bi-*, eat food from the gardens, participate in activities, speak to an affine (although never loudly or in anger), and to go above them and behind them (although never for aggressive acts). Shells given to deceased affines are placed on their grave.

These affinal taboos serve immediately to separate the married from their married and unmarried kin as well as from their affines. Typically, newly-married couples move to a hut in a garden clearing and reside there. Since males marry late in life, most have established gardens to which they can retire with their new bride. If there is no garden in which they may be isolated, either the groom's kin or the bride's will allow immediate removal of some of the necessary restrictions so that the couple may reside with or close by them. The restraint between affines also works to marginalize the married couples from too close or prolonged daily contact with either group of living affines, and from their place of burial.

Finally, separation of married from unmarried is also marked with a change in reference and address kin terminology used between siblings and that used between parents and children. A married sibling is called by and referred to by a distinct set of terms depending on the sex of the speaker. A married child is called by and referred to by the same terms as those he/she uses for parents of the same sex. These terms are initially used when it is known or assumed that the sibling or child is sexually active in the marriage.

While marriage marginalizes the couple in relation to the central clearing with which they affiliate, it is also true that married couples are placed in a medial position between clearings or *bi-*. Because of the prohibition of any acts of aggression between affines, some marriages are deliberately arranged in order to achieve a peaceful relationship with another formerly hostile local group. These 'marriage alliances' and the peace they reflect only serve to affiliate the married couple with the two local groups thus achieving limited integration. However, the couple does have emotional ties to both of these groups, mediating between the respective kin, and consequently helping to suppress aggression. At the very least the couple itself will not participate in any outbreak of conflict between the groups for fear of injuring an affine. It is important to emphasize here that the alliance between married individuals and their respective affinal kin is reflected in mutual interest both groups take in the children the couple produces. The children as replacements of their parents may choose to affiliate with either set of relatives.

Marriage is only one type of alliance relationship between individuals of different local groups. Exchange partnerships independent of affinal relationships are of even greater importance to the political fabric of the society. Such exchange relationships are most frequent between individuals of the same sex, but may also occur between males and females. They must be cultivated and nurtured through repetitive acts of exchange or the relationship ceases to exist. Men and women usually make only one marriage relationship in their lifetime, although some men may manage several, either concurrent or successive. However, through trade and shell transactions everyone may create and maintain 'alliance' networks far more extensive than those they can make through marriage, and trade partnerships are less hedged with behavioural restraints and less inherently dangerous to health and life.

Although all or most women marry, not every man will take this route to achieve fame and fortune. While obviously some men enjoyed being chased and courted by girls and would use love magic to attract attacks and pay out large amounts to satisfy the girls, many would flee from marriage, its permanence, restrictions, and increased health hazard. Extremely late marriage for males was not unusual and some men remained unmarried throughout their lifetime. The path to fame and fortune for a male was through production of taro, pigs, and other transactable items, through developing extensive trade networks and through the successful management of a *bi-* and the activities of its affiliates. If one attracted residents into one's *bi-*, their cooperation would help achieve prestige for all. A successful manager used to attract married as well as unmarried kin to affiliate or to cooperate on a regular visiting arrangement. A number of men expressed the view that sisters and mothers were far more reliable female helpers than most wives, and less competitive than brothers. However, it was also acknowledged that a good wife, one who worked hard and productively, could also be an important element in a man's success as well as in her own.

With little necessary sexual division of labour in the production of garden products or in the raising of pigs, a man could become successful on his own with only temporary help from male and female kin when necessary. Some men did manage to achieve considerable fame as big men, managers of *bi-* with many active affiliates, without entering into marriage. Such men endeavoured to attract a sister's son, or a brother's son to bury them when they died, and take over management of the *bi-*. Nephews, however, were not considered to replace their uncles' identity.

Women on their own behalf traded and transacted with kinsmen in other locales. Through such activity they gained fame and were acknowledged as *polamit*, or big women. Producing and caring successfully for many children brought recognition for both women and their husbands, as did having a big garden and raising many pigs.

Women as well as men attended rituals involving the killing of pigs and transacting in pork. In the night of singing prior to the morning transactions, women joined the singing with men, without distinction. In large intercommunity affairs, however, the women of all groups took an intermediate position between the separated groups of men as they danced in lines. Before the colonial period, fights, which were said 'always' to accompany such affairs, included women as well as men in the battles, in extreme cases.

## Conclusions

The contrast between clearing and forest is an important distinction informing Kaulong life. We must now consider in what aspects this concept helps us to understand the following Kaulong categories: peoples/demons, male/female, and single/married.

The Kaulong have two main concerns or desires for personal achievement; 1) immortality through reproduction of identity, and 2) self-development through production and social activity. Because immortality requires human beings to engage in animal-like sexual intercourse in contrast to spontaneous plant-like reproduction through cloning, human reproduction is physically separated from plant and tree replacement and production, and takes place in the forest away from garden and central clearing. Self-development is displayed in the central clearing. It is in the pork distributions and singing that all may see the tangible and intangible results of extension of self.[17] Self-development is expansive, the develop-

17  Rarely is any forest product offered to exchange partners. Chief items are manganese oxide (black) and ochre (red), and water from a single source having special powers to cause illness or death to those who lie. Other natural resources of importance for occasional exchange are lizard skins for drum heads, wild piglets, and sometimes feathers for blowgun darts.

ment of an ever bigger self and more extensive personal trade network, while replacement of personal identity is maintenance, a one-to-one replacement of individuals.

With these dual concerns of immortality through reproduction of identity and self-development through production and exchange, Kaulong are faced with continuous decisions concerning self and identity management. They must decide whether to pursue one or both goals, then time and balance their activities to achieve their desires. Women may be seen as more equally balancing this duality, in that they are normally involved in both concerns for longer periods of their life. Men prefer to emphasize self-development over identity replacement in their early and middle life.[18]

The dual concerns and activities of adult Kaulong are also contrastive in that one is considered typical of human beings (self-development) while the other is typical of non-humans (reproduction of identity). Self-development places one in the centre of a network of socially active kin and trade partners while reproduction of identity isolates one from all save a sexual partner, husband or wife. At death there is a reversal of placement as the self leaves the body and the clearing, eventually residing in the deep virgin forest of the high mountain tops, while the person who replaces one's identity takes his or her place at the centre, in the *bi-*, and often in the social network of trading partners as well.

Married individuals are ambiguous as well as marginal because they are involved in both 'human' and 'non-human' activities. In non-human (reproductive) activities they cooperate only with each other for life, while in human (productive and transactional) activities they act as individuals, co-operating with kin or affine as they desire. Because there is no rigid division of labour based upon gender in productive activities the meaning of marriage for Kaulong is centrally located in the reproductive act, and not in production nor development of self.

It is only in aspects considered related to sexuality and reproduction (e.g. menstruation, childbirth, courtship and marriage) that gender distinctions are significant and necessitate the spatial relocation of those involved in relation to clearing and forest. This relocation involves at times men as well as women as each alone or together is isolated on the margins of clearing. Self-development on the other hand is not gender specific.

It is possible to propose a simple model of the Kaulong world as follows:

18  It is not entirely right to say that reproduction of identity is more dangerous to men. Female informants frequently discussed with me the difficult and sometimes fatal instances of childbirth and consider that a woman's womb should be fully developed (by the mid-twenties) before she can safely bear a child. Sexual activity is differentially dangerous to men and women; however, it does make them both equally weak.

culture      :   nature
clearing     :   forest
single       :   married
production   :   reproduction

It is not possible to fit male/female into such a model, nor would a Kaulong consider the attempt worthwhile. Far more significant to the Kaulong is how to surmount life's greatest dilemma, how to achieve both self-development, fame and fortune in this world, and immortality in the future — an immortality which is dangerous to life and health, thus counteracting the achievement of fame and fortune throughout a long life span. For the Kaulong the model is more appropriately drawn as follows:

human         :   animal
life          :   death
production    :   reproduction
*bi-*: garden :   forest

The central symbols in this model are those of permanent clearing (*bi-*) and natural forest, with garden as a temporary or intermittant clearing, in an ambiguous medial position between *place* and *forest*. Place (*bi-*) is envisioned as a very small clearing surrounded by a threatening and ever encroaching forest, a clearing requiring constant human activity to maintain, else humanity itself is lost in the forested world. To reduce this philosophy to a simple opposition of nature and culture is to understand little of what informs the behaviour of Kaulong in relation to their environment.

## Bibliography

Chowning, Ann and Jane C. Goodale. 1971. 'The Contaminating Women'. Paper presented at American Anthropological Association Meeting, Washington DC.

Forge, A. 1972. 'The Golden Fleece', *Man* (N.S.) 7, 527–40.

Goodale, Jane C. 1973a. 'The Kaulong Gender'. Paper presented at Association of Social Anthropology in Oceania, Annual Meeting, Orcus Island.

1973b. 'The Rape of the Men and Seduction of Women among the Kaulong and Sengseng of New Britain'. Paper presented at Association of Social Anthropology in Oceania, Annual Meeting, Orcus Island.

1976. 'Big-Men and Big-Women: The Elite in Melanesian Society'. Paper read at American Anthropological Association Annual Meeting, Washington, DC.

1977. 'The Management of Knowledge among the Kaulong'. Paper presented in Symposium on Knowledge in Oceania. Association of Social Anthropology in Oceania, Annual Meeting, Monterey, Calif.

1978. 'Saying it with Shells in Southwest New Britain'. Paper presented in symposium: Symbolic Exchange in Melanesia. American Anthropological Association Annual Meeting, Los Angeles.

1980. 'Siblings as Spouse: The Reproduction and Replacement of Kaulong Society', in Mac Marshall (ed.), *Siblingship in Oceania: Studies in the Meaning of Kin Relations*. ASAO Monograph no. 8, University of Michigan Press, Ann Arbor.

Huntsman, J. and A. Hooper. 1975. 'Male and Female in Tokelau Culture', *Journal of the Polynesian Society*, 84, 415–30.

Ortner, Sherry B. 1973. 'On Key Symbols', *American Anthropologist*, 75, 1338–48.

1974. 'Is female to male as nature is to culture?', in *Women, Culture and Society*, edited by M.Z. Rosaldo and L. Lamphere, pp. 67–88. Stanford University Press.

Panoff, M. 1968. 'The notion of the double-self among the Maenge', *Journal of the Polynesian Society*, 77, 275–95.

Shore, B. 1978. 'Ghosts and government: a structural analysis of alternative institutions for conflict management in Samoa', *Man* (N.S.) 13, 175–99.

Weiner, A.B. 1979. 'Trobriand Kinship from another point of view: the reproductive power of women and men', *Man* (N.S.) 14, 328–48.

# 7    Images of nature in Gimi thought

GILLIAN GILLISON

## Introduction

The proposition that nature is to culture as female is to male fascinates us because it seems to explain women's secondary status. It suggests that women everywhere are seen as more animal-like, as "more enslaved to the species than is the male" (de Beauvoir 1953:239), and therefore as sub-human. This formula ties the origin and meaning of gender, not to the interaction between men and women, but to a theory of how culture is different from and superior to nature. The way a people conceptualize their relation to animals or to the uncultivated environment becomes the true subject matter of gender, its 'deep structure' so to speak. We are offered an explanation of sexual segregation and antagonism that dispenses with any consideration of human sexuality and concentrates instead upon the logic of indigenous classification: what is not male (woman) is linked to what is not human (nature). From this perspective, the awe or disgust which surrounds menstruation and parturition is engendered — not by what these bodily functions represent in women — but by the non-human world with which they are universally associated.

The beliefs of the Gimi people of the Eastern Highlands of Papua New Guinea do not conform to this cultural logic.[1] The debasement of Gimi women cannot be attributed to their symbolic association with the surrounding rainforest because that realm is regarded as a male refuge from women and from ordinary life within the settlement. The Gimi wilderness is an exalted domain where the male spirit, incarnate in birds and marsupials, acts out its secret desires away from the inhibiting presence of women. Gimi men's mundane existence is degraded and their mortal potential is unfulfilled because of the inescapable nearness of women inside the hamlet and of the powerful contamination which female

1 Between October 1973 and September 1975, together with my husband, David Gillison, an artist and photographer, and our then six-year-old daughter, Samantha, I carried out the fieldwork upon which this paper is based. In this endeavour I gratefully acknowledge the financial support of the National Science Foundation and the Canada Council.

sexuality exudes. Men's fear of menstrual blood, their obsessive efforts to avoid contact with women through the foods they eat, the places they sleep and the subsistence tasks they undertake, are not explained by an underlying contempt for lower forms of life in nature nor by a drive to control them. On the contrary, men's ambition, as expressed in their rituals, is to identify with the non-human world and to be revitalized by its limitless, masculine powers. Men's desire to escape from women 'into nature' suggests that sexual conflict determines rather than reflects the dichotomization of the Gimi universe.

The idea of "the wild" is central in Gimi thought. It refers to pure forms of plant and animal life which occur "spontaneously"[2] in the rainforest but which originate from an immortal human essence. The fantastic variation and abundance of the Gimi wilderness demonstrate the infinite creativity of this transmogrified male spirit. Both the uncultivated and the after-life are designated by the word *kore*: "wild pandanus fruit" is *kore hina*, "wild pig" is *kore ugunu*, and "ghost" or "ancestor" is *kore bana* (literally, "wild man"). After death, men's spirits collectively constitute a forest reservoir from which emerges the animating life-force of new generations. *Kore* is an honorific title, like Sir, used to address men of advanced status or age in recognition of the magnitude or imminence of their posthumous contribution to the other-worldly sources of existence. Very old women are sometimes also addressed as *kore* because, by achieving old age, they manifest indestructible or spiritual (and therefore masculine) traits. Yet female ritual experts and other women of exceptional ability — women whom Gimi men say are "like men" — rarely receive the honour of becoming *kore* after death. The word *dusa* appears in Gimi myths as the opposite of *kore* but is rarely used in other contexts. *Dusa* means "this worldly" or "ordinary" and connotes the domesticated forms of plants and animals and the constraints of human social existence. If as a methodological device (cf. Strathern), we violate Gimi usage by translating *kore* as 'nature' and *dusa* as 'culture', then Gimi associate the former with the transcendent male and the latter with the profane interactions between men and women.

## The Gimi

### I  *Subsistence and the sexual division of labour*

Gimi is a language spoken by about 10,000 people who inhabit an isolated

2  Throughout the text, inverted double commas are used only around words or phrases actually uttered either by the Gimi or by other authors. Inverted single commas indicate that a word or phrase is meant symbolically rather than literally, usually as part of my interpretation of the Gimi meaning.

region of the Eastern Highlands Province of Papua New Guinea. A Gimi hamlet is made up of some 20 compounds, each housing around eight to 20 adults. The men and initiated boys of a compound are ideally patri-lineally related and sleep together in one or two large oval men's houses that dominate the clearing. Married women normally live virilocally, each with her mother-in-law or co-wife, her young children, unmarried daughters and several pigs, in smaller round dwellings at the compound's edge. The rule regarding marriage (by a male ego) to a second cross cousin (i.e. to a real or classificatory MFBSD or FFZSD) may be thought of as perpetuat-ing the relationship initiated by an 'original' exchange of sisters among at least three unrelated pairs of brothers.

The climate of this high forested region is continually humid with a brief drier season from June to September. The slight seasonal alternation and the altitudinal range of lands exploited by the Gimi together produce a subtle spatial and temporal pattern of subsistence activities. Teams of men cut into the forest and clear gardens at the beginning of the wet season (in October). Women escort their pigs below the garden sites into uncultivated groves of mid-mountain oak and chestnut to fatten them on the nuts that litter the ground. The pigs may roam at this elevation into semi-cultivated orchards of red-fruited pandanus (*Pandanus conoideus*) to root for grubs and wild taro. As the wet season advances, pigs forage on higher ground, digging up small tubers of sweet potato deliberately left unharvested in abandoned gardens. In drier weather, women plant the cleared land in such a way that crops of cucumbers, greens, bamboo, maize, beans, pumpkin, the staple sweet potato, taro and tobacco ripen sequen-tially. Bananas and sugarcane, planted by men, ripen last. As the dry season progresses, pigs scavenge in higher forest for larvae which infest the rotting pineapple-shaped clusters of white, nut-like fruit that falls from huge wild pandanus trees. A closely related species (*Pandanus brassii*) cul-tivated above the upper limits of the settlement and reserved mainly for human delectation also ripens at this drier time of year.

Men compare their freedom to enter the unfenced, outlying orchards of "wild" (semi-cultivated) pandanus with the confinement of women to individual plots inside fenced gardens. Men remark that they keep women in separate gardens (apart from rivalries with other women) and inside the hamlet (apart from the forest). When they say this, men may be remember-ing their mothers' bedtime stories which tell of the *kore badaha* (literally, "wild/spirit women") who temporarily escape domesticity. In one tale, a woman flees her worldly (*dusa*) husband by entering the den and becoming the cohort of a marupial possum. In the forest, she acquires stupendous powers to nurture children and to cultivate crops in open expanses. Even-tually, men of her husband's lineage shoot her and bring her back to ordinary life within the settlement. The fantastic powers which the *kore badaha* enjoys in the wild have a masculine character: "Sir Woman" loses

her freedom after receiving a wound (literally, "a mouth") which some
informants likened to a castration.


Men and the forest: the escape from women

Gimi society and the non-human life outside it are both dominated by men.
Men's social, domestic and sexual interaction with women creates order in
human life but it pollutes the male being, forcing him to seek a higher,
purer form of existence without women. Ideally, men organize and construct the boundaries within which women care for children, pigs and sweet
potatoes, while men alone venture outside those limits to wage war or to
secure alliances with the men of other settlements. Men climb into the high
moss forests to hunt birds and marsupials whose plumages, fur and meat
they will use during the rituals and ceremonial exchanges of the dry season.
As they climb, the hunters mimic bird calls and answer the echoes as
though being welcomed to a male sanctuary, and scrawny dogs that range
behind and ahead of the group respond noisily to the scent or sight of forest
animals. A dozen men may capture or kill 30 to 40 tree kangaroos, wall-
abies, marsupial cats and possums in three days or two men may take ten
to 12 animals after five or six days in the bush. Until several generations
ago, when Gimi began to acquire domesticated pigs in substantial numbers,
"wild meat" was used for ritual meals.

At about five- to ten-year intervals, men of two or three clans joined by
marriage initiate their respective 'sisters' sons', whom they exhort to be
"true men like the Birds of Paradise (*Paradisaea raggiana salvadorii*)!" The
men say that they model their rites of initiation upon the emergence from
its nesting hole of the fledgling Hornbill (*Aceros plicatus*). The bird's
"father", as the men report, calls upon all the other birds of the rainforest
to gather in celebration of his "son's initiation". The female Hornbill,
sequestered for many weeks with her sole offspring, is now released by the
male Hornbill who breaks away with his beak the mud barrier covering the
hole. As the female emerges, the male enters. Moments later, with the
fledgling perched on his back, the male Hornbill flies out. As he alights on
a branch nearby, say the men, the assembled birds of many species squawk
and call to honour the occasion. The parallels in men's rites — the seclusion
of the initiates, called "birds", inside men's houses referred to in song as
"nests", the boys' confinement together with their maternal uncles whom
they address as "mothers", the 'violent' emergence through a shattered
doorframe of initiates hoisted on men's shoulders and decorated with
gorgeous plumages, the assembly of spectators from distant villages — all
are said to be staged in imitation of the birds' behaviour.

Things in the wild exist in their original, eternal and in that sense perfect form. The stated aim of men's initiation rites is to achieve the 'ideal
type' in nature. By decorating their bodies elaborately with feathers, the

boys 'become' birds: their purpose is to be changed by sharing an avian existence rather than to change the birds by bringing them under human control. In the songs and rites of male initiation, the stages of men's existence are symbolically identified with elements of the natural universe (*korena*): the fruit of trees (adult men) is food plucked by birds (initiates or spirits of the recently dead). Trees grow out of mountains (the no-longer-individuated ancestral mass) from which issue rivers (the flowing and prolific ancestral fluid, *kore abe*, literally "male spirit urine", a euphemism for semen). The rivers' headwaters are abundant sources of birds and flowers, symbols of the initiates' gorgeous, emergent manhood. Trees (men in their prime) form the productive core of this system: the fruit at their "heads" feeds the bird-initiates and the rich decay of falling detritus nourishes the ancestral mass beneath them.

Life in the forest is a world to which men and their spirits flee as 'like unto like'. Even those creatures with female associations such as the possum (whose fur and marsupial pouch men liken to pubic hair outside the uterine cavity) are compatible with men. They represent feminine characteristics *detached from actual women*. The female symbolized in nature is a male-owned element. When a man dies, his body is placed inside his mother's house but his spirit escapes into the forest to dwell among the possums. His male relatives hunt dozens of the animals to use in "secret" divination rites they will conduct out of women's sight. Because of a 'uterine' tie to the spirit of the dead man, the marsupials can 'speak' the name of his killer. Later, when the death is avenged, the man's spirit comes to lodge with the birds. For this reason, unsuccessful hunters say they unwittingly offended particular male ancestors who warned their cohorts of the men's approach. Gimi men's rites of divination and initiation represent attempts to nullify the boundary between human and non-human, so as to transcend mortal existence.

## Women and cultivation: the symbolic incorporation of the male

Men's work is seasonal and sporadic but women work steadily and repetitively throughout the year. Both sexes say that women's intense and prolonged physical and emotional attachment to infants, pigs and crops has uniquely nurturant properties. Women breast feed shoats as well as babies and they often sleep embracing both their young. The vigour and fruition of all nurtured life is believed to depend upon exclusive attachment to, or symbolic incorporation by, individual female caretakers. While planting, weeding and harvesting vegetables and tending her pigs, a woman sings a large and partly secret repertoire of magically nurturant songs which proclaim the intensity and uniqueness of her relationship to each plant and pig in her care. The spells conclude with an emphatic refrain: "I speak of no one else – to no one else – but *you* my darling vegetable (pig)!" Their imagery suggests that the reciter's tie to her non-human dependants is modelled upon the bond of motherhood, especially as it exists *in utero*. In one incantation, a newly planted tuber of sweet potato is tenderly encouraged to "enlarge like the echidna, sleeping inside its warm nest, lodged within the dense and entangled roots of the huge fig tree" (symbolizing, the spell's creator allowed, the silent growth of the human foetus encompassed by its mother). In order to take root and prosper, new life must achieve a state of union with the female. As one man expressed it: "In song, the woman's *auna* ["life-force"] and the food's *auna* are made one. That is how the food grows bigger!" In this sense, all domesticated fertility is symbolically allied to the processes of human gestation.

Although Gimi men formally own the land and the livestock, decide what land to clear, how to divide the land under cultivation among various crops and female gardeners and calculate the optimum size and composition of pig herds, and although informants of both sexes state that a man's semen alone forms the foetus (cf. Glick 1963:100), women's special bond to the different kinds of living male property tends to contradict the social rule of men's ownership of resources. Female nurturing power is of a contradictory nature: it fosters growth toward a viable independence (the goal for all life) by means of an intense attachment to the 'mother'. Because it is founded upon attachment, women's nurturance tends to 'turn back on itself', i.e. it tends to promote then inhibit the development of separate entities (cultivated goods and human beings) which men can detach from women. The female tends permanently to retain and in that way to destroy (i.e. to re-absorb) what she nourishes. Interestingly, the Gimi verb "to plant" (*fa*) also means "to kill".

The negative potential of female nurturing power is consummated whenever crops or pigs — once women's cared-for/gestated 'children' — are 'again' taken inside the body. As foods, these lives women cultivated are now terminated. I would argue that, to varying degrees, eating any of the products of women's 'labours' is symbolic cannibalism. Actual cannibalism was traditionally practiced by the Gimi, supposedly only by women (and young children) and only upon men.[3] Men were the prototypical children-of-women who became food.[4] Conversely, then, cultivated foods may tend to be symbolically associated with the male, particularly with the state of his incorporation by the female. Let me go back and arrive at this interpret-

---

3   Starting in the late 1950s, the Australian Administration vigorously suppressed the practice of cannibalism. To my knowledge, it did not occur during the period of fieldwork. My account is based upon first-hand testimony by informants of both sexes.

4   As revealed by their myths, women also fear being devoured by women who are portrayed as cannibalistic grandmothers (like Little Red Riding Hood's) or as bisexual monsters.

ation again after examining how Gimi men themselves describe their fear
of women.

So pervasive is the female danger, men say, that they avoid frequent
contact with women through commensality, sexual intercourse, touch or
eating foods with particularly strong female associations. During the period
before marriage when men become warriors, they must not eat anything
grown by their mothers (only the products of special gardens cultivated by
men) nor are they allowed to eat greens cooked in bamboo containers that
split longitudinally in the fire, their contents being rendered "like something from a mother's vagina", nor raw greens whose pungency will make
the lips pucker and involuntarily utter "*nahora* (my vagina)", nor red pandanus which is like menstrual blood, nor wild mushrooms that smell like
vaginas, nor wild sugar cane whose stalk swells like a pregnant woman's
torso. For a year after their first initiation, adolescent boys must not venture into the forest because marsupials bounding overhead from tree to
tree may place the unwary initiates below in a position "between female
thighs". Edible insects that burrow in the ground are tabooed because
their interment is like a menstruating woman's seclusion. Only in old age
can the male again eat frogs that squat and move like women, or flying
foxes, owls and other birds "without noses" (i.e. without penises), or
hawks, swallows and bower birds that frequent inhabited areas or dwell
upon the ground. These birds, like any species shot near water, have
female qualities: they frequent populated areas, they are "low-lying
creatures", or they "menstruate" (i.e. they are about to wash away menstrual blood).

According to Gimi of both sexes, the threat to male purity and
superiority created by the proximity of women emanates from a particular
feature of female sexuality — the regular occurrence of menstruation. The
vagina (or anything which is thought to resemble it) is feared as the site of
bleeding. Objects touched by a menstruating woman are bound to deterio-
rate rapidly: wooden bowls will crack, stone axes will misbehave in the
hands of their male owners and inflict upon them otherwise inexplicable
wounds, crops will wither and die, even the ground over which the menstruator steps will lose its fertility. Menstrual blood is "dead womb blood",
the result of a "striking" or "killing by the moon", every Gimi woman's
"first husband". Gimi liken menstruation to a pregnancy which culminates
in death rather than in the emergence of a separate, living child. It is
always caused, they say, either actually or symbolically by a "husband".
"A woman does not menstruate for no reason!" said one Gimi man. "Her
husband enters her and the blood flows out along the path he creates."
But men's fear of menstruation is based upon a contradictory, unspoken
premise: that the female (not the male) genital is the 'killer'. The male
places a living part of himself (his penis) inside the female who, when she
menstruates, delivers 'back' something dead that is associated with the

penetrating male. In these terms, we may compare Gimi men's attitude to menstrual blood with the horror of gangrene: contact with it may cause the *rest* of the male body to die.

During boys' initiation rites and in daily life, men continually express the fear that menstrual blood, lodged invisibly under women's fingernails from their handling of blood-soaked moss tampons, will settle in the food they cultivate and will quickly kill the men who eat it. By re-examining Gimi attitudes to the female nurturing role (see page 148), we may see another connection between cultivated food and menstrual blood. Women are considered uniquely adept at making things grow because the female reproductive process can be extended to domesticated plants and animals. Women raise crops or pigs by symbolically incorporating them: cultivated foods have been 'ingested/gestated' by female nurturers. Unless men inter-fere in this suction-like 'internal cultivation', the female will retain and kill – she will re-ingest – the foods she produces. By the same token, what she retains and kills may be considered 'food'. In this sense, menstrual blood is the ingested, edible product of women's rampant retentiveness. It tends to be mixed into other foods because it is produced by the same incorporative method of 'cultivation'. When a man eats the blood, his body (by impli-cation equivalent to his penis), symbolically retraces the path travelled by what he ate, is taken back inside the female and devoured (i.e. he/his penis is 'killed' or 'reduced to menstrual blood'). The eater 'places himself back inside the female' where he becomes her 'child', her ingested 'food'. The eater of menstrual blood is himself 'eaten'.[5] In these terms, the overt fear of menstruation contains at a deeper level the fear of being devoured by women. These fears do not presuppose that those who menstruate or devour are of a different species. On the contrary, they suggest that female and male have too great an affinity, are too easily brought together and unified. Menstrual blood originates inside women but is associated with the wounding penis/the retained 'food'/the cannibal meal: it represents the destruction of the boundary between male and female, the end of men's separate existence in the world.

Gimi men say that eating itself is "dangerous" and that each time a man overeats he hastens senescence and death. During their initiation, men are taught cane-swallowing to induce vomiting as a means to rid their bodies of polluting "mothers' breast milk and all mothers' food" – parts of their mothers' bodies which the initiates have swallowed. By expelling food, men dissociate themselves not merely from something female, but from something female that symbolically is, or once was, the men themselves (from something that represents the male *within* the female). By disgorging

5  Much of this discussion applies equally to women who eat menstrual blood. In this sense, the 'eater' who becomes the 'devoured child' is always symbolically male because the child is an entity separable from the female and therefore categorically opposite to her.

Plate 7.1 On ceremonial occasions men prepare the earth oven, a pit dug in the ground, lined with hot boulders, filled with vegetables and meat, and covered with banana leaves and moisture-retaining ferns. When the food is cooked, men will serve it to the waiting women. This division of labour reverses the daily pattern in which women prepare and cook the food, and serve it to the men.

food, men disidentify from those whose state of being is 'to have food inside'. To be men, the Gimi initiates 'have food outside' their bodies: they
create by externalizing, as trees put forth fruit for birds in their upper
branches (see page 147) and as men give food as ritual gifts to women.
Eating is an appropriate public activity only for women who, on most
ritual occasions, sit in long rows to receive foods ostentatiously presented
to them by the male leaders of the rites. The men eat later, inside the
men's houses (and, despite appearances, consume the larger and choicer
portions). Their public abstinence may be interpreted as a denial of their
symbolic status as comestibles: not to eat food is not to be food, not to
travel where cultivated foods (and men themselves) have been during their
inception and where they will go upon their demise – inside women. Food
tends to become trapped within an endogenous female cycle of production
and consumption. Menstrual blood, as the 'prototype' of cultivated foods,
represents the deadly consequences of that entrapment.

These interpretative statements about the conceptual grounds of sexual
antagonism among the Gimi take for granted different kinds of symbolic
associations. They are based upon equations which were stated to me (e.g.
that first menses is a pregnancy and a wound inflicted by the penis), others
which were implied (e.g. that each loss of menstrual blood is like a death)
and those which were neither stated nor implied by informants but which
emerged from a consideration of the data as a whole (e.g. that to eat menstrual blood is to return to the womb as a dead child – as a 'devoured
penis'). I do not make explicit the distinction between "symbols of
identity" in which, for example, menstrual blood is felt metonymically to
be a dead part of the male body, and "symbols of representation" in
which, for example, red pandanus fruit is recognized as a ritual metaphor
for menstrual blood (cf. Segal quoted by Tuzin 1972:243). In other words,
what we might call conscious, preconscious and unconscious associations
are run together. I interpreted as a single text informants' statements about
their beliefs, many versions of myths, my observations of rituals and the
exegeses elicited by these observations. When I looked for the unspoken
logic connecting the whole, I found that it rested upon implicit identifications among conceptual categories based upon their underlying sexual
content (e.g. crops cultivated by women = gestated foods = foetus = male
body; and male body = penis = 'food eaten by the vagina and killed' =
menstrual blood).

  The notion of the Gimi male as an endangered species and of the female
as his ubiquitous enemy cogently summarizes the content of men's ritual
but it gives a distorted view of their feelings about women in other contexts.
Although Gimi men genuinely fear menstrual blood, speak of women with
contempt and go to great lengths to avoid them, they are also attracted to
women's dangerousness. Sitting around the fire inside a hunting lodge, men

discuss the delights of heterosexual sex. Their songs celebrate the eroticism of menstrual blood: "I follow the River ___ to its source. As I climb along its course, I see blood staining the rocks. As I round the bend I see you standing naked in the water, beautiful red blood streaming down your shiny black legs! When shall we have sex? Now? In a moment?" Indeed sexual intercourse often took place inside menstrual huts built (before missionaries prohibited them) at the outskirts of the settlement in order to isolate women for the period during the month when they supposedly reach their peak as a source of danger to the community. According to female informants these huts were routinely used as the sites of assignations arranged by men (in the way that garden rain shelters are used today).

I emphasize the often wide gap between stated and practised norms because the following treatment of Gimi rituals may make it appear that men follow their own rules (or are constrained by their logic). If menstrual seclusion were honoured and if women were avoided to the degree men say is necessary, then women would have some autonomy. The effects of men's fears might give women the potential to dominate social and political as well as cosmological affairs. However, several women told me they often cannot convince their husbands or lovers to stay away from them while they are menstruating and uncomfortable (cf. Lederer 1968:25–6). Hence, men's behaviour in 'coming close' to women deviates from their stated beliefs about avoiding them and robs women of a certain negative power invested in them by men's ideology.

## II  The Gimi cosmos: the cyclic regeneration of life

In the next sections, I examine a small part of the ritual which follows cannibalism and first menses and conclude that the rites, supposedly designed by men and forced upon women (but actually the result of what I see as a tacit agreement between them), are intended to re-establish the separation of the sexes which women's eating of the male corpse and menstrual bleeding are thought to deny. The performance of the rites perpetuates the cosmic cycle by preventing the male body (the source of the cosmos) from becoming a permanent part of the female body, no longer separate and alive. Menstruation occurs 'naturally' in women but cannibalism is 'assigned' to them: it is as though by consuming the male and being ritually forced to release his spirit, women enact an antidote to their natural condition in which they incorporate and kill the male being. The performance of men's rites is predicated upon a set of oppositions that we may for the moment state as: female : male : : merging of the sexes : separation of the sexes : : cessation of life : cyclic continuity of human and non-human existence.

When men participate in life in the rainforest (while hunting, fighting or in death) they are at one with the reproductive forces of the Gimi universe. Their identity is merged with the ancestors' whose spirits collectively produce the forest reservoir from which re-issues the domesticated human world. Contrary to his wish, the male cannot move unimpeded at death into the realm of *kore* and from *kore* again into life in society because the Gimi female must first release him from inside her body. Because of her capricious and insatiable character, she may at any time refuse to 'let go'. In these terms, the essence of what men fear is that, by retaining the male, the female would be 'sated' – 'filled up' – and therefore unwilling to accept the male back again out of the collective *kore*, preventing his re-birth into an individuated human society. By her satiation, the female would stop the cyclic continuity of birth and death in the male universe. Trapped forever inside woman, indistinguishable from her, the male could never 'enter' *kore* so that there could *be* no *kore*, no resource from which to regenerate Gimi society. In that case, there could be no society, no world: life would become 'dead' (like women's menstrual blood).

To understand this complex sequence of symbolic events we explore the mythic origin of *kore* in the flutes – paired, side-blown, bamboo aero-phones, the objects of a secret male cult similar to those found among other Eastern Highlands language groups (cf. Langness 1974) (see plate 7.2). Using the story of the flutes, I set forth a series of five mythic stages or premises which dramatically describe the Gimi life cycle and the relation of women to the male realm of *kore*.

*1. Women enter the spirit world of the forest as "owners of flutes" (penes). Men steal the flutes and banish the women.* Whereas it was vitally important that a man died and was eaten on his clan territory so that his individual life-force (*auna*) might escape and be absorbed into the locally-situated store of clan essence in the forest (*kore*), it was a matter of indifference whether a female corpse was eaten. Women did on occasion consume the bodies of women. But unless the dead woman was greatly revered, the men dispensed with those parts of the ensuing cannibal ritual designed to release the entrapped *auna* from inside the woman and to ensure its eventual incor-poration as eternal *kore*.

Despite their exclusion from the forest after-life, Gimi women yearn to escape there. One of the women's myths describes how a wife, foully tricked into marriage, takes revenge upon her husband by feeding him their child, disguised as a suckling pig. When the man realizes he has eaten his own son and turns in rage to his wife, she transforms herself into a gorgeous red-and-black bird and vanishes into the forest. She forces upon her husband the female role of cannibal and herself assumes the guise of a bird, the prime symbol of the erect penis and of the transcendent male spirit. The "birds" in men's myths are the bamboo flutes (repositories of all cosmic power) which were invented and owned exclusively by one or two *kore badaha* (see page 145) in the era before men created Gimi

Plate 7.2  Side-blown bamboo flutes played by men in a sacred grove of the forest out of sight of women. The haunting sounds of these particularly large paired aerophones are heard only during a late phase of male initiation.

society. The original "wild woman" (or two women) did not menstruate and kept the sacred instrument — "the bird" — hidden under her bark-string skirts.

One day, the woman's brother heard strange sounds, like a child's crying, and grew insatiably curious. He hid in the tall grass until his sister had gone to her garden, crept into her house, and stole the flute which she had left at the head of her bed. When he picked it up to play, he did not notice that the flute's blowing hole was stuffed with his sister's pubic hair which she used as a plug when the instrument was not in use (cf. Dundes 1976: 230). Because of the brother's inattention (in not removing the plug), a beard grew around his mouth so that today all men have beards which are really, so the men say, female pubic hair transferred. The woman who invented the flute died without telling other women what had happened. "Today, whenever we show the flutes to young boys during their initiation, women think, "I wonder what it is — some strange bird, perhaps — hiding inside the men's house and crying?" But, in truth, it was once something that belonged only to women. It wasn't ours! We men *stole* it!"

The flutes are symbolic penes with which women were once uniquely endowed. By implication, the genitals of the original "wild women" were a combination of the male and the female apparatus such that the hollow female penis — the flute — functioned as an external continuation of the birth canal in which the "crying babe" was trapped. When, in the myth, the brother stole the flute from his sister, he liberated her "flute-child", creating a separate male being. The woman was left "wounded" and began to menstruate. Ever after she was secluded each month inside a menstrual hut. The huts are called "flute houses" because, men say, the theft of the flutes is the "true cause" of menstrual bleeding. When we compare this statement with others which attribute menstruation to sexual penetration by a woman's "first husband, the moon" (see page 149), it seems that the menstrual wound is inflicted in opposite ways — by a woman's 'receiving' a penis and by her 'losing' one. We again encounter contradictory premises: (1) the stated idea that men are the causes of menstrual bleeding; and (2) the unstated implication that menstruation occurs spontaneously in women. We may infer that when a woman is sexually penetrated, she loses something (a penis) which she *already possesses* — something which she brought with her in marriage as a virgin.[6]

6  When a bride arrives in her husband's village, she carries two bamboo tubes inside a net bag hung over her head. Supposedly, she believes they are containers of salt, part of the marriage prestation. Actually, the men reveal, the bamboo tubes are "flutes" belonging to the bride's father who (the men explain) says symbolically through his acts, "I give the woman with the flute." Further, the men state that the decorative incisions around the flute's blowing hole — its "mouth" — are identical to tattoos applied around the bride's mouth some weeks

2. *As cannibals, women regain the male element. Men again arrange its release from women and its escape into the forest.* When I suggest that certain Gimi beliefs can be understood as parts of a drama in which conflicting ambitions lead each sex to devise "secret" ritual manoeuvres to get possession of the flutes, I emphasize that the competition is acted out by mutual consent. By the time they reach early middle age, Gimi men and women seem to know the whole ritual cycle and to cooperate in enacting their conflict of interest. From this perspective, women's cannibalism is a means to avenge their symbolic castration: by eating the male body the women 're-acquire' the mythic penis they lost when the flutes were stolen. But the original deprivation makes the female permanently insatiable so that she not only (actually) eats men when they die, but she also (symbolically) 'kills the men she eats' (i.e. she 'converts' their penes to menstrual blood) as the means to replace within her what her brother stole.

Men say that cannibalism was entirely "women's idea". At the conclusion of the week-long mourning period, men of the dead man's mother's clan traditionally carried him on a litter from his mother's house (where he was placed immediately after death) to his garden where they laid him to "sleep" upon a roofed-in platform. In two or three months, men calculate, decomposition was complete. Then they collected his bones, using sticks to lift the "powerful" remains in which the man's *auna* (personal life-force) still resided, and placed them inside the hollow trunk of a hoop pine, inside a mountain cave and in other places in the forest associated with the regeneration of *kore* (collective male life-force). But, as male informants quickly add, this orderly sequence of events was interrupted at a time in the past and forever changed. Women and children, after following the corpse and watching it installed on the garden platform, came back to their compounds, made excuses to the men about "garden work", scattered and hid. "The women made a pact among themselves!" say the men. Secretly, they returned to the dead man's garden, dragged him off his bed and, without ritual, cut him up to eat. "You see, the women do not want the men to *see* them and to say, 'I think they are cutting up this man!' The women are ashamed . . . But they trick us! They shove the meat into bamboo containers together with wild green vegetables they secretly collected.[7] Inside

before marriage. The bride's tattoos give her the appearance of having a beard which, according to the flute myth (see page 156), is 'actually' female pubic hair. If we infer that the flute's blowing hole is similarly surrounded by pubic hair (that it is a vaginal orifice which has been newly created), then we may say that the flutes the bride carries inside her net bag symbolically represent her own 'detached penis'. "Whether we cut [i.e. send] the bride far away or near," say the men, "we cut [i.e. decorate] the bamboo at the same time."

7  The eating of the male body together with wild foods is a means to ensure its regeneration as *kore*. Such details in men's accounts reveal that the women themselves take steps to ensure the transformation of

the men's house of the dead man, the women consume the pieces of his body . . . and their husbands come home and *see*! 'Ah! They are eating!' "

Women say that they had too much compassion for the dead to let them rot away in isolation. When men's bodies were brought home from the battlefield, women sang: "Come to me lest your body rot on the ground. Better it should dissolve inside me!"[8]

Once the women had stolen the corpse, cut it up, cooked and ate some parts and loaded the rest into their net bags, they left the dead man's garden and went to his men's house to 'reveal' their deed. The men detained the women there (in a place tabooed to them at all other times) until their meal was completely consumed and digested (a period of about four or five days).[9] Because the cannibals are treated as men by being allowed to sleep in the men's house and to see the flutes, I suggest that symbolically the women have penes — invisibly, inside them. Momentarily, in 'ritual time', the women become what they have eaten.

Recounting the cannibal deed, men describe how the women of a hamlet, ecstatic with grief, descended willy nilly upon the corpse. They imply that the chaos created by women was a pretext for men's intervention:[10]

one man, a "nothing man", a man "without a name", like D ___ or B ___ (men of exceptionally low status) and a small boy, too, can go and watch and split firewood and help the women to prepare the stones (for the earth oven). Men like K ___ or O ___ (big men) would *never* go to watch! All the women and the "nothing men" together eat the dead man.

One or two of the women also watched the proceedings with the "nothing man" so that later, inside the men's house when their human meal was digested, they could report to the brothers and sons of the dead man who ate what part of his corpse. Before the women were allowed to emerge from seclusion in the men's house, each had to accept from these men portions of "wild meat" (marsupials or, in the recent past, pigs) that were anatomically identical to sections of the man's body she reportedly consumed. The marsupials, whose fur men equate with female pubic hair, may

the male. In their own renditions of cannibalism and in their myths, women say that the elevation of the male as spirit is a prime purpose of their acts.

8   Although the practice of cannibalism is now suppressed, this song is still sung during theatrical re-enactments of the cannibal meal performed during marriages and initiations.

9   This length of time seems to have been determined not by any calculation of the duration of human digestion but by the time it took a number of men to hunt the requisite number of marsupials (see page 146).

10  According to female informants, the actual dismemberment and distribution of the corpse was not disorganized. Several senior women cut up the body into large sections, each of which they allotted to a woman who was responsible for cutting and further dividing it.

represent in this context the hairy plug stuffed inside the flute's blowing hole by the "wild woman" (see page 156). The possums, I suggest, symbolize the contents of the flutes – the "crying child" – liberated by the woman's brother. These "wild children" are not born of women but are hunted by men in the forest: they represent something "female" which is separated from the female. By feeding them to the women as incarnations of ancestral *kore*, the men attempt to replace with an equivalent and thereby to 'force out' what is inside the cannibals' bodies. As a condition of their emergence from seclusion, the women had to release the spiritual essence of the man they ate. In effect, the men repossessed the flute (the penis/spirit-child) held inside the women as the residue of their meal.

After the women disposed of the soft parts of the male body, the men took possession of the "indestructible" bones and placed them in mountain caves and in the trees of overgrown gardens so that, as disused gardens revert to forest and as water emerges from mountain crevices, a man's lasting spirit will someday re-issue in new human life. But that day will not come until men ritually arrange it by themselves taking male spirit out of the forest and 're-depositing' it in the female. At first menses men initiate the bride.[11] They 'force' her to drink 'ancestral semen' (water taken from a river owned by her husband's clan) and to eat a 'spirit child' (a possum shot in the husband's clan forest and encased in sugarcane and vines, symbols of the penis). The father of the initiate's husband enters the menstrual hut (the "flute house") where the girl is secluded and carries a decorated length of bamboo. He dances up to the girl, offering her water from the bamboo in a teasing gesture. She sings in response that she is thirsty only for "the water of my father". Eventually, parched by her ordeal, the initiate accepts "the gift of my husband's water" and a later prestation of the possum meat. If she does not ingest these ritual foods (representations of her husband's ancestral spirit), her father-in-law says she will not bear his son's child.

Like the cannibal ritual, the public portion of female initiation enacts a cannibal meal in which marsupials (or pigs) 'replace' the male body. Women must eat what men capture in the non-human spirit world (*kore*) in order to induce the male spirit (*auna*) which once animated the corpse but which is now held inside the women to leave their bodies and to remain inside

11 Female initiation cannot be celebrated before the initiate's marriage arrangements are complete. Ideally, the rites occur about a year after the wedding when the bride begins to menstruate (often not until age 18–19). The season and the economic ability of the families of the newlyweds to stage the rites also determine their timing. It is unusual for the one or two initiates actually to be menstruating. The vivid details of the rites (e.g. the burning of odoriferous branches to counteract the "bad smell" of the blood) reveal the degree to which they are symbolically rendered.

the men's house in men's possession. The remains of the women's meal are the spirit-ridden bones which, once men disperse them in the forest, eventually 'become' (or are symbolically associated with) stones, boulders, mountains and all that dwells thereupon (e.g. the possum-child) and therein (e.g. the river water-semen). The 'cannibal' rite of female initiation reverses this journey and allows the male spirit (after a forcible entry) to begin its passage back through the body of the female novice into the social world of human life. The initiate's consumption of wild spirit-foods allows her husband's semen to take root inside her and to become a foetus.

*3. While men possess the flutes, the life cycle is uninterrupted.* According to the logic of men's rites, the symbolic role of the Gimi female is to re-cycle the male — to move him through the female body and simultaneously through the universe. Passage through the female digestive/procreative system transfers the male from this world into the other world. Once released from inside women, the spirits of dead Gimi men flee to join the clan reservoir of life-force in the wilderness. Men escape as birds from the polluting and inhibiting life they live "on the ground" close to women. But the men's flight is temporary because male spirit, in order to become human again, must find a way to re-enter the female cannibal cycle.

This configuration of Gimi belief (figure 1) is based upon the assumption that the flute myth is an organizational idea upon which Gimi culture as a whole is constructed and which its members (both male and female) accept as axiomatic because it is founded upon other ideas which are largely unconscious. A premise of such profound and extensive cultural importance must be interpretable in multiple and contradictory ways. The supposed combination of the processes of digestion and procreation in the female may either facilitate the transmigration of the male or it may prevent it. According to the phase of the myth selected, the female passage may be opened (like the flute's blowing hole) so that the 'eaten-and-excreted' male spirit moves unimpeded through it; or, the passage may be closed (plugged up like the flute before men stole it) so that the male spirit — the crying babe — is trapped inside. If procreation and digestion are continuous, women 'keep their bellies full' by endogenously producing and consuming their own male element. Menstrual blood and women's incorporative methods of cultivation (see page 148) symbolize the male's entrapment in the female: in the accounts of both sexes, women actually went to the garden to eat the male body.

This supposedly orgiastic event is recapitulated in mortuary and menstrual rites during which women eat marsupials as replacements for the body. The cannibals must later eat food captured and killed by men in nature, in the non-human spirit world (*kore*), as substitutes for the food created and nurtured by women in the domesticated world of flesh and blood. Women who digest and retain what they themselves produced are

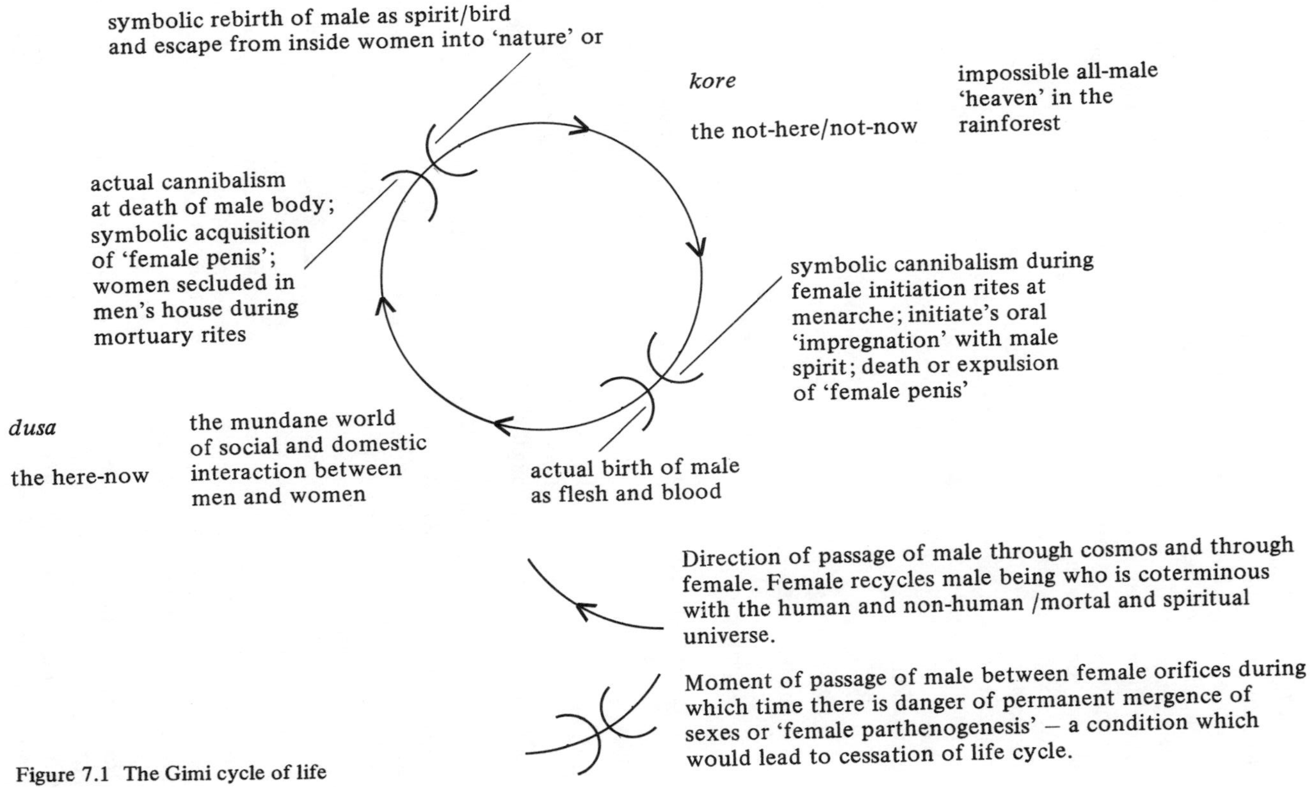

symbolic rebirth of male as spirit/bird
and escape from inside women into 'nature' or

impossible all-male
'heaven' in the
rainforest

*kore*

the not-here/not-now

symbolic cannibalism during
female initiation rites at
menarche; initiate's oral
'impregnation' with male
spirit; death or expulsion
of 'female penis'

actual cannibalism
at death of male body;
symbolic acquisition
of 'female penis';
women secluded in
men's house during
mortuary rites

actual birth of male
as flesh and blood

*dusa*

the here-now

the mundane world
of social and domestic
interaction between
men and women

Direction of passage of male through cosmos and through
female. Female recycles male being who is coterminous
with the human and non-human/mortal and spiritual
universe.

Moment of passage of male between female orifices during
which time there is danger of permanent mergence of
sexes or 'female parthenogenesis' – a condition which
would lead to cessation of life cycle.

Figure 7.1  The Gimi cycle of life

self-sufficient or flute-holding. In the sense that the marsupials symbolize the contents of the flutes (see page 159), their intestinal passage through women opens the flutes and detaches them from women. The "female" marsupials induce the departure from women of a *feminized* male spirit. The elevation of the male to the realm of *kore* depends not only upon his escape from women's bodies but also upon his absorption of female spirit. The male can pass through the female and not lose himself there because he takes the essential part of her with him, so to speak.

By acquiescing in men's rites, women acknowledge that they do not internally possess (but must be fed) the bisexual spirit (*kore*) which animates all forms of life (including garden products). In effect, women acknowledge that they have no flutes; that they are not self-sufficient or 'phallic'. Implicit in this hypothetical narrative is the following set of associations:

| | | |
|---|---|---|
| male spirit/<br>flutes owned by women | : | female spirit/<br>flutes owned by men |
| phallic female | : | phallic male |
| cultivation of gardens | : | spontaneous regeneration of<br>rainforest and human spirit |
| absorption/death of male<br>(foetus formed by<br>menstrual blood) | : | separate existence/life of male<br>(foetus formed by semen) |

*4. Possession of flutes is eternal question. Men's efforts to 'steal' them imply female ownership.* As I interpret it, Gimi cosmology presents an insoluble contradiction: although men's bodies and spirits are uniquely the matter of human and non-human life, men do not control the meta-processes of life's continuation. To perpetuate existence, men must 'go inside' women — with their whole bodies at death or with their penes during sexual union. This unavoidable entry into women has two outcomes. Men may pass through women unimpeded. This ideal outcome abstractly describes the received Gimi theory of procreation which gives all the credit to semen and treats women as 'sterile vessels'. The second possibility is that men who go inside women stay there: the male disappears but the female becomes phallic. This 'outcome' describes an unarticulated counter-dogma of procreation which suggests that the Gimi female is parthenogenetic, i.e. that menstrual blood represents an invisible, internal penis which occurs spontaneously in women.

*The mother as 'sterile vessel'.* In response to questions about the contributions of the living mother and father to the inception of uterine life, Gimi of both sexes state that a man's semen alone forms the body of the foetus (cf. Glick 1963:100). My suggestion that it might feed and grow on menstrual blood was usually greeted with horrified denials: such 'food' would surely kill the unborn. Burial practices for breast-fed infants (who do not eat other foods) indicate that a child's body is considered still a part of its father's seminal fluid. During the terminal illness of a nine-month-old male, the mother scrupulously collected the baby's watery feces in coleus leaves and kept them in a net bag. When the child died, she buried the leaves in a separate grave to prevent the feces rotting and being mixed together with the decomposing corpse. Such a posthumous combination of substances would, she said, kill her husband: it would be tantamount to introducing her breast milk (the unweaned baby's feces) into his semen (the baby's corpse). "Having a child," said her husband, "is something that comes from men. It doesn't come from women! Men give the child to women, women become pregnant and they must look after what men give them [the semen]" by protecting it from contamination.[12]

We have seen how the bride-initiate is made publicly to eat wild foods which represent her husband's ancestral semen and his spirit-child. By implication she will serve merely to incubate a foetus whose body is derived from its father's semen and whose animating life-force is derived from the *kore*. Even a female child is symbolically male in the sense that it is wholly derived from the father or his ancestors.

*The phallic (parthenogenetic) mother.* Relying on men's and women's statements and on their public rites, we may infer that Gimi consider the active female role in procreation to be unimportant or non-existent (cf. Read 1952:14). But this inference is not sustained by an examination of secret initiation rites which men conduct in the forest.[13] After the initiates are married and fathers of two living children, clan elders intern one or two of the men at a time[14] inside a "menstrual hut" or "flute house" rapidly constructed in a clearing from palm fronds and wild banana leaves. Inside the hut, an older man applies a tourniquet made of peeled banana stems to the upper arm of the initiate and "shoots" a protruding vein at the inside of the elbow with a miniature bow and obsidian-tipped arrow. As the blood spurts up and falls onto a bed of edible greens, the men shout threats at

12  The same informant pointed out that in the past when mothers ate their dead babies, it was impossible for a child's feces inadvertently to become mixed together with its corpse so endangering the life of the father.

13  My knowledge of this rite and of the participants' explanations is based upon fieldwork conducted by David Gillison. The interpretation is the product of both our efforts.

14  Unlike the first male initiation, when groups of ten to 16 youths (aged about ten to 14 years) are secluded simultaneously in two or three men's houses, these later rites for married men are held — like the rites for married women — for one or two initiates at a time.

the novice, telling him they will kill him if he reveals the secret they are about to reveal to him. The initiate's blood and the greens are wrapped in a large banana leaf and hung to steam over a slow-burning fire. The men leave the initiate and go outside the hut to decorate their heads and bodies lavishly with leafy bamboo vines (see Plate 7.2 page 155). They return in a procession, two of them playing flutes made from the wide base section of a large bamboo. After some fanfare, these most sacred flutes, called "the Mother of the Birds" (cf. Salisbury 1965:71), are laid in the initiate's lap. Again the men threaten the initiate with an ugly death and hold an axe at his throat as they extract an oath of secrecy. When the flutes are stowed away, all the men, including the initiate, eat the meal of his cooked blood and elatedly make their way back to the settlement.

Combining our knowledge of the flute myth with explanations given by the participants, we may say that the initiate is treated as female: 'she' is secluded inside a menstrual hut and wounded with an arrow by a man. 'She' is 'castrated' and loses 'her' penis. But the penis — the flute — is returned to the initiate by the men. Because of the way the men 'give it back' — *as a detached and male-created thing* — the initiate is 'reborn' as a man from men. By this interpretation of the Gimi rite, predicated on the 'secret idea' that menstrual blood betokens women's original ownership of the penis, we may explain "one of the most difficult and troublesome theoretical questions with respect to initiation rites . . . Does initiation make men of boys or does it make women of boys? . . . Initiation rites make boys into men, but they do so by means of feminising the initiates (cf. Hiatt 1971:88)" (Dundes 1976:232). From the time of their first initiation (at about 12 years) Gimi youths are called "new vaginas" by their initiators; their 'castration' is the first stage of their "rebirth *from men*, not women" (ibid.: original emphasis). Masculinity is wholly achieved when the married Gimi initiate successively assumes the ritual identities both of female (menstruator) and male (flute-owner) and of mother (supplier of uterine food) and child (eater of uterine food). To attain full male status the initiate symbolically *acts as his own creator.* He is *mother* to himself: he menstruates like a woman and loses the blood ('kills the penis'), then ingests it and so negates the loss ('gives birth to his own penis'). When I suggest that the men's secret ritual is an imitation of female digestive/ reproductive functions (cf. Mead 1970:259), I mean that its purpose is to appropriate the phallic (i.e. *endogenously* child-creating) role of women — to "steal" it from them.[15] The rite implies an equivalence between the

15    It will strike the reader that here I interpret a ritual built around the imitation of female body functions as men's attempt to deprive woman of her procreative role — to "steal" it from her — and in that sense to diminish the female. On the other hand, I interpret the imitation of birds' behaviour (pages 146–7) as men's attempts metonymically to share an avian existence and thereby to elevate the male (but not correspond-

penis and the *creativity* of menstrual blood in this sense: *once menstrual blood is taken away from women (by men who menstruate) its phallic power is 'restored'.* Female attributes that are deadly in women become life-producing when they are detached from women and owned by men. Men's rites of imitation which aim to disendow the female paradoxically suggest her reproductive superiority (see plate 7.3).

My interpretation of the Gimi flute myth and rites of male initiation which are supposedly kept secret from women implies that men view the female both as 'phallic' and as 'castrated', as once having possessed the penis (the flute), as having now lost it, but as retaining rights of original possession. "If the [flute] is phallic . . . why should this need to be kept secret from women? Women are surely aware of the existence and nature of the male phallus" (Dundes 1976:223).[16] But, according to the Gimi myth (see page 156), women are not aware that the phallus – the flute – once belonged to them. Men may fear that if women had this knowledge they would reclaim what was originally theirs: the flutes would 'again' be attached to women. Why should men fear an impossibility? Perhaps, contrary to what they say (but consistently with their "secret" rites), Gimi men suspect that menstrual blood is synonymous with child-bearing power and that it occurs spontaneously in women. If women were partheno-genetic, then men, having no role, would cease to exist separately from women. Women's phallic power would be 'restored'. If flutes were attached to women, the male spirit could not travel through the female body because it would be 'closed'. Dead Gimi men, trapped inside phallic women, could no longer provide their spirits to fill the clan reservoir of life-force in the rainforest and so could not animate new generations of clan members. Life in the world would cease.

Why Gimi men characterize women as primordial possessors of flutes, as eager cannibals, as eternally reluctant relinquishers of men's spirits and of their living children, as the only barren sex, are questions which cannot be broached here. I indicate only that the men's attitude is consistent with certain "secret" parts of female initiation which precede by several days the men's public celebration of a girl's first menses. During these closed sessions the older women teach the novices "blood songs" to arrest the menstrual flow – an aim which I suggest reveals a female wish to 'keep the flute' or to 'remain parthenogenetic'.

ingly to devalue the bird). Apparently, similar ritual procedures do not produce similar results when the contents of the rites differ radically.

16 Dundes' question is posed with regard to the bullroarer. However, "a number of scholars have observed that flutes are sometimes substituted for bullroarers" (Dundes 1976:231). Because the bullroarer is also "something which is produced by women and is stolen by and for men" (1976:225), the substitution seems especially apt in this case.

Plate 7.3 Belying the assertions of men and women that the details of each other's secret ritual performances are unknown to the opposite sex, young men dressed as female initiates enact in the forest a scene from the women's "secret" rites. They are rehearsing a mime to be performed at night inside the men's house where male initiation rites (from which women are rigorously excluded) will be in progress.

*5. Women's secret rites contain symbolic attempts to 'keep the flutes'.* The imagery of the women's songs implies that the female body can be 'sealed up' so that the blood remains inside. As one woman put it: "The song says to the blood, 'You cannot come outside! You must stay inside! I say to my husband . . . ' I am like the cordyline leaves whose redness is nothing more than a shine (i.e. whose redness is static or contained inside the leaves, not flowing out, like blood)." The blood which the women induce to remain inside the menstruating initiate belongs to the girl's father or, collectively, to the men of his lineage (many of whom are named by the women in successive verses of their songs). As another woman explained: "What the moon kills (the menstrual blood) is the red lorikeets' nose-water. It is the blood from the noses of our brothers. Those boys give us their blood." The birds (the red lorikeets) are the girl's lineage brothers who "menstruate" by having their noses bled in a forest stream as part of a "secret" site of male initiation (cf. Read 1952; 1965). Because birds' noses are explicit symbols of male novices' penes I infer that the "nose-water" — the boys' "menstrual blood" — also represents their semen.

Considering women's statements that the source of the initiate's "first pregnancy" (i.e. first menses) is the blood of her paternal lineage, blood extracted from the noses of her 'menstruating' lineage brothers, I suggest that the women are inverting the logic of the men's flute myth. Whereas, in the myth a man "steals" his sister's flute (her penis), in the women's rites the sister is "filled up with" *his* menstrual blood. Combining the logic of myth and rite we may say that the female initiate internalizes what she has lost and thereby denies the loss: she denies the theft of the flutes. If, following from this, we establish the equation: menstrual blood = father's/ brother's semen = female penis, we may see another inverted parallel between men's and women's initiation rites. In both cases, the initiates "menstruate" and lose a 'penis' (see page 164): the male initiate's 'lost penis' belonged originally to his mother or sister;[17] the female initiate's 'lost penis' belonged originally to her father or brother.[18] Whereas men 'replace' the 'mother's penis'[19] lost by the male initiate with his own

17  According to the flute myth, the original penis belonged to the sister, but, according to men's rites, separation is sought from the initiate's mother. The initiate receives the bamboo flute and sacred flute tunes from his mother's brother who, one may presume, 'took' them from his sister. In other words, the flute originates with the sister of the bestower and the mother of the recipient.

18  I realize the speculative nature of these formulations. In order to present an overview of Gimi cosmology in a small space, I have had to omit detailed analyses of ritual and of other ethnographic material upon which I base my conclusions and which alone make them fully convincing.

19  Many facets of men's rites indicate that 'mother's penis' (the flute)

penis (a flute which he himself will possess), the men replace the 'father's penis' lost by the female initiate with her husband's penis (symbolized during the rite by the "children of his flute", the wild foods taken from his clan forest which men of her husband's lineage ritually force the initiate to eat (see page 159).

In these terms, female menstruation is a substitutive process in which the 'deposits' of one man (the father or, collectively, his lineage) are destroyed and replaced by the 'deposits' of another man (the husband or his lineage). The thwarted purpose of women's preceding rites is secretly[20] to oppose the exchange which the men publicly engineer to prevent the 'emptying out' of their bodies. According to informants of both sexes, the appearance of menstrual blood results only from sexual penetration – "a killing by the moon". Several of the women's blood songs implore the moon to "turn to stone". A husband/moon of stone, one woman explained, has no fluid to release: he cannot penetrate the initiate, 'open her up' (as the stolen flute was cut and opened) and cause her to 'lose what is inside'. The idea that the girl's 'internal contents' are derived from her father or his lineage is consistent with informants' statements that every Gimi child is an embodiment of its father's semen (see page 163) and is animated by its paternal ancestors.[21] In this sense, the blood the initiate loses during her

may refer to mother's breast. The most obvious of these is that there are two flutes. As the breast is the source of food for the newborn, the flute is the source of food – the male initiate's "menstrual blood" – which will 'feed' (i.e. give birth to) his own penis. Tentatively we may suggest that the equations 'flute = penis = breast' and *'men's* menstrual blood = food-from-the-penis = semen = mother's milk' have the effect of 'replacing' the initiate's female mother with a "male mother" – first his mother's brother (see note 17), then himself (see page 164).

20    Discussing and enacting their rites of initiation, Gimi men and women continually refer to the secrecy of particular myths or ritual sequences. Women conscientiously post guards during portions of their night-time celebrations to ensure that no male is lurking in the bushes to spy on them. Yet my interviews with informants of both sexes indicate that adults have intellectual (if not visual) knowledge of the entire range of so-called "secrets". By calling something secret, Gimi seem to refer to that part of their myth or ritual which expresses aims or wishes that are implacably opposed to the aims or wishes of the opposite sex.

21    From the foregoing analysis it appears that the premise of female initiation rites is that 'the child [i.e. the initiate] is wholly derived from the penis of the father'; and of male rites, that 'the child [i.e. the initiate] is wholly derived from the penis of the mother'. That Gimi ideology contains these and other "secret" or conflicting premises (see note 20) is an implication of my work whose complexity is only touched upon in this paper.

first menses symbolizes the birth of the father's dead child (cf. Salisbury 1965:72). It is as though the introduction of husband's semen creates an intolerable excess of male substance inside the body of the bride-novice and induces the departure or death of father's semen, which appears outside the initiate's body as menstrual blood. Here is a striking difference from male initiation: whereas in women's rites semen inside the female body is changed into blood and killed, in men's arm-bleeding and nose-bleeding rites (see pages 163—4) menstrual blood inside the male body is 'changed back into' semen, its life-giving power restored.

When women endeavour through the efficacy of song[22] to restore the virginal capacity of the initiate's body to contain the blood, I suggest that they are symbolically attempting to forestall the 'initial' transformation of semen into blood. If she could turn the murderous moon to stone, the initiate could exclude her husband's 'lethal' ejaculations and so retain the 'father's child' she possesses from birth — as a virgin — as a 'sealed *and filled* vessel'. The men who publicly 'force' the initiate to eat the foods which symbolize her husband's semen and his child effectively deprive her of this internally-created father-derived 'food'. They kill it, causing it to appear outside the body as blood. In a sense, the men deny that menstruation occurs spontaneously, that the initiate is parthenogenetic, that she has flutes inside her. The men who represent her husband undo the initiate's efforts, expressed in the blood songs, to keep the products of her body unseparated from her and unseen by the outside world.

## Conclusion

In this brief analysis of Gimi thought, the myth of the flutes serves as a premise around which the culture is organized. Its central event — the stealing of flutes from women — is treated as a symbolic solution to men's greatest fear: that they would remain, like the foetus, merged with the female and indistinguishable from her, or that they would live, like the newborn, as her phallic appendage. In the condensed symbolic terms in which I have presented a Gimi view of the world (mainly a male Gimi view), I suggest that the theft is intended to save men, and in a more complex sense, women too, from an internal (incestuous) attachment to women whose fatal consequences are symbolized by menstrual blood.

22  Special incantations that accompany each stage of planting and weeding of sweet potato, taro, greens, yams and the raising of pigs (see page 147) together form a women's anthology of nurturance, rich in metaphoric allusions. "When we take young women into seclusion," said one Gimi woman, "we give them spells to care for pigs, to plant new gardens and to rid them of menstrual blood. We close our doors and the men do not hear the things we say . . . The spirit of marriage [rites] and of female initiation [rites] is the spirit [*auna*] of food."

Although the theft of the flutes stands for the decisive separation of male from female and of an all-male preserve in the forest (*kore*) from a profane existence with women, in themselves the flutes and the realm of *kore* represent a state of union with the female. Rather than be absorbed by women, the Gimi male appropriates from women an expurgated female element. The hollow tubes that "cry" represent the combination of male and female characteristics in a parturient phallus. In the same way, female elements in the forest symbolically represent their separation from actual women and incorporation within an aggrandized male realm. As the climactic moment of revelation of the flutes to adolescent male novices approaches, the symbols of the body in men's initiation songs, which up to this moment have been unequivocally masculine, now become bisexual. Trees are phallic projections which not only have "heads" that feed birds (symbols of the erect penis, the gorgeously befeathered initiates and the transcendent spirit of dead men) but they also have hollow trunks inside which nest "female" marsupials (symbols of women's pubic hair, initiates when they are called "new vaginas", and the ancestral spirit-child). Headwaters are not only clear streams of male effusions but are also, according to the singers, the issuances from fissures in rocks and from inside mountain caves. The dark cavities of trees and rocks, Gimi men say, are like vaginas; the rivers, like menstrual blood.

The secret of the flutes and of the wild — of *kore* — is that their total maleness includes attributes of the female. A true man is pan-sexual and therefore is capable of reproducing himself without recourse to women. To achieve this ideal state, men appropriate women's powers of endogenous creativity. The spontaneous occurrence of these powers in women, the women's loss of them, and the fatal consequences of women's *retaining* them are together symbolized by menstrual blood. Men 'discard' the female by taking possession of her parthenogenetically-created child — the flute — and thereby paradoxically imply that she has the potential to reassert her omnipotence. In Gimi thought, the power to create is derived from the union of sexual opposites *in a male form*: the hollow penis is also a womb; menstrual blood is also semen when it emerges from a real or symbolic penis (the noses or arms of male initiates). Once these opposite forces coalesce (in ritual or in the mythic past) they become an indissoluble object, symbolized by the flute, which can be possessed at any moment only by one sex or the other (i.e. by forces which are in daily life distinct). But this formulation is a precarious fantasy. The perfect all-male forest after-world (*kore*) created by the flutes is fully attainable only in death. Its magnificent sounds, shapes and colourations are part of a universe which inverts the one men fear women want — an internal world where the processes of life are silent, invisible and inaccessible and where males exist only insofar as they are incorporated by the omnipotent and phallic (flute-holding) mother.

Because the flutes — the realm of *kore* — were stolen from "under women's skirts", their mode of reproduction invertedly parallels the female digestive/procreative mode. Inside the rainforest, the dead and the unborn exist as male spirit; inside women they exist as digested or gestated flesh and blood. Men's relations to the forest and to women are similarly envisaged as participatory and cyclic. Before birth and after death men's other-worldly existence is indistinguishable from the life in nature, as it is indistinguishable from the life in women's bodies. But men's ritual has the opposite intention toward women to that which it has toward the wild. While men seek complete union with the *kore* they try to arrange complete separation from women (in whom the *kore* originated). The combination of male and female characteristics *in the male* is the secret of male dominance; their combination in the female is men's doom. The stealing of the flutes represents both the violent leave-taking from actual women and the creation of a forest world where the male safely approaches a purified — i.e. a masculinized — female element.

We cannot account for the institutionalized expression of men's fear and hostility to women by the notion of a primordial cosmic split — a 'big bang' theory in which everything categorized with the 'here-now' or the self (e.g. culture and the male) is valued above everything categorized with the 'there-before' or the discarded other (e.g. nature and the female). Rather, we see the Gimi cosmos as a continually occurring "regeneration of elements" (Weiner 1979:329) wherein the separations in existence (self/ other, male/female, human/animal, etc.) are repeatedly destroyed in order that they may be repeatedly created. From this perspective, sexual antagonism is a conflict over who controls the *indivisible* power to reproduce the world, a power which resides in the body because "the important aspects of the cosmos are inside man's body, not outside it" (Newman 1965:82). The contested issue is whether women's power to 'absorb the male' — to negate body boundaries through cannibalism and menstruation — surpasses men's ritual power to release the male spirit and to elevate it through the absorption of female elements.

In my view, the opposition between culture and nature represents an externalization of the relation between mind and body or between consciousness and instinct. It originates primarily in the tendency of some structuralist anthropologists to extrapolate universal cultural categories from an unspecified theory about the internal operation of the mind (cf. Lévi-Strauss 1969:3–11). Characteristics which we ordinarily impute to 'human nature', such as baseness and rampant uncontrollability, the nature/culture model of explanation attributes to native conceptions of the environment. Human nature is driven out of the body into the wilderness and deprived of its sexual content. If we view the model as a distorted version of psychic relations, then we see that it 'confuses' the control which human consciousness exerts upon our inner selves with the intended purpose of culture, as expressed in ritual, to triumph over the productions of the non-human environment (Ortner 1974).

Through ritual men may abdicate control or seek union with the higher authority of gods or totemic ancestors who inhabit unpopulated regions, are part-animal or are in other ways 'part of' or 'closer to nature'. Rather than to demonstrate human autonomy, the purpose of ritual is often to perpetuate a connection between a human and a non-human world when the latter is in the ascendancy. If culture's understanding of its supremacy is not universally demonstrated, then the argument for using that attitude as the underlying metaphor for men's subordination of women cannot be easily made. To say that cultures are centrally concerned with dominating their environments is drastically to underrate the complexity of indigenous cosmologies and to deny the importance of different obsessions.

## References cited

de Beauvoir, Simone. 1953. *The second sex*. New York: Bantam Books.

Dundes, Alan. 1976. 'A psychoanalytic study of the bullroarer', *Man* (N.S.) 2, 220–38.

Glick, Leonard B. 1963. 'Foundations of a primitive medical system. The Gimi of the New Guinea Highlands'. Unpublished PhD thesis. Graduate School of Arts and Sciences, The University of Pennsylvania.

Hiatt, L.R. 1971. 'Secret pseudo-procreation rites among the Australian Aborigines', in *Anthropology in Oceania*, ed. L.R. Hiatt and C. Jayawardena, pp. 77–88. Sydney: Angus & Robertson.

Langness, L.L. 1974. 'Ritual, power and male dominance in the New Guinea Highlands', *Ethos*, 2, 189–212.

Lederer, Wolfgana. 1968. *The fear of women*. New York: Harcourt Brace Jovanovich.

Lévi-Strauss, Claude. 1969. *The elementary structures of kinship*. Boston: Beacon Press.

Mead, Margaret. 1970. *The mountain Arapesh volume II: arts and supernaturalism*. Garden City: The Natural History Press.

Newman, Philip L. 1965. *Knowing the Gururumba*. New York: Holt, Rinehart & Winston.

Ortner, Sherry B. 1974. 'Is female to male as nature is to culture?', in *Woman, culture and society*, ed. M.Z. Rosaldo and L. Lamphere, pp. 67–88. Stanford: Stanford University Press.

Read, Kenneth E. 1952. 'Nama cult of the central highlands, New Guinea', *Oceania*, 23, 1–25.

1965. *The high valley*. New York: Charles Scribner's Sons.

Salisbury, Richard F. 1965. 'The Siane of the eastern highlands', in *Gods, ghosts and men in Melanesia*, ed. P. Lawrence and M.J. Meggitt, pp. 50–77. Melbourne: Oxford University Press.

Tuzin, Donald F. 1972. 'Yam symbolism in the Sepik: an interpretative account', *South-western Journal of Anthropology*, 28, 230–54.

Weiner, Annette B. 1979. 'Trobriand kinship from another view: the reproductive power of women and men', *Man*, **14**, 328–48.

# 8    No nature, no culture: the Hagen case

MARILYN STRATHERN

## I Introduction

In describing some of the symbols to be found in their decorations and
spells, we have asserted that the Hagen people of the Papua New Guinea
Highlands make an association between two pairs of contrasts, wild and
domestic things, male and female (A. and M. Strathern 1971). Other Highlands ethnographers have reached similar conclusions. But one of them,
Langness, has also specifically questioned the analytical status of such
constructs. He writes:

It seems plain that the distinction between the domestic and the wild . . .
is widespread in the New Guinea Highlands (Bulmer 1967; Newman 1964;
Strathern and Strathern 1971). Perhaps it is a universal dichotomy (Lévi-
Strauss 1969). But whether universal or not, does it have the symbolic
significance we are now attributing to it? And is it as symbolic to 'them' as
it is to 'us'? . . . Even if we knew that a wild—domestic or *nature—culture*
dichotomy was universal, and that it always had some symbolic significance, what about other symbols that do not appear to be directly associated with it? [1976:103; my italics]

Barth discusses Baktaman (central New Guinea) ideas with much the same
scepticism. Referring to 'the Domestic : Wild : : *Culture : Nature* dichot-
omizations claimed for pig and marsupial symbolism, in areas of the Highlands (cf. Strathern 1968)', he notes that there is little to indicate either
as basic constituting dichotomies in Baktaman cognition. ' "Culture" does
not provide a distinctive set of objects with which one manipulates
"Nature" ' (1975:194—5; my italics).

This presents something of a problem in cognition. Neither author is
happy with the terms *nature—culture*, but in our case at least they are
criticizing concepts we never employed. What, then, is the source of their
equation? Why extrapolate from wild—domestic to nature—culture?

They provide some clues. Langness's comments arise in the context of
discussions about male—female relations in the Highlands,[1] and particularly

1    In the same volume a similar extrapolation is made, with some reser-
vation, by Meggitt. He suggests that the oppositions which emerge
from Mae Enga stories between demons in the forest and humans in

notes Lindenbaum's account of the Fore (1976). These Eastern Highlanders make an explicit connection between resource management and social control:

The [Fore] opposition of the domestic and wild . . . has to do with control and safety which comes from regulation and management, in contrast to the danger which lies in the uncontrolled, unpredictable, and unregulated. Just as South Fore groups depend on regulated access to forest resources, so they depend on regulated access to women . . . Women's sexuality is the dangerous 'wild' which men must bring under control [1976:56].[2]

Barth's observation that Baktaman do not recognize a nature—culture dichotomy rests partly on the lack of any clear distinction between settlement and forest, persons and pigs moving freely between these domains, and on the readiness of Baktaman travellers to confront new environments without the aid of luggage, tools or weapons. All places, species, processes are of one unitary kind: nature is not 'manipulated'. Both writers are assuming certain meanings here, Langness in using the concepts of nature and culture, and Barth in dismissing them. Their chain of associations includes elements such as a boundary between settlement and forest,

> settlements 'may perhaps be an expression of a more general view of a dichotomy between nature and culture' (1976:68). But he adds that he would not want to push the suggestion too far. Buchbinder and Rappaport comment on an explicit Maring opposition between the wild and cultivated, between the bounties and danger of nature and the cultural order, although they note that 'cultivated' or 'domestic' is an incomplete gloss for the opposite of 'wild'. Fecundity is an aspect of the wild, and they describe an ornamental plant which is set around a ritual oven 'for the benefit of women, domestic pigs and gardens' as lashing 'sociocultural ends onto natural processes' (1976: 30). The same plant is put on graves, the fecund and the mortal being combined as female elements in opposition to male. They write: 'The conflation of vagina and grave is not unique to the Maring, and the identification of men with culture and spirituality and women with nature and fertility . . . is widespread' (1976:32).
>
> 2 Lindenbaum does not herself summarize these attitudes as a matter of nature and culture, though she does argue: 'In a sense, female menstrual cycles provide a physiological regularity, like the annual ripening of the pandanus fruit, which is an ecological given. For a society which can profit from an increase in numbers, it is adaptive to observe this regularity . . . Yet the order in this case poses a threat, since it is a structure provided by women, not men, a phenomenon Fore and other New Guinea groups attempt to neutralize by male rituals of imitative menstruation . . . performed characteristically during initiation . . . Men have taken on themselves the task of orchestrating the balance among continually fluctuating environmental, biological and social variables' (1976:56—7).

notions of control and manipulation, and culture as the works of man against the natural environment or human biology.

Insofar as such notions of nature and culture belong to a specific intellectual tradition within our own culture, some interesting issues are raised by attributing this dichotomy to the thought systems of other peoples. In the sense apparently intended by these writers, there is no demarcated 'nature' or 'culture' in Hagen thought. Hageners' own distinction between the domestic and wild is therefore worth examining in detail.

The exercise is illuminating for one reason: out of all the meanings which 'nature' and 'culture' have in the western world, certain systematic selections are made when the same ideas are imputed to others. There are at least two drives behind the selections manifested in the handling of New Guinea ethnography. One comes from ecological interests, which sees an analytical relationship between ecology and society echoed in other people's contrasts between the wild and the domestic. The second characterizes that area of feminist writing preoccupied by the relationship between biology and the man-made, a concern which echoes the way in which notions about male and female are in our own culture articulated with those of nature and culture.

These two viewpoints substantially impinge upon and draw support from each other. Indeed, I would solve the problem Langness and Barth set up by suggesting that a non-western wild—domestic dichotomy triggers off an interpretation in terms of 'nature—culture' *in the presence of* explicit themes of environmental control or of male—female symbolism. It is even arguable that a male—female distinction in western thought systems plays a crucial role as symbolic operator in certain transformations between the terms nature—culture. That we presented the Hagen categories wild—domestic in direct association with their own gender symbols accounts for, I think, the plausible but in this context ultimately absurd extrapolation that we were talking about nature—culture.

## II  The idea of nature—culture

*What do we mean by nature and culture?*

Langness refers the nature—culture dichotomy back to Lévi-Strauss. There is no doubt that impetus to incorporate these terms in symbolic analysis stems from their currency in structuralism, and the arguments of Edwin Ardener and Sherry Ortner, with which this book is partly concerned, acknowledge the background inspiration of Lévi-Strauss.

MacCormack offers a critique of these concepts within the structuralist frame, as from their different perspectives do Gillison and Harris. My own account bypasses the question of underlying structures, and the usefulness of these terms for apprehending the workings of the human mind. Rather it is addressed to those styles of interpretation *which impute to other people* the idea of nature—culture as a more or less explicit entity in their mental representations. Whatever status these concepts have within 'rationalist' discourse, there has been demonstrable 'empiricist' (cf. Leach 1976) appropriation of them.

Nature and culture tend to acquire certain meanings as categories of analysis when those working mainly in an empiricist tradition turn to the exegesis of cognitive systems. First, they are given the status of surface components in the system under study — that is, explicitly or implicitly they are interpreted as substantive principles which make sense of indigenous categories in their own terms (metonymically), as 'consanguinity' or 'pollution' or 'initiand' may be said to do. Second, nature and culture are understood in an essentialist sense: that is, peoples apparently entertaining notions of this order may be thought of as wrestling with the same problems of control and definition as form the content of these terms for ourselves.

Such solipsism has been fully discussed by Wagner: although we allow, he says, that other cultures comprise sets of artefacts and images which differ in style from our own, we tend to superimpose them on the same reality — nature as we perceive it (1975:142). The point to extract is simple: there is no such thing as nature or culture. Each is a highly relativized concept whose ultimate signification must be derived from its place within a specific metaphysics. No single meaning can in fact be given to nature or culture in western thought; there is no consistent dichotomy, only a matrix of contrasts (cf. Hastrup 1978:63).[3] The question then becomes how large a part of *the total assemblage* of meanings must we be able to identify in other cultures to speak with confidence of their having such notions.

Perhaps the problem tends to be ignored because the social sciences themselves commonly employ certain constituents of the nature—culture matrix, including those concerned with ecological systems and their environments, society and the 'individual', and the whole view which Sahlins (1976) has described of culture as production. Burridge (1973) points to that distinctive tradition in European thought long concerned with the opposition between things as they are and things as they might be; separation of subject from object and the construction of ideal or alternative forms of society are part of a dialectic between participation and objectivity. The combined capacity to participate in 'otherness' and treat that otherness as an object (of study) has made anthropology. This process depends upon a central conviction that man 'makes' culture, and insofar as this is true can also stand outside his own 'nature'.

3 Some of the historical changes involved are discussed in chapters 2 and 3.

Indeed, Goody (1977:64) notes that nature and culture have penetrated so deeply into cultural analysis that we regard their opposition as inevitable ('natural'). He directly questions whether such corresponding pairs of concepts are always to be found in other cultures, logically comparable to other conventional classifications such as right–left or male–female. To include a nature–culture contrast along with these where there are no explicit equivalents inadmissibly combines both actor and observer classifications. He characterizes the dichotomy itself as a 'highly abstract and rather eighteenth-century' (1977:64) piece of western intellectualism. If so, we need to account for its twentieth-century currency. In Sahlins' words: 'all our social sciences participate in the going conception that society is produced by enterprising action' (1976:52).

Jordanova and the Blochs demonstrate some of the ways past thinkers in the western tradition have employed such ideas. My own treatment will be essentially ahistorical, and draws on my understanding of our twentieth-century interest in these same terms. Let me sketch the main constituents of them in the empiricist styles of interpretation with which I am concerned, and start with the point that in our own thought nature and culture cannot be resolved into a single dichotomy.

When thinking of culture as common to the species we may refer to it as a manifestation of 'human nature': when thinking of it as particularizing mankind in relation to the rest of the world we envisage culture as an ingredient adding refinement to a given 'animal nature' we share with other species. As Benoist puts it: 'Is culture rooted in nature, imitating it or emanating direct from it? Or, on the contrary, is culture at variance with nature, absolutely cut off from it since the origin and involved in the process of always transforming, changing nature? The matrix of this opposition between culture and nature is the very matrix of Western metaphysics' (1978:59). Culture is *nomos* as well as *techne*, that is, subsumes society as well as culture in the marked sense. Nature is equally human nature and the non-social environment. To these images of the 'real' world we attach a string of evaluations – so that one is active, the other passive; one is subject, the other object; one creation, the other resource; one energizes, the other limits.

These values are not held in a fixed relationship but may adhere to either category. The location of the active agent shifts (cf. Wagner 1975: 67; Schneider 1968:107f.). At one point culture is a creative, active force which produces form and structure out of a passive, given nature. At another, culture is the end product of a process, tamed and refined, and dependent for energy upon resources outside itself. Culture is both the creative subject and the finished object; nature both resource and limitation, amenable to alteration and operating under laws of its own. It is rather like a prism that yields different patterns as it is turned – through it at times either nature or culture may be seen as the encapsulated or the encapsulating element.

To gain analytical insight from these terms, the prism has to be kept momentarily rigid. For depending on our philosophical standpoints we can employ various parts of this matrix in support of certain evaluations — and do so by reducing involute combinations to a series of oppositions. One way of proving to ourselves that we have constructed a real dichotomy between nature and culture is to project aspects of it onto the societies we study. Such a projection may be encouraged by the discovery of indigenous symbolism which appears to set up parallel dichotomies between male and female or domestic and wild. This is the significance of the substantivist homology: when male versus female carries connotations, say, of collective versus individual enterprise, or when the domestic refers to a village in the clearing and the wild to bush around, we too easily assume the presence of a clear, objectified polarization between culture and nature.

In other words I would see ideological intention — there from the beginning according to the Blochs (p. 39) — in the desire to produce a dichotomy (nature vs. culture) out of a set of combinations (all the meanings that nature and culture have in our culture, rich in semantic ambiguity). It is the same logic which creates 'opposition' out of 'difference' (Wilden 1972). In selecting from our own repertoire of overlapping notions certain concepts envisaged in a dichotomous or oppositional relationship (nature vs. culture), we are at best making prior assumptions about the logic of the system under study, and at worst using symbols of our own as though they were signs; as though through them we could read other people's messages, and not just feedback from our own input.

I have already referred to certain modes of interpretation which illustrate this tendency. The essentially ecological model of the type Sahlins discusses in terms of 'practical reason' approaches culture as modifying the environment or adapting to it; it thus sets the creativity of culture against the givens of nature. 'Naturalism understands culture as the human mode of adaptation. Culture in this view is an instrumental order' (Sahlins 1976: 101). A homology may be perceived between the subject matter of nature and culture in indigenous thought and the observer's analysis of the place of that society within its environment. The reality with which we endow our own interaction with nature is thus imputed to the systems of those we study — even to the extent that an indigenous distinction between village and bush may be rendered as reproducing our evolutionary understanding of human society in terms of technology modifying resource. 'Nature' as 'environment' is the particular concern of these ideas. A second model is sometimes employed by those interested in relations between the sexes as a history of a power struggle: they see in the association of cultural artefacts and male creativity a process which by relegating woman to a natural status has deprived her of social identity.[4] 'Human nature' with its problems of consciousness, identity, and mind—body dualism is centrally at issue here.

Another set of assumptions holds a common place in both formulations. These posit a link between nature=environment, resource, limitation, and human nature=universal capacities and needs. The (biological) 'individual' as opposed to 'society' can thus come to occupy a position analogous to nature as opposed to culture. When social science sets up the problem of conversion, from the (natural) individual to the role-playing person, it entertains a notion of human nature as raw biological matter to be moulded by society. The 'feminist'[5] equation of culture as man-made can invert the values sometimes implicit in this position. (In feminist arguments of the 'expressive' type (Glennon 1979), the created is male, artificial, colonial, while females remain an uncontaminated 'human' resource.)

Each model thus sets up a dynamic opposition. The one sees primitive society as grappling with the same concerns for control over the environment as preoccupy the industrial west; the other demonstrates the insidious manner in which men's control over women is built into a notion of culture's control over nature, reason over emotion, and so on. They hold in common the idea of a *relationship between* nature and culture that is not static, but always involves tension of a kind. There is more than the notion of nature and culture as the halves of a whole (dichotomy). It may also be imagined as a continuum — things can be 'more or less natural', there are 'lower' and 'higher' degrees of what is cultural (civilization). We may think of a process. Nature can become culture — a wild environment is tamed; a child is socialized; the individual as a natural entity learns rules. And we may think of hierarchy. This can take an evaluative form — as in the claim

4    E.g. Reiter (1975:19) prefaces a collection of essays on women: 'These essays subject our notions of male dominance to specific analysis, and push us to understand that it is anything but natural. As an artifact of culture, such patterns have undergone changes that we can analyze, and are amenable to changes for which we can actively work.' Biology (science/fact/the innate) is important to one type of feminist argument. By showing that there is no biological basis to our own cultural symbols of male and female we can 'prove' that the symbols are 'false' (i.e. constructs which do not properly represent nature). From a different approach, however, insofar as humanity may be said to transcend nature, natural justifications for cultural discrimination cease to be valid (Firestone 1972).

5    There is, of course, no single 'feminist' position, and I use the term here as a shorthand for certain types of arguments (see Glennon 1979 for a discussion). It is equally a 'feminist' viewpoint that so-called personal and individual relationships cannot be differentiated from political ones, and that it is an attribute of a male-dominated ideology to separate out 'political' and 'personal' spheres of action.

that culture is everywhere seen as superior to nature; or it can be a matter of logic — thus nature, the higher order category, includes culture, as the general includes the particular.

These western nature–culture constructs, then, revolve around the notion that the one domain is open to control or colonization by the other. Such incorporation connotes that the wild is transformed into the domestic and the domestic contains within it primitive elements of its pre-domestic nature. Socialization of an individual falls as much within this scheme as taming the environment.

In spite of the fact that Lévi-Strauss's own suppositions about the relationship between nature and culture ostensibly deny hierarchy or incorporation, it is constructs of this kind which arguably lie behind much anthropological investigation, and which come to be ascribed to the cultures being studied.[6] This is a point the Blochs (see chapter 2) also make. To link indigenous categorizations which appear to oppose something like culture and nature and our own interpretation of social forms is almost another instance of the totemic illusion. Other people's images of nature and culture are held to reflect the degree of control which actual societies achieve over their actual environments. The same imagery of control is repeated in the 'feminist' conviction that society is to be understood as imposing itself upon the (authentic/natural) individual, as men dominate women. In the concepts we attribute to others, we are seeking confirmation of our own motivated oppositions: and issues to do with 'control' (of the environment, of people) trigger this off.

Lévi-Strauss uses a wild–domestic dichotomy in relation to the human mind; but the types of homologies dealt with in *The savage mind* (1966) suggest that mythical thinking may locate men in a very different relationship to 'nature' from that they occupy in our own world (cf. Godelier 1977:208f.). The striking thing about 'empiricist' exegesis is the attempt to reproduce the *same* location of natural elements as informs certain versions of our own nature–culture constructs.

6  For example, Errington suggests that the Karavaran (New Britain) view of human nature constructs it as compounded of greed and violence, 'characterized by the untrammeled exercise of individual interest. The expression of unrestrained human nature is seen as a chaos of conflicting desires and activities' (1974:21). Social order is imposed upon disorder. These ideas are presented as very close to a nature–culture dichotomy, as emerges from the Karavaran claim that a time of total disorder ended at a specific historical point (when the first missionary landed and turned the hot sea water cool, bringing with him principles of social division and shell money), but that the state of disorder is ever-present as a condition of humanity; and from their use of male–female symbols as images for the 'domestication' of this disruptive condition.

Sahlins writes: 'reduction to biology . . . characterises the best of evolutionary anthropology. Yet in this respect our science may be the highest
form of totemism. If totemism is, as Lévi-Strauss says, the explication of
human society by the distinctions between species, then we have made an
empirical science of it' (1976:53). I would add to this. The type of
nature–culture dichotomy I am discussing takes for its 'natural' (=real)
relationships not categories within nature but the domination of nature
itself. Whereas totemic societies may use nature as a source of symbols to
talk about themselves, 'we' use a hierarchical contrast between nature and
culture itself to talk about relations internal to society, predicated on
notions of transformation and process that see society as 'produced' out
of the natural environment/individuals.

If control/adaptation as themes in other cultures' enterprises is one
trigger which releases in us notions about nature–culture, another is symbolic ordering in male–female relations.

## Gender as operator

Our own philosophies have brought contrasts between male and female
into deliberate relationship with nature and culture. Simone de Beauvoir's
description of woman as 'the privileged object through which [man] sub-
dues Nature' (1972:188) – object to his subject, other to his self, and at
the same time 'the fixed image of his animal destiny' (1972:197) – is a
brilliant rendering of *one* of the ways in which we mesh together nature–
culture, male–female, with all the elements of contest and subjugation (cf.
Harris p. 70). It is a constitutional paradigm: culture is made up of bits
from nature, and we contain within ourselves a nature prior to culture.
Male–female symbolism can sustain the same opposition as those notions
of 'control' and (conversely) 'adaptation', which set up a subject–object
relationship between culture and nature.

Thus we use 'male' and 'female' in a dichotomous sense. They represent
an entity (the human species) divided into two halves, so that each is what
the other is not. The division makes clearest impact in biological reproductive terms, so that there is constant endeavour to collapse behavioural
differences into biology. Yet insofar as we do not simply conceive of nature
and culture as opposites of one another but also bring them into various
relationships (continuum, process, hierarchy), these are re-directed back
onto the male–female dichotomy to produce a whole series of *non*-
dichotomous statements about men and women. Hence, from an equation
between female and nature can flow the notion that (1) women are 'more
natural' than men (at a particular point in a continuum); (2) their natural
powers can be controlled by cultural strategies (as the natural world can
be domesticated, a matter of process); (3) they are evaluated as inferior

(value hierarchy); and (4) have a generalized potential in relation to men's particular achievements.

Indeed gender may be the crucial metaphor in western culture which enables us to shift from a cultivated—wild contrast to a society—individual one and imagine that we are still talking about the same thing (culture and nature). Both can be rendered in terms of a male—female contrast — males are the creators and social/females biological and infrasocial. As Mathieu writes: '[An] absolutely essential point about . . . notions of "masculine" and "feminine" [in our society] is that they do not involve a simple relationship of "complementarity" . . . but rather of hierarchical opposition' (1978a:4).

Yet the male—female, culture—nature combination is seemingly so energizing that we find it hard to hold it steady. A scheme of this kind, as we shall see, underlies Ortner's persuasive presentation (1974). That particular hierarchical relationship has been criticized by Rogers (1978:134) as 'only one of several cultural perceptions, and certainly not universally accepted . . . Even within American culture, women are by no means always associated with "nature". The ideology of the American western frontier includes the notion of women as "cultural"-bearing or civilizing agents, who eventually subdued those rowdy anti-social males who had tended to revert to nature before the arrival of the "gentler sex". American sexual imagery portrays man with his "natural" animal lust channelled by more responsible and civilized women' (1978:134). Ortner herself had noted 'inversions' to her general scheme, including 'some aspects of our own culture's view of woman' (1974:86), to which she adds 'European courtly love, in which man considered himself the beast and woman the pristine exalted object' and an example from Brazil (nature/raw/maleness : culture/cooked/femaleness).

Certainly, in our culture, to make male—female symbolism 'work' and sustain culture—nature as a dichotomy we constantly have to shift its terms of reference, a characteristic Jordanova has already put in a historical context. Thus males may be seen as attuned to cultural needs, females to biological ones: an equation we *also reverse* in the image of males as self-expressive, capable of displaying base nature to the female's other-orientated artifice/sociableness. We say that in being closer than males to a pre-cultural state of nature females represent the general over men's particular achievements. Or, on the other hand, that in respect of their imperfect socialization they represent particularistic personal interests against men's social concerns. There is both constant effort to reproduce these concepts as oppositions, and no overall consistency (see fig. 1).

The apparent paradox at the heart of the equations — male can flip from representing the cultivated to the savage, culture can flip from being subject to object — rests, I believe, on genuine problems in our perception *male—female as symbols for culture—nature*

|   | m | | | f |   |
|---|---|---|---|---|---|
|   | creativity | | | instinct |   |
|   | man-made | | | innate |   |
| c | society | | | individual | n |
|   | cultural | | | biological |   |
|   | cultivated | | | savage |   |

|   | savage | | | cultivated |   |
| n | basic nature | | | superficial artifice | c |
|   | self-expressive | | | other-orientated |   |

*culture—nature as symbols for male—female*

|   | c | | | n |   |
|---|---|---|---|---|---|
|   | doing | | | being |   |
|   | public | | | domestic |   |
| m | cosmopolitan | | | confined | f |
|   | active | | | passive |   |
|   | subject | | | object |   |

|   | object | | | subject |   |
|   | tame | | | powerful |   |
| f | subdued, restrained | | | violent, energetic | m |
|   | cultured | | | animal-like |   |

*Note.* This is a crude schematization of certain ideas I believe to be common to western formulations of gender and nature—culture. Here is not the place to properly demarcate the semantic fields concerned, and the rough nature of my suggestions is indicated by the haphazard grammatical status of the various words.

Fig. 8.1. Some metaphors in western culture

of the material world as resource and energy. It also turns on a crucial ambiguity in relation to concepts of the 'individual' – both naturally limited and naturally resourceful, both culturally moulded and the free agent who creates culture. And I would finally hazard a conjecture that in the relationship between male and female we also prefigure that combination of social rank/economic resource which informs notions about class. Both Wagner and Sahlins see the pursuit of production as the 'western' project. In this view we can perhaps account for the fact that of all the ways in which we employ male–female symbolism, an equation of female with nature is particularly salient.

## Critiques of gender analysis, and a further critique

'Seeing woman as "natural" has, more or less explicitly, fascinated the Western world' (Mathieu 1978b:63). What prompts this observation is a critique of Edwin Ardener's original article on 'Belief and the problem of women' (1972).

Ardener suggested that in constructing their boundaries around 'the social' Bakweri men locate women in nature. Mathieu, noting in passing that Bakweri men are also thought to 'dominate' nature, suggests that Ardener's analysis 'stems from the same location of the female category in "nature" as he attributes to those he is studying' (1978b:63). Ardener (1977) has forcefully denied he ever intended an equation between woman and nature, and instead emphasizes the bounding problem presented by women when 'society' is defined by men. In a reply to Mathieu he reiterates the view that: 'In the conceptual act of bounding "society" there is a fortuitous homology between the purely ideational field . . . against which "society" is defined as a *concept*, and that part of the actual, territorial world which is not socially organised – the "wild" ' (1977:23; italics in original). Ardener's central concern is with the conceptualization of structures, and there is more to his account than can receive justice here. Perhaps his using 'nature' and 'culture' as vehicles through which to talk about muted and dominant structures is another 'fortuitous homology'. Nevertheless it is something of a puzzle that he should repeat the point: 'In rural societies the equation: non-social = non-human = the wild = "nature" is easily concretized', is a powerful metaphor (1977:23). Such a retreat into a symbolized ecology actually reproduces the same essentialist equation which Mathieu was criticizing. 'Their' non-social or wild can be read as 'our' nature.

This is not the place to go over ground already covered by MacCormack and others in this volume; nor do I intend to more than acknowledge the seminal importance of Ardener's paper. It is a masterly piece; so, with a very different orientation, is Ortner's paper, which addresses not a conceptualization of society but of culture itself.[7] Here we find the view that in the interests of its own delimitation culture employs a symbolized gender. I cite this account yet again merely to substantiate the contention that of all the terms we use in cross-cultural translation 'nature—culture', by virtue of their polysemy in our own culture, cannot be attributed to others in an unanalysed manner.

Ortner's propositions directly develop the notion of a culture—nature contrast whose constitution is the result of process.

Every culture . . . is engaged in the process of generating and sustaining systems of meaningful forms (symbols, artifacts, etc.) by means of which humanity transcends the givens of natural existence . . . In ritual . . . every culture asserts that proper relations between human existence and natural forces depend upon culture's employing its special powers to regulate the overall processes of the world and life . . . every culture implicitly recognizes and asserts a distinction between the operation of nature and the operation of culture . . . the distinctiveness of culture rests precisely on the fact that it can . . . transcend natural conditions and turn them to its purposes. Thus culture (i.e. every culture) at some level of awareness asserts itself to be not only distinct from but superior to nature . . . it is always culture's project to subsume and transcend nature [1974:72—3].

And she goes on to suggest that women's position in the symbolic order is to be interpreted as their being 'less transcendental of nature than men are' (1974:73).[8] Women are 'seen' as closer to nature, they 'represent' a lower order, are 'symbols' of something every culture devalues. Even though she notes (1974:75) that this perception may be unconscious, it is clear that women's 'association' with the domestic and the 'identification' with the lower order (1974:79) as well as their symbolic ambiguity are to be taken as indices of a nature—culture hierarchy whose terms lie close enough to the surface to be described as part of people's self-awareness.

The culture/nature distinction is itself a product of culture, culture being minimally defined as the transcendence, by means of systems of thought and technology, of the natural givens of existence. This of course is an analytic definition, but I argued that at some level every culture incorpor-

7  Given the degree of polemicization which characterizes many debates, I record here my personal admiration for the work of Ardener and Ortner alike. Indeed, to paraphrase Ortner herself, it is less their arguments which I quarrel with than some of the things their arguments stand for, or have been made to stand for in the works of others!

8  Rosaldo and Atkinson note that an emphasis on biological fertility seems absent from Ilongot (Philippines) preoccupations (1975:63), and suggest that in societies which stress sexual functions, the celebration of female fertility 'implies a definition of womankind in terms of nature and biology; it traps women in their physical being, and thereby in the very general logic which declares them less capable of transcendence and of cultural achievement than men'.

ates this notion in one form or other, if only through the performance of ritual as an assertion of the human ability to manipulate those 'givens' [1974:84].

I would make the following comments.

(1) Her account ignores the multivalent nature of our own categories of nature and culture, taking the shifting boundaries between their semantic fields to be embodied in an actual fence. Ortner is thus able to present us with a dichotomy between nature and culture. (2) This dichotomization is logically necessary because she wants us to concentrate on the notion that nature is a 'force' which is acted upon by culture. That is, there is a specific subject—object relationship here, and one, as Gillison notes, she uncompromisingly represents in terms of hierarchy: 'The universality of ritual betokens an assertion in all human cultures of the specific human ability to act upon and regulate, rather than passively move with and be moved by, the givens of natural existence' (1974:72). Control — regulation — is the essence of the relationship between the two terms. (3) She assumes that conceptualizations of an interplay between nature and culture are *both* made by 'every culture' *and* correspond to what we recognize as nature and culture. (4) In the way in which she refers to women being 'seen' as closer to nature, as 'symbols' of what culture devalues, we are also meant to take it that these notions are relatively accessible constructs of people's own thought systems. The overall implication is of every culture's *self-awareness* of 'the' relationship between nature and culture. (5) Finally, she suggests that the actual symbols used are everywhere the same — viz. relations between male and female.

Quite apart from the question, then, of what we ourselves might mean by nature or culture, is the level at which we attribute comparable notions to other people.

## Culture as classification

Lévi-Strauss writes that the contrast of nature and culture 'should be seen as an artificial creation of culture, a protective rampart thrown up around it' (1969:xxix). Ardener further comments that in the cause of this intellectual effort 'men have to bound themselves in relation to both women and to nature . . . If men are the ones who become aware of "other cultures" more frequently than do women, it may well be that they are likely to develop metalevels of categorization that enable them at least to consider the necessity to bound themselves-and-their-women from other-men-and-their-women.' Boundaries between societies thus comprise a stage in respect of the aboriginal demarcation of culture as such from nature. 'The first level is still recognizable, however, in the tendency to slip back to it frcm the metalevel: that is, to class other men and their wives with nature' (1972:142).

If we believed our division between nature and culture reflected an external 'reality', the issue of the extent to which other people might share such a notion could indeed be phrased as a matter of self-consciousness: how they represent their own boundaries. Differentiation of man from animal, social life from the wild and so on, might appear as explicit verbal concepts (like our own 'individual' and 'society'); be expressed through symbol and myth and thus be known in a less explicit though perhaps equally emphatic way; or be uncovered as properties of modes of classification and cognition which shape the actor's world view but are not known to him as principles or values logically separate from it. These degrees of self-consciousness would classify the kind of structure we attempted to describe.

In spite of their different intentions, in suggesting that societies may class themselves, and men and women, on a nature—culture axis, Ardener and Ortner both imply some indigenous self-awareness. These ideas are to be found at the first two 'levels' as well as perhaps at the third. In other words, through symbols, stereotypes and the treatment of the sexes, people are making known to themselves certain perceptions of culture and nature. Thus we can talk of such perceptions being part of this or that particular culture as relatively accessible constructs.

This is the level at which I approach Hagen ideas.[9] Can we speak of Hageners operating a contrast between nature and culture formulated in verbal idiom or as an axis for symbol and metaphor? Do we require these ideas in order to make sense of ritual and what people say about their actions? If they represent their own society to themselves, is it done through an idea of man's achievements (culture) being superimposed on/ controlling 'nature'; in particular, is the place of male and female in the symbolic and social order to be understood in such terms?

But another problem of level remains. Since our concern is with the way nature—culture has been related to male—female contrasts it is pertinent to ask whether we might be dealing with only male or only female models. Ardener raised this issue (1972) when he suggested that it is men who are particularly motivated to draw boundaries. Shirley as well as Edwin Ardener (1977) have since extended the notion of mutual and dominant models in relation to women whose representations of society they would argue are invariably englobed by men's. It is the dominant model to which the anthropologist has most ready access. E. Ardener (1977:24) writes: 'if the male perception yields a dominant structure, the

---

9  We do not have to search for a 'deep structure' (for example, the
   Ardeners' p-structures (S. Ardener 1977)) in which nature or culture
   might be motivating elements. My concern is with ideas reasonably
   articulate or accessible.

female one is a muted structure. It is an empirical contingency that the immanent realizations of muted structures are so often equated in this way with the nullity of the background, of "nature" '. In other words the dominant model has built into it a definition of its own bounds as a model, accommodating the subdued articulation of other models as one of its own terms (manifestations of nature). I am not sure that Hagen men's and women's differing perspectives are most usefully considered as differently constructed models (cf. Strathern 1981); however, this is not a point to pursue here. I am concerned with dominant and accessible concepts. An exclusively male source might skew the gender images these notions project, but the Ardeners do not postulate that only men would make a division into culture and nature.

Wagner (1975; 1978) has cogently argued that 'culture' is our invention, and that other peoples' ideas of the self and society may set up different dichotomies. He therefore provides us with something of a commentary upon the obsession which western culture has with its own self-definition. We visualize our culture through a conventional symbolization which 'defines and precipitates a sharp distinction between its own symbols and orders on the one hand and the world of their reference and ordering on the other' (1978:23). This is to be contrasted with self-signifying symbolization, as in the construction of a metaphor, which assimilates the symbolized within its own construction. All cultures employ both, but whereas our own tradition sees conventional symbolization as a legitimate realm of human action in the precise and orderly classification by human beings of the natural world they inhabit, other traditions regard the conventional order as innate.

The whole matter of which *kind* of [symbolization] is considered the normal and appropriate medium of human action (the realm of human artifice) and which is understood as the workings of the innate and 'given' is important . . . It defines the accepted and conventional form of human action . . . what things and what experiences are to be regarded as prior to [an actor's] actions and *not* as a result of them. We might call this collective orientation the 'conventional masking' of a particular culture. In the modern American middle class Culture of science and collective enterprise, with its emphasis on the progressive and artificial building up of collective forms, conventional masking amounts to an understanding that the world of natural incident . . . is innate and given. And in the world of the Daribi . . . with its stress on the priority of human relationships, it is the incidental realm of nonconventionalized controls that involves human action, whereas the articulation of the collective is the subject of . . . conventional masking [1975:49–50; italics in original].

He goes on to argue that cultures which conventionally differentiate approach the world with a dialectic logic that operates by exploiting oppositions against a common ground of similarity; whereas those, such as our own scientific traditions, which conventionally collectivize appeal to consistency against a common ground of (natural) differences.[10]

Wagner is primarily concerned with symbolic form; at a very different level I take up what he also tells us about the content of various formulations. His argument is germane since the 'other tradition' which he describes most fully is that of Daribi, another New Guinea Highlands people. The Daribi contrast between what is innate and what is artificial holds a different position to processes of particularizing and collectivizing from its place in western culture. Thus the collective conventions of Daribi social life are regarded as given components of humanity and the universe, in respect of which individuals improvize, differentiating and particularizing themselves, whereas 'we' stress collectivizing controls which constantly have to work on individuating, innate motivation. For Daribi there is no 'culture' in the sense of artefacts and rules which represent a summation of individual effort; no 'nature' on which these are brought to bear.

Much the same can be said for Hagen. What renders this material particularly interesting are certain very explicit categorizations which Hageners make: a distinction between *mbo* ('domestic') and *rømi* ('wild') is brought into conjunction with that between things appropriate to men ('male') and those appropriate to women ('female'), a difference sometimes found in oppositional form as social versus personal orientations.

The Hagen domestic—wild distinction (*mbo—rømi*) is itself innate in the sense that it is treated as an attribute of the given world. It is affirmed or discovered, but not made, in contrast to our manner of constantly 'making' culture and in so doing re-making the relationship between culture and nature. Indeed, the lack of consistency demonstrable in our own images of nature and culture, or our own uncertainty as to which is encapsulated and which encapsulates, can be attributed to the way in which we struggle with the very distinction as an artefact, in Lévi-Strauss's phrase (p. 187). We make conventional symbolization a matter of human creativity. Hageners, who take the relationship between the symbols *mbo* (domestic)

10  'Consciously and purposively we "do" the distinction between what is innate and what is artificial by articulating the controls of a conventional, collective Culture. But what of those other peoples who conventially "do" the particular and the incidental, whose lives seem to be a continual improvisation? ... By making invention and hence time, growth and change a part of their deliberate "doing", they precipitate something analogous to our Culture, but do not and cannot conceive of it as Culture. It is not artifice, but the universe. The conventional, be it grammar, kin relations, social order ("norm" and "rule"), is for them an innate, motivating, and "creeping" (thus unaccountable) distinction between what is innate and what is artificial' (1975:87). In Wagner's view Westerners create the incidental world by trying to systematise it; tribal people create their universe of innate social convention by trying to change it or impinge upon it.

and *rǫmi* (wild) and what they stand for as axiomatic, do not imagine that the one can be collapsed into the other.

For us, nature is given and innately differentiating. Thus we locate the ultimate differences between the sexes 'in nature'. Like 'the individual', these are of a biological order. Yet we regard 'culture' as putting these facts to varying use. At the same time, then, our collective endeavour to demarcate our human, cultural selves off from nature also creates the notion of irreducible, non-cultural differences, in the same way as seeing society as an artefact produces the 'problem' of its separate, constituent individuals. Since these distinctions are open to human definition, nature and culture are in a true dialectic − their meanings shift in relation to one another depending, as I have suggested, on the formulation of control or influence between the two domains. I have further suggested that what we perceive as an irreducible difference in nature (sexual differentiation) may be used to construct a differentiation between nature and culture itself as though it too were a given in the world. In other words, while the very construction of the notion 'culture' implies that the relationship between nature and culture is an artifice, we further try to legitimate that artifice by grounding it in nature itself. Gender is a crucial operator in this transformation.

Gender in Hagen also acts as a symbolic operator, though not in a uniform manner. Similar to the domestic−wild distinction, physiological differences constitutive of the person are regarded as innate and axiomatic, not subject to human intervention. Yet, insofar as aspects of gender behaviour can also be regarded as 'created' or actively sustained by individual action, certain other distinctions between male and female hold a very different epistemological status. Thus 'male' and 'female' can refer to a domain of human behaviour, how men and women act in their relationships, where boundaries are more open to manipulation. In this sense, like the Daribi, Hageners conventionally differentiate, and 'male−female relationships . . . can be seen as acts of conscious differentiation against a background of common similarity (the "soul" and other collectivities of culture [e.g. the notion of humanity] ), and thus as a dialectic between the particular and the general, man and woman, and so on' (Wagner 1975:118− 19). So when 'male' and 'female' are in this kind of opposition, there is a dialectic between the terms (the possibility that persons or things classified as one may be disturbed or influenced by the other), whereas *mbo-rǫmi* and gender as physiologically constitutive generally involve a simple notion of difference. The following account uses 'contrast' in a weak sense to cover either of these logical relationships.

## III The Hagen case

### *The domestic:wild dichotomy*

A pair of terms in the Hagen language can be translated as domestic and wild. *Mbo* refers to things which are planted. Used in ordinary parlance for a cutting pushed into the ground,[11] and breeding pigs which represent a new point of growth, it also applies to people, who are 'planted' in clan territory.[12] Major named social groups (tribes, clans, subclans) are referred to as being 'one stock' (*mbo tenda*) and the autochthones or owners of territory as *pukl wamb* ('root/base people').[13] Personal kin networks, extending beyond the clan, are one's *pukl* ('root/base people'). Indeed, the vegetative emphasis of this idiom is on rooting a piece of plant taken from its parent stock into ground that will nourish it — a matter of general potential for growth, rather than of the parent plant finding its particular replacement, as in Kaulong (p. 134).

In a contrastive framework *mbo* signals all that is human and associated with human activity as distinct from spirit (*kor, tipu*) or the wild (*rømi*). Thus 'human beings' are *mbo wamb* in contrast to ancestral ghosts and other spirits (*kor wamb*). 'Spirit' is not to be equated with 'wild', however, for spirits themselves are divided into *mbo kor* (the ghosts of once living people and still human) and others who lack the epithet *mbo* and among whom there is a class of 'wild spirit' (*kor rømi*). *Mbo kor* are associated not only with human activity but with human purpose and intention. Wild spirits on the other hand inhabit forests and tracts of otherwise uninhabited land around settlements. In comparison with people 'grounded' in relationship, wild spirits are either solitary ('one-sided', or with forest moss on their backs) or exist in undifferentiated plurality.

Such spirits are thought of as tending wild plants and animals as people do their domesticated varieties. By no means all plants have wild and domestic counterparts; but the chief tubers, taro, yam, sweet potato, are found in wild (*rømi*) form, divided in some cases into named varieties, and generally identified as *kit* ('bad') or *rakra* ('bitter').[14] Wild plants are notably inedible by contrast with the 'true' (*ingk*) cultivated varieties (*kae*, 'good'; *tingen*, 'sweet').

An inedible—edible axis does not apply to all aspects of the *rømi—mbo* classification. In the case of pigs (domestic pigs are generally *mbo*, as well as the specially marked *kng mbo* intended for breeding), the focus of differentiation is the tameness of the domestic animal and the ownership people exert. They are truly creatures over whom human control is mani-

11   The main cultigens are propagated from cuttings (sweet potatoes), from the original base (taro, yam, banana) or a node (sugar cane).

12   Cf. A. Strathern (1972:19—20; 1977). One idiom for describing the clan is *pana ru*, 'garden segment/ditch' (A. Strathern 1972:101).

13   *Pukl* also refers to ownership of any resource, i.e. the *pukl wua* ('owner man') is the 'source' or 'origin' of the item in question.

14   Cf. M. Strathern (1969). *Note*: I make citations to our own work not on authoritative grounds but to indicate other contexts where Hagen ideas have been discussed.

fest, from the early days when their caretakers familiarize them with human smells and feed them tubers by hand to their ultimate fate on the ceremonial ground, to which they are brought by rope in squealing protest. Quite apart from the wild pig itself, other creatures of the forest such as marsupials may be thought of as the 'pigs' of wild spirits, and these are, with due precaution, hunted and eaten (almost exclusively by men). They have their own 'sweetness'.

These idioms do not really envisage man in his enclosure surrounded by a 'natural environment'. While woodland and bush is a source of *rømi* things in contrast with settlements and gardens, the concepts do not focus on a spatial division between (say) bush and settlement, nor designate discrete domains with the connotation of the inhabited area having been carved out of the wild. Indeed, there is no boundary between a wild and domestic area in a geographical sense. Most clan territories include tracts of bush, and the area over which men have control is not systematically opposed to 'wild' land.[15] For land itself is neither *mbo* nor *rømi*, though human exploitation of its resources is marked in a contrastive manner: thus gardens may be demarcated as human rather than spirit property, whereas men hunting in forest seek products prized because they are wild. *Mbo–rømi* differentiation is in terms of the essence or character of certain resources. Nevertheless they incorporate the distinctions

| cultivated | : | wild things |
| social | : | solitary/non-social attributes |

We are certainly dealing with some kind of image of social life. I identify at least three different areas of concern: internal control; influence or the meeting with external sources of power; and a definition of humanity through idioms of nurture. They emerge separately in relation to pigs, spirits and plants.

(1) Hageners do not attempt to tame wild pigs – these are hunted only. They do sustain the domestication of tame animals by deliberate association – piglets are kept in human company, fed by hand and so on. But since pigs generally lack the complete minds (*noman*) which people possess, there is a limit to what can be internalized, and in the last resort pigs are

15   Certain sparsely populated areas, such as the Jimi valley, which yield a concentration of *rømi* things, come near to being considered a wild domain. Note that Hageners do not live in villages, but in homesteads and settlement clusters scattered over clan territory. Gardens are equally scattered, though there is often (not always) a general boundary between the total area of garden or fallow land which has been under cultivation and woodland or grassland not regularly used. Cordylines may be planted on garden boundaries to signify both particular territorial claims and the fact that the land has been made a source of human sustenance in which wild spirits should not interfere.

controlled by force. Unlike their *rømi* counterparts, then, *mbo* pigs are subject to control.

(2) Interaction with the wild spirits as owners of forest creatures and uncultivated land revolves around a rather different point, the meeting of interests. People attempt not to subdue but to come to terms with them. When they hunt in the forest or clear gardens in wild places people disturb the spirits' spheres of influence, and may seek the support of ancestral ghosts to protect them from spirit hostility. The ambiguities of the situation are resolved to some extent by a division of wild spirits into 'good' and 'bad' forms. Whereas the latter attack with caprice, provoked by the simple presence of human beings, the former may also protect people's wandering pigs. (Analogously, of all uncultivated land — including swamps, riverain pastures, grassland — forest and mountainous areas are of special significance as the source of plants and creatures whose powers can be activated in spell or cult. Forest resources may thus be 'good' *rømi* whereas swamps are 'bad' *rømi*.) Wild spirits have affinity with named Spirits, who are the subject of cults, and with the nebulous Sky-Spirits. These Spirits were never people, though to some extent they embrace human intention and welfare within their aims. Indeed, the more accessible of such Spirits to whom appeal may be made in cults are sometimes referred to as *mbo* ('planted').[16] At the same time their sources of power are definitively non-human. The division into 'good' and 'bad' wild spirits partly reduplicates this contrast, playing on a difference between those wild spirits who incorporate human ends within their own motivation and those whose intentions are sheer caprice.

(3) The primary plant category picked out by *mbo–rømi* comprises tubers. Although luxury crops, banana and sugar cane, which grow tall and bear above ground may also appear in *rømi* form, at the same time the high foliage of the planted varieties can itself provide cover for malevolent spirits intruding into the settlement. But if classification here is ambiguous,

16  Spirits attended to in cults are distinguished from ancestral ghosts. Their origin is quite separate — they are not rooted in the ground but have affinity to Sky-beings (*tei wamb*), an appropriately cloudy category (A. Strathern 1970:573). These beings are a source of growth which lies beyond human capacity but is brought to bear upon it: thus in some parts of the Hagen area the *tei wamb* are spoken of as founding the essential *mi* substance (divination 'totem') of tribes. On this creative axis, *tei wamb* and named Spirits are distinguished from *møi wamb* ('ground beings') (cf. A. & M. Strathern 1968:190). Vicedom (1943–8:2: ch. 15) refers to the *tei wamb* as first holding foodstuffs and pigs which they 'threw down' to men. The Female Spirit may be referred to as a *mbo mel* ('planted thing') i.e. an entity with whom there is a relationship of care-giving ('We look after the Spirit and kill pigs' etc.), but at the same time all non-ancestral spirits have affinities with the wild, and wild objects are used in her cult.

other plants are simply irrelevant to it. There is a whole range of green-stuffs, as well as minor animals and insects, which is eaten but not subject in any marked way to the *mbo–rǿmi* classification. These miscellaneous items may either be planted or picked wild, and to that extent be classed as *mbo* or *rǿmi*, but unlike the various tubers are not held to constitute different forms, in the way that 'wild' and 'planted' varieties of sweet potato are paired. The particular significance of this pairing perhaps lies less in the importance of these crops as subsistence items (since the subsistence–luxury classification actually cuts across them, taro and yam being associated with banana and sugar cane as luxuries) than in another characteristic: the edible part of tubers are all produced underground. A train of association links together the ground in which crops grow – the consumption of food – the creation of substance – and the development of human beings attached to territory (cf. A. Strathern 1973:29). Territory is soil upon which people are grown and a common source of sustenance produces in people a common social identity.

Indeed, 'domestic' seems rather a tame rendering of the Hagen *mbo*. *Mbo* refers to the human properties of consciousness and self-awareness, to the domain of human interaction, where control is internalized, as distinct from the caprice and isolation of wild spirits, or is seen as grounded in a common source of sustenance. Ardener identifies the Bakweri wild as a non-social domain. The wild is 'nature' (1972:141), and men bound off 'mankind' from nature (1972:143). Although the village–forest contrast provides concrete imagery for the Bakweri boundaries here, he argues that these boundaries are in the first place conceptual: the wild ('nature') is the 'non-social' (1977:23). If we accept for the moment that *mbo* in Hagen carries connotation of the social, is *rǿmi* really nature?

### Is rǿmi nature?

Nature (in the empiricist definition described earlier) is for us a pre-condition of existence which provides the raw materials for life, including

*n. 16 cont.*

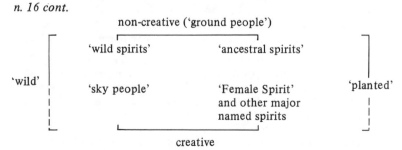

Categories of spirit being

bodily structure and capacity, and thus human needs and instincts, and a
non-social environment. Nature sets limits to what men can do, as well as
making requirements, but is open to manipulation. Degrees of culture can
thus be measured in terms of the extent to which the natural environment
is altered or subjugated. An important part of this view is the imputation
of regularity (cf. Lewis 1975:200). Nature is not merely acted upon but a
system with laws of its own, and it is these laws that limit the possible.
Our constitutional idiom points to an ambiguous notion of control: on the
one hand we are part of that system, and on the other able to use its laws
for our own purposes, which render them separable and ourselves transcendent.

*Rømi* in Hagen comprises neither a domain of given features in the
environment nor innate propensities in people. Missing is the crucial link
between the 'natural' world and human 'nature' which for us sets up a
homology between artefact and rule, between the material world men
create and their social life, and which produces (Wagner 1975:21) the
western notion of 'cultivation'. For through refinement and breeding we
imagine that men can also domesticate themselves. Thus the one can
become a measure of the other: the greater the refinement of artefact, the
more advanced the civilization. *Rømi* is certainly about control. But it
works in a very different way.

In no sense does *rømi* connote all that is given or innate. In some contexts *rømi* things are inimical to people's doings, in others they represent a
source of power men can tap. These are powers which stand in antithesis
to the ordinary bonds human beings create among themselves through
nurture. Conceptualization of the wild thus serves to locate nurture, sustenance and the furtherance of social relationships as essentially 'human'
characteristics.

Hagen ideas would seem to lie much closer to Daribi,[17] that sociability
is innate. Although at birth individuals lack full awareness of their humanity,
the child grows into social maturity rather than being trained into it; and
is certainly not *rømi*. As its body takes in food it responds to nourishment.
acquires identity, relationships with others and eventually self-awareness.
Consciousness of humanity comes to the child less through acquisition of
skills, or even ability to keep rules, than through appreciation of what
relationships with others involve.[18] So in their development Hagen children

17  Clay notes that among the Mandak of New Ireland 'social groups are
    constituted positively through the articulated variants of nurturing
    relationships . . . I found no indication . . . that the Mandak believe
    their social life to be fundamentally disordered, as Errington suggests
    for the Karavarans' (1977:150). See p. 181, n. 6.
18  Cf. M. Strathern (1968:555). The rare children who are markedly
    stunted in growth and/or mentally retarded may be called *rømi* — not
    because they display undeveloped or modified human nature, but

Plate 8.1 A garden is freshly made from old fallow. The casuarin trees in the background have been planted on the site of old gardens which will be brought into future production. The land belongs to the natal kin of the woman who is making plots from the section she has been allotted by her brother, here preparing strings to align the ditches.

are not thought of as recreating the original domestication of men. They are less 'socialized' than 'nurtured'.

This is all expressed in the gradual way children are thought to acquire *noman* — mind, conscience, consciousness, though not particularly speech, by which the Laymi mark maturity (pp. 72–3). *Noman* functions through being embodied in social relationships; it has no other context. *Noman* marks people out as human, *mbo*; the point is that *rφmi* is not here used as a counter image of the pre-human. A concept of the pre-socialized child as 'nearer to nature' does characterize some western for-mulations, as Ortner describes ('One can easily see how infants and chil-dren might themselves be considered part of nature . . . Like animals they are unable to walk upright, they excrete without control' 1974:77–8).[19] Conversely there is no real counterpart in Hagen thought to our ideas that humanity lies in the propensity to make culture.

Insofar as we formulate human nature thus, we may mark off this uni-versalizing ('cultural') aspect by thinking of our *given* natures as animal-like.[20] Needs, body build and emotional states held in common among people comprise our animal nature. When we denigrate certain behaviour as making the person 'like an animal', we bring to mind not only com-parison with creatures whose existence is not regulated by culture ('the animals') but imply that the person has given in to impulse, thereby expressing what is normally regulated. Hageners use the same idiom ('like an animal') of someone who crosses a boundary; the import is that he is behaving in a non-human way, has lost the awareness of what relationships mean, and this has turned him, figuratively speaking, into something else (*kara ponom*, 'gone headstrong', *timbi ranom* 'changed into a wild pig'). He has assumed an appearance *at odds with* his fundamental identity. There is no particular idea that anti-social propensities lie beneath the sur-face of every socialized human being; nor, I think, do Hageners have any theory of human needs.

because they are metaphorically derived from non-human stock. People commenting on these characteristics may refer to them as changelings, the offspring of wild spirits substituted for the human child.

19  From the Hagen point of view we can make sense of Read's (1955) discussion of the person among the Gahuka-Gama (Eastern Highlands). For 'us', basic humanity comprises common and universalizing features of 'the human condition', a nature not embedded in culture but thought of as prior to it (and thus paradoxically, in a non-religious world, also as 'animal nature'); for the Gahuka-Gama basic humanity is expressible only through social relationships, so that morality appears to attach not to 'man' on universal criteria but to 'men' in particular roles.

20  The topic of Willis' book (1975) is the use to which notions about 'animal' are put in the classification of social existence and selfhood.

This puts the issue of control into a certain light. Our own analogies between human nature and the environment use the terminology of domination — we 'tame' nature, 'fight' its hostile manifestations, 'carve out' domains from virgin land. When Hageners cut new gardens on the edge of cultivated areas or in stretches of forest they may be apprehensive about disturbing a local wild spirit, if one is known to lurk nearby, or upsetting the troops of *kor wakl* ('little spirits') found in swampy places. They are equally cautious of ghosts, if it is near a cemetery. But their intention is less to dominate such forces as to come to terms and prevent them from interfering with the venture in hand. A hunter, entering the forest, may through his ancestral ghosts send sacrificial meat to wild spirits, and in the past in certain areas offerings were made directly to *kor wakl*. A fresh garden can disturb the sphere of influence of local spirits; cordyline boundary markers indicate the lines of new ownership — to other men and spirits alike. Yet we cannot interpret these as outposts of a domestic domain colonizing the wild.[21] They are not a defence because areas of cultivation and social life are not thought of as under inevitable and generalized attack. Wild spirits do pounce on people, but such attacks are hazards or misfortunes rather than a manifestation of an on-going battle between wild and cultural forces. It is noteworthy that when sickness specialists pitch their own powers against these spirits and expel them or their weapons from an afflicted body, the wild spirits are not destroyed but are *sent back* to the areas where they belong.

It is clear that the *mbo–rømi* classification partakes of elements which inform our culture–nature distinction. But the intention of the opposition is different. Although we could translate one term as nurture (*mbo*) its counterpart is not really 'nature'. *Rømi*, the 'wild', is best thought of as a category of power located outside the bounds of those relationships which rest on control and nurture. And only in a very restricted sense can what is defined against *rømi* (wild) be thought of as 'culture'.

## Is mbo 'culture'?

As opposed to what grows wild, *mbo* signifies the act of cultivation. But its social connotations diverge from the western notion of the cultivated. We stress the orderliness of garden and field, the selective breeding of desired strains, a total process from modification of given resources to the profit

21  Wild pigs are no longer a hazard in the main Hagen areas, though they are still hunted in the Jimi valley. Fences and ditches round cultivated land are erected against the predations of *domestic* pigs which roam free during the day. (Pigs normally typify behaviour that is not under the guidance of mind (*noman*). Insofar as some pigs, like dogs, learn to recognize their owners, they may sometimes be said to possess *noman*.)

our energies yield in the form of produce. *Mbo* by contrast remains attached to a notion of planting,[22] does not refer to any other horticultural stage, and is not applied to ground, gardenland as such nor to the tools people use (except in the general sense of 'pertaining to people'). Its connotations are of rootedness, the tethering of people to land and relationships. When used of breeding pigs it points to domestic growth and increase. *Mbo* makes no particular play on the possibility of taming elements that are by origin wild.

A. Strathern (1977) describes the very specific manner in which people are thought of as 'planted' in clan territory and the rituals which express this. The idiom of implanting may be used for teaching. 'Knowledge here is seen as a slip or cutting taken from the original stock' (1977:506).

If knowledge may be objectified as planted, aspects of material culture are also seen as things possessed. 'Our way of doing things', 'our customs' mark off regional variations between peoples in terms of house-styles or customary procedures at bridewealth. Through present-day contact with outsiders,[23] these forms of self-definition have become increasingly prominent. 'We Hagen' are self-defined as people who 'make *moka* ('ceremonial exchange')'. Hageners also contrast people sleeping in houses with wild creatures in the open. On all these counts we may say they have a concept of 'culture'. In the sense of different cultures differentiating peoples, the analogy with our own is close. The same idea also differentiates human beings from wild animals. What is missing is the cumulative, produce and profit connotations of our 'culture' which *put it in a particular relationship with 'nature'*.[24] The sense of culture as 'building something out of' nature is not there. Differing styles of life of neighbours or spirits or animals serve to define what is Hagen or human. They are not in addition measures of achievement and production.

It is true that Hageners like to see evidence of people and their works. Cleared, inhabited areas are *kona kae* ('good places') as opposed to the bush (*kit*, 'bad'); but this is a matter of habitation versus desolation. Thus the coastal city of Port Moresby may initially strike migrants or visitors as *kona kae*, and they praise the scale of building and numbers of people. This first impression frequently gives way to criticism when these do not turn out to be indices of nurture — local food is poor, money is hard to

---

22    *Mbo* is used for the activity of planting even when ordinarily 'non-domestic' plants are involved — e.g. forest trees set about a ceremonial ground.
23    Europeans have been in the area since the 1930s. Hageners nowadays know about the 'customs' of many other Highlands groups, as well as people outside the region altogether.
24    Godelier (1978:764) comments on how rarely 'labour' in other cultures contains 'the idea of a "transformation" of nature and of man'.

Plate 8.2 A woman soothes a pig and marks it with a streak of clay to signify it is committed to *moka* (ceremonial exchange). This was a small showing of pigs, and the ceremonial ground has been only roughly cleared.

find, the soil is bad (= does not yield resources as a basis for wealth). They
have been deceived.

Our own equation of 'culture' is not only with 'cultivated' but 'domestic'.
There is fascinating ambiguity in the word 'domestic' which throws up a
number of problems in the path of any attempt to assign domestic—wild
dichotomies to a culture—nature axis.

On the face of it, domestication and cultivation in western parlance are
homologies: the taming and rendering of (natural) resources for (cultural)
use. Creatures brought within the human circle become 'of the house', and
we use the former term generally for matters to do with the household and
private family life. Housework is thus domestic work. Yet domestic work
is not culture. Far from it; for us, the domestic sphere may be actually
opposed to a public domain where issues of cultural and social significance
are to be found.

This discussion began with Langness's and Barth's analogy that the wild
is to the domestic as nature is to culture (domestic = domestication =
cultivation = culture). Ortner equates the domestic with nature. She does
this by setting up different equations altogether, interpreting the public
and the social as culture so that its opposite, nature, has to be a private,
semi-social domain of domesticity (domestic = house-bound = infra-social
= nature). In her argument that women are everywhere seen as closer to
nature than men, Ortner is drawing on certain specific suppositions (see
pp. 86—7). Culture's transformation of nature is rendered encompassing:
the control of natural forces, the control of personal nature and control over the human body. In this (western) view it is feasible to find
within culture certain elements only partially transformed, as human
nature itself is only imperfectly domesticated. Thus she argues that the
frequently found opposition between domestic and public spheres of
action reflects a universal awareness of domestic life — focussed on the
biological family and fragmenting, particularistic concerns — as infra-social
(1974:78—80). Women, through association with the domestic sphere, are
thus symbolized as representing lower-level concerns, the nature which
culture seeks to modify.

The steps in this argument contain one highly significant premise: that
the transcendence of 'social' issues over the needs and wants of 'the individual' is an aspect of the culture—nature conversion.

Hageners appear to make similar equations. They certainly contrast
things of the house with the concerns of the wider social world. Domesticity is thus denigrated in relation to the public domain. But neither *mbo*
nor *rǿmi* nor the contrast between them are activated in relation to this
dichotomy between social and domestic. A rather different association of
domesticity with confinement, the mundane, dull, ordinary things may,
however, be pointed up by a contrast with *rǿmi* in the sense of the exotic.
Foreign, extra-social sources of power are thus *rǿmi*. But their counter-

part is understood to be the mundane — which may or may not be referred to as *mbo* in this context. Semantic focus is on the exotic as such.

Hageners thus oppose (in the strong sense) (1) domestic and social, and (2) domestic and exotic. *They do not, however, encompass both sets of meanings in a mbo–rǿmi framework.* Thus evaluation of the domestic (= private) and the social (= public) finds readier expression in a distinction between things which are rubbish (*korpa*) and things of prestige (*nyim*).

In some of our own versions of nature–culture, metonyms for evolution, we do compress all these ideas into aspects of a single transformational sequence. An enabling metaphor, I suggested, lies in the male–female dichotomy. Hagen culture also uses male–female as symbols for a whole range of ideas. It is to these that I now turn. Unlike Gillison, whose discussion is drawn from a specific domain (how Gimi conceive their 'life cycle'), I rather unsatisfactorily use a number of different kinds of data. My rendering of Hagen gender images (both how the sexes are thought of, and how sexual qualities then come to be applied to other formulations) is thus composite. At the same time, my intention is to show that neither 'male' nor 'female' in Hagen usage can be reduced in an essentialist way to match some single overarching ideational principle in Hageners' view of their world. Whereas Gillison points to potent ambiguities at the heart of Gimi notions of genital identification or the role of the sexes in procreation, I follow Hageners' rather differently located preoccupations and describe the place of sexual idioms in other — and thus various — domains of social life.

## The implications of gender symbols

Hageners bring together notions of male and female, *mbo* and *rǿmi*, but not in a single dichotomous frame (see figs. 2 and 3); Hagen men may be associated with either the wider social world or with the wild; women while prima facie confined and 'domestic' can also appear wild.

Culture in the empiricist formulation is the process, tools and results of transformation. While each individual must from birth be socialized, and while lack of responsiveness to control is always a threat to civilization, the works of men are cumulative, so that we speak of artefacts or social forms as evolving. If Hageners have a culture they define it against a non-cultural world rather than postulating that culture incorporates the wild within it. Theirs is not a colonizing metaphor: the domain of *rǿmi* (wild) is not seen as being subjugated by things *mbo*.

It follows that the domestic sphere, which they distinguish quite emphatically from a public domain, is not 'natural' or 'wild' or even subcultural. Indeed, in one sense it is the heart of nurture, the place where food is prepared and consumed. Females and the household, nonetheless, symbolize affairs which are infra-social. They do represent particularistic, personally-oriented interests, against the public interest of males. This opposition between individual and social turns on the problem of control among people. It uses male and female as symbols, but not a metaphor of nature and culture.

Yet *mbo—rømi* may contain something of a contrast between the social and the non-social. The focus, I suggested, lay in the areas of control, influence and sustenance. Let me return to these. (1) In the case of pigs it is the *domestic* animal which is seen as subject to control. Their wild counterparts are merely hunted.[25] The control of things domestic thus appears as a matter internal to social organization, and does not encounter an opposing force in nature. (2) In dealings with wild spirits, the aim is to influence them to keep out of the way, not tame or subjugate or kill them. (3) In the case of food crops it is the sharing of sustenance, nurture predicated upon dependency (on parents, other kin, clan land), which creates bonds. Animals who forage for themselves, spirits who snatch, are creatures without bonds. People (temporarily as anti-social, permanently as insane) ignoring the conventions of nurture, are greedy or irresponsible. Their acts are those 'of a pig', 'of a dog', or they have become *rømi* (wild). This is interpreted as a masking or transformation of behaviour, not an expression of human nature in some elemental, primitive form. Naming certain acts wild constitutes an attempt to recall the person to his or her senses, a reminder that he or she is not *rømi* and should not behave thus. When public interests are set against narrower ends, these are seen to be con-

male is to female

as

| | | |
|---|---|---|
| wealth, oratory | : | poverty, speechlessness |
| *nyim* (prestigious) | : | *korpa* (rubbish) |
| transaction | : | production |
| public | : | domestic |
| clan | : | family |
| social interest | : | self-interest |
| safety | : | danger |
| life (cults) | : | death (pollution) |
| spiritual | : | non-spiritual |
| exotic | : | mundane |
| the wild | : | domesticated |
| birds | : | pigs |

Fig. 8.2 Some Hagen contrasts involving gender symbols

25  Cassowaries are caught in the forest and brought back into the settlement. There is little attempt to tame them: the birds are cooped up in small cages, fed wild fruits, their wildness preserved for the very reason that they will be presented in an exchange as exotica. If you go near a cage people will comment on their fierceness.

cerned with the management of people's minds (*noman*) rather than with basic anti-social 'natures'.

Women (in evincing 'female' behaviour) are regarded as less amenable to social control than men; they symbolize the autonomous individual with self-referring interests, and are more prone to wild behaviour. This does

| *mbo* | *rǿmi* |
|---|---|
| planted | uncultivated |
| belonging to people | belonging to wild spirits |
| settled area | bush |
| help from ancestral spirits | encounter with wild spirits |
| human intellect | non-human, animal-like |
| nurture | greed |
| relationship | solitariness |
| edible and/or accessible | inedible and/or inaccessible |

*no male−female contrast operates*

| | |
|---|---|
| point of growth in human affairs | source of extra-social energy |

*men* are agents for tapping extra social energy
brought to bear on social ends

↓

attached to a *male−female* contrast are:

| male | female |
|---|---|
| the wild | domesticated |
| free to roam | confined to house |
| hunting | gardening |
| cults, etc. | pollution, etc. |

| social | individual |
|---|---|
| clan ends | personal ends, anti-social behaviour |
| *nyim*, etc. | *korpa*, etc. |

Fig. 8.3. Connotations of the *mbo−rǿmi* contrast: the boxed categories are both marked as associated with *rǿmi*.

not put them closer to nature, because one does not attempt to control 'the wild'. Moreover the fact that wayward women may be likened to wild pigs of the forest does not thereby make the forest a female domain. In any case the same epithet may be used of men. A group of recalcitrant clansmen who moved away from their home area, and were 'lost' to the clan, were likened to 'wild pigs'. There is a double metaphor here — that women or men are wild and that they are like pigs. One possible aspect of the Hagen 'wild pig' symbol, however, is the cryptic identification of woman and pig which in their domestic state are more or less biddable.

Now the wild does not merely have characteristics which are non-social — it is also a source of extra-social power. Seen in this light, it is men who are associated with wild things, who bring exotic powers to bear upon an ordinary world, who represent their individual achievements as the ability to step beyond social bonds.[26] Men have an access to the spirit world women do not enjoy. They travel, fetch valuables from strange places, hunt in the forest and on mountain slopes. But if men are associated with the wild, it is not in opposition to women who represent society or 'culture' — it is in opposition to women who are tied to the house, rooted indeed to the ground in which they tend their crops, to circumscribed paths and a mundane life. When male power is seen to come from outside society, this does not mean that females are associated with society, only that they do not have this power. A girl's upper teeth develop first, Hageners say, because they grow down, towards the ground over which women are always bent. A boy cuts his lower teeth first, shooting upwards, for men are like tall trees that grow towards the sky or like the birds flying there. Yet we cannot extrapolate from these metaphors into a generalized contrast, with women more rooted than men, more 'cultivated'. From the point of view of territory and clan substance, it is women who become rootless, moving from one area to another, while men normally remain planted. Through the perpetuity of the clan, ancestor worship and their spirit cults, males represent social continuity, whereas females are said to have brought death into the world.

On the surface Hagen mythology seems very little concerned with the beginning of things. The relationship between the forest and untoward events, between false/true appearances of wild or human beings, are certainly important themes in the stories collected by Vicedom (1977). But there are no culture heroes as appear, for example, in Hallpike's description of the Tauade (non-Highlands Papua) (1977). There, a dialectical relationship between the wild and the domesticated, he argues, is fundamental to the Tauade world-view. The domestic he translates as the tame, both in the sense of cultivated or controlled and without creativity or

26  To signify success at ceremonial exchange, a clan will top its gifts of valuables with exotic wild animals (snakes, cassowaries and so on).

Plate 8.3 Ceremonial exchange: the pig is transferred by a stylized gesture and shout. The donor has removed most of his decorations, but his bustle is evident, ornamented with forest (*rømi*) plants. He has an axe in his belt, spear in his hand.

excitement. Women are depicted 'as the preservers of culture and social life, as opposed to the destructive force of the men' (1977:135). Men are destructive, but also creative, powerful, seekers of glory. 'The Wild is not merely the destructive alternative to social order, but is the source of life and of creativity in general . . . the primary forest is seen as the source of most of the domestic forms of plants' (1977:254). It is women with whom fire, cooking, string bags and the useful arts are associated; they are 'portrayed in the legends as the inventors and sustainers of culture' (1977:254). However, men control most magic, and through this means they promote the production of gardens, pigs, children and so on, the magic itself belonging to a domain of 'wild', non-human elements. Men thus promote an extra-social creativity, and have access to forces and energy which lie beyond the manufactured material culture with which women are associated. Hagen men enjoy similar powers, but not in antithesis to women as culture-creators.

Women in Hagen are a source of symbolism for what is 'female'. The definition of 'female' finds confirmation in the way 'women' are treated. As females, women constantly present to men certain problems of management. But controlling people from within society is very different from harnessing the 'wild' to social ends. Indeed the possibility of influencing or directing the minds of others is a fundamental premise of nurture. Nurture is manifested in two kinds of control. First, the subordinate, the dependant, who is fed as pigs are fed by hand, is in a way 'owned' by the person who feeds. A big man's male dependants (metaphorically 'fed by' him) are liable to be ordered about. These are people without, as women are without, wealth in their own name, who lack the powers of oratory and persuasion which enable important men to influence others. Women thus are directed by men, and, if recalcitrant, coerced. Runaway wives, one is told, in the past might be returned home slung from a pole as pigs are carried (M. Strathern 1972:187). On the other hand, in specific household roles, the sexes form a complementary relationship over land and food: wives feed (cook for) their husbands, even as they are fed (with produce off his land). Second, nurture also creates relationships based on common substance. An identity of interests such as binds clan members gives rise to joint action and concerted effort. Women, who at marriage normally change residence, are thought by men as more prey than themselves to conflicting interests. It nevertheless remains true that, between spouses, men's control over women exists in part in the husband's ability to present his wife with certain aims and the wife's own willingness to make those ends her own. Men appeal to women's minds (*noman*), to their volition and commitment to the relationships in which they are enmeshed. Management thus lies in influence over the intentions of others.

Male and female are used by Hageners as symbols of motivation. Males are assumed to have social interests at heart, whereas females are prone to pursuing narrow personal ends. This is not simply a positive and negative evaluation: a high value is put on personal autonomy, and social goals are thought of as always involving alignment of personal orientations. For the Mandak of New Ireland Clay (1977:151) says: 'nurture does not eradicate individual antisocial motivations, but it opposes them in intentions and results'. Individual tendencies, she suggests, are 'harmful'. In Hagen the definition and preservation of the individual as an autonomous being is of great importance. Thus collective action must be seen to come from multitudinous personal decisions. The 'individual as antisocial' is simply a marked constituent of this overall category.

In presenting their aims to themselves men and women use idioms of status – devotion to clan affairs is a matter of prestige (cf. M. Strathern 1978). It is the rubbish who do not strive for eminence in this way. Females may be categorically 'rubbish' by contrast with males: household concerns and horticultural labour do not carry the prestige of group enterprise. When they define themselves as interested in prestige, committed to the clan, and thus rooted in society, males set their gender off from the potentially irresponsible and 'wild' propensities of females. Categorically (though not in terms of individual ascription, quite another matter) females are of lower status than males. In power terms, however, male supremacy is much more ambiguous. The dangers which they locate in females are a source of threat to themselves. In preserving autonomy, moreover, they have to allow autonomy in others. Here possibly is some of the significance of men's mystical access to the exotic 'wild'. In the latter context they assert a strength to which there can be no challenge, because the mystical forces harnessed through cult or rite stand in innate opposition to the weaknesses and harms of the mundane world. The Female Spirit cult, for example, is said to protect men from menstrual pollution: it defines male strength against that of the female.[27] It does not seek to cleanse the female or banish pollution, as in other cultures witch hunts seek to banish witches.

In short, where power is at issue men stress their extra-social strength,

27  Participation in Spirit cults is one of the key elements of men's claims to spirituality/wildness. Further discussion on this point can be found in M. Strathern (forthcoming). Access to ancestral ghosts is another dimension of men's power, from which women are largely excluded, but the ghosts are also nearer to home and are concerned with women's as well as men's everyday affairs. Hagen women do not have any special links with the spiritual world. Compare, for example, Polynesian Tokelau (Huntsman & Hooper 1975) where men's strength and control of both the social and extra-social world (animals and spirits) is set against women's sedentary 'inside' life on the one hand and on the other their entanglement with spirits – women have connections with animals and spirits which give them an innate mystical power.

Plate 8.4  Ceremonial exchange: a line of bewigged men dance as a clan, facing an audience composed largely of women (evident with their hands raised to their heads to steady netbags). Ignoring them, a further group of girls and young women shriek above the men's chanting and execute a dance of their own.

where status is at issue they stress their social orientations (pursuit of clan goals) and cultural superiority (ownership of wealth, ability to make speeches). Hagen men thus locate maleness equally in social organization (their control of women, of things domesticated) and in extra-social forces (their access to the spiritual and the wild). Hagen women may locate femaleness at the heart of nurture, and in drawing men's ultimate responsibilities towards themselves and their children also individuate their interests from the 'social' pursuits of men.

Now these operations employ gender as a symbol in two distinct ways. On the one hand, it is used dialectically to structure different patterns of behaviour; yet, on the other, it posits that genital sexuality is an innate condition of the given world. The first employs elements of the *mbo–rømi* contrast in a differentiating mode to typify appropriate action; the second states that the physiological distinction between male and female is as much a given, and thus of the same logical order, as that between *mbo* and *rømi*. I treat these in turn.

There is great focus on manipulable aspects of gender identity based on ascriptions of behaviour. Whether people behave in a 'male' or 'female' way is linked to the evaluation of activities likely to bring prestige or rubbishness. Such maleness and femaleness are presented in turn both as a matter of choice (it is up to the individual whether he or she sets sights on social goals) and of no-choice (males have an innate capacity to perceive such goals against which females suffer a handicap). This is an idiom through which men attempt to influence one another and to interest women in their affairs. Control (directing others in the way they act), transformation (inducing certain states of mind), manipulation (structuring values in such a way as to impel participation in social events) are all notions applicable to behaviour. They rest on involvement and commitment among individuals. The manipulation of behavioural gender attributes is thus part of nurture, of how people act out their relationships. It differentiates: individuals can cross the boundary (low status men are 'like women', women of prestige are 'like men'). A change in status (a big man failing, a woman proving she is man-like) is always possible.

The mystical power of the wild which males bring with them, by contrast, is at a remove from control in inter-personal relations. This power is set against female characteristics, as the 'wild' is set against the domestic, an antithesis which marks a boundary no-one can cross. Or, if crossed, it is in appearance only — ultimately one's 'nature' as a denizen of the wild or as truly human cannot be changed; this is the theme treated frequently in myths. Hence, as far as celebration of the Spirit cults is concerned, men gain power but not identity. It is a male attribute to perform in the cults, as it is to hunt, but these activities do not make a person more male, only demonstrate the strength maleness entails. For sexual demarcation here rests on physiology; the sexes as genitally and functionally distinguished are givens in the world. Genital identity is not open to 'creation'; there is no initiation ritual — as, for example, in Sherbro and Kaulong — and thus no endowment of the sexes with the appurtances of their physical development. The differentiation of cult participants (all males of a clan, whatever their status, join in, all females are excluded) reflects an absolute cleavage. Genital sex is not open to change. There are no ritual transvestites in Hagen, no forces linking role to sex, no suggestion, for example, that men's organs came first from women. Sex is 'innate' and immutable. Maleness and femaleness are in this sense non-manipulable. On this axiomatic base women are excluded from the mystical domain. Within the Papua New Guinea Highlands, this particular contrast between what is given (physiological, genital sex) and what is open to alteration (gender characteristics as evinced in behaviour), is possibly restricted to Hagen and some of their neighbours. Elsewhere, especially in the many Highlands societies which have initiation rituals focussed on sexual identity, physiology is to some extent 'created'. The Gimi described by Gillison are a good example, though unusual in the Highlands for holding female as well as male ceremonies. This is not the place for a comparative review. I merely note that the Hagen concern with what is innate and what is manipulable is not anchored in the male:female idiom itself (e.g. males associated with creation, females with uncontrollable givens). Goodale (see chapter 6) has quoted Forge's comments, that in New Guinea women are considered a part of nature, and that their powers of reproduction and creation are considered natural and innate, while men to be creative have to be so culturally, mainly by the performance of ceremonial.[28] The point applies

28  Aside from the question whether 'natural' and 'cultural' are appropriate extrapolations, I would not, on the other hand, want to rule out this contrast between the innate and the created as a component of the symbolic systems of other Highlands societies. There is considerable concern, for example, in the Eastern Highlands region with the relationship between human reproduction/growth and death, physiological process being seen as linking human beings to the vegetable and animal world. Identity of physical substance may be the focus of ritual to an elaborate degree (as in initiation ceremonies), and possibly thus played upon, manipulated, 'created'. See Poole's (1981) account of Bimin-Kuskusmin (non-Highlands) interest in physiology, and the attachment of male and female qualities to bodily substances that can to some extent be exchanged between the sexes. An Eastern Highlands case of physiological crossing of boundaries is described by Meigs (1976). The Hua use a marker, sexual fluids, which classifies male and female states independently of genital ascription, though they remain of a manifestly physical nature. Elements of similar ideas are found situationally in various Hagen contexts, but not as a prime focus of cosmological attention. I am grateful to Gillian Gillison for discussion on this point (and see chapter 7).

no more to Hagen than it does to Kaulong. Hagen notions of female reproductive 'power' bear this out further.

It is men who give evidence of being able to harness the power of wild
or spiritual elements. They derive a strength from outside society which
females never match. Their manipulation of this power is done in the name
of women as well as men, but also sets men off against them. Among
various reasons given for women's exclusion from central rites in the
Female or Male spirit cults is the fact that females are impure, they menstruate. This capacity is linked equally to fertility and death. This is a
condition to be handled and met with, but little is added to our understanding by labelling it a 'natural' feminine power. It is certainly not
referred to as a 'wild' characteristic. Women's capacity to bear children has
no bearing on the situations in which females are associated with being
*rømi*, although it is hedged with danger for men.

Female fertility is neither more nor less innate than the power males
evince in interaction with ghosts and spirits. The reason why Spirit cults
which have fertility as a theme are organized by men to the exclusion of
women has to do with the association of males with social ends and females
with personal interests: what is at issue is a conversion of fertility individually manifested into fertility for the clan. Thus in the Female Spirit cult
fertility itself is defined transexually: the aim is increase for people and
their stock/gardens together. Men are the sole human participants not
because they are trying to make a female power into a male thing – but
because as males they are in touch with forms of extra-social energy represented in the manipulation of *rømi* items (forest products and so on) which
they bring to bear on the forces of growth within the domain of *mbo* (cf.
A. Strathern 1970; 1979). Male sexuality is a theme of the Male Spirit cult,
less often enacted. Here an explicit phallicism goes along with an emphasis
on copulation, and the partial inclusion of women in the cult celebration.
An assertion of the male role in human procreation is combined with an
emphasis on clan solidarity. Women are in the background, but the genital
complementarity of the sexes is quite unambiguous.

At an abstract level, then, Hagen men demonstrate their own powers of
fertility, to which they bring an association with wild things. Their powers
are expressed as a different order from women's. But men's capacity to act
thus is as much a given of their sex as women's capacity to bear children.
So while female sexuality may contextually be impure ('bad' or 'rubbish')
it is not marked as 'natural' in contrast to male endeavours. Oppositions
enacted through the cults do not stem from a necessity to bring natural
forces under cultural control or from an assignment of the sexes to
opposing sides of such a dichotomy.

Contrasts between men and women cannot be squeezed into a single
social–non-social, let alone culture–nature set. By no means all Highlands
ethnographers who have reported on a domestic–wild contrast have done

this. The elaborate antithesis between forest and horticulture which sustains Karam treatment of certain creatures and crops (Bulmer 1967) is linked chiefly to the definition of kinship roles and rights, setting certain claims off against others. Bulmer stresses that cassowary and pandanus, the prime elements of the uncultivated wild, 'are not merely undomesticated but *may not be* domesticated' (1967:17; his italics). The Hagen association of maleness with extra-social sources of power emphatically by-passes domestication. This power is efficacious precisely because it is non-tameable. Magic which incorporates objects taken from the wild cannot be represented as a control of nature, any more than domesticity is culture. I reiterate the point that 'the wild' is encountered and dealt with but not subdued. Wild forces are defined in antithesis to the domestic, rather than being thought of as potential components of it. The use of wild creatures and plants in spells and in cults is thus less a matter of 'control' being exercised over these items than a demonstration of differentiated power between human agents. Through males, extra-social forces brought to bear on human endeavours endow them with exotic efficacy.

Our empiricist nature—culture dichotomy in relation to that of male—female contains a significant component which Hageners formulate separately. This is the contrast between individual—social. On this axis, *when we equate social = cultural*, female can be linked to lower-level, individuating naturally-based concerns as against the higher order 'social', culturally-induced interests of males. Let me summarize what I understand to be the very different Hagen formulation.

(1) In the definition of humanity, through notions of sustenance and nurture, *mbo* and *rǿmi* (planted and wild) carry connotations of human and non-human, the collective and the solitary. On this axis male—female do not appear as discriminators.

(2) In the definition of internal social control versus personal autonomy, self-seeking and socially destructive behaviour may be called *rǿmi* (wild). Its opposite is the social orientation of the *noman* (mind), which is an attribute of being human (*mbo*). Females are seen as more prone to anti-social individualistic behaviour, more often as *rǿmi*, than males.

(3) There are also what I have called extra-social sources of strength sometimes thought of as *rǿmi*, and here as mediators men have a prerogative of access. In this sense *rǿmi* is a male domain. The contrast is with things of the house, definitely associated with the circumscribed orientations of women, but not particularly *mbo*.

(4) Possibly most illuminating of all is the fourth nexus, most salient in everyday reference and comment. This defines orientating values — prestige and status — and the contrast between the public and the domestic/private. In our own society, prestige, public achievement, cultural creativity and civilization all run together. In Hagen a contrast

between things which are prestigious (*nyim*) and rubbish (*korpa*) is intimately tied up with symbols of male and female. But *mbo* and *rǿmi* fail to enter the configuration.

*Mbo−rǿmi* alone (1) is essentially a relation of difference (non-hierarchical). Gender differences as innate physiological givens are of the same logical order here as *mbo−rǿmi*, which therefore cannot be differentiated by them. The other three categorical relations, however, which all involve idioms of gender, create notions of opposition and tension. For gender is here being used to differentiate styles of human activity. To a greater or lesser extent it may recall the immutability of physiological sex or the creation of behavioural patterns. In the contrasts between social and personal interests (2) and the exotic and mundane (3), *rǿmi* (wild) tends to be the marked category. There is a cross-over in the application of male−female imagery, however, in the one case it being females and in the other males who are wild (cf. fig. 4). This is significant: in a dialectical mode

|     | | | | |
| --- | --- | --- | --- | --- |
| (1) | *rǿmi* | : | *mbo* | *definition of* |
|     | (wild) | : | (domestic) | nurture−humanity |
|     | non-human | : | human | |

|     | | | | |
| --- | --- | --- | --- | --- |
| (2) | *rǿmi* | : | social | internal social control |
|     | autonomous | : | social | versus |
|     | female | : | male | personal autonomy |

|     | | | | |
| --- | --- | --- | --- | --- |
| (3) | female | : | male | power relations/external |
|     | non-spiritual | : | spiritual | sources of strength |
|     | mundane | : | *rǿmi* (exotic) | |

|     | | | | |
| --- | --- | --- | --- | --- |
| (4) | female | : | male | |
|     | rubbish | : | prestigious | orientating values and status |
|     | (*korpa*) | : | (*nyim*) | |

| | | | | | | |
| --- | --- | --- | --- | --- | --- | --- |
| (1) | *mbo* : *rǿmi* | : : | human : non-human | | | |
| (2) | social : autonomous | : : | *mbo* : *rǿmi* | : : | male : female | |
| (3) | mundane : exotic | : : | *mbo* : *rǿmi* | : : | female : male | |
| (4) | male : female | : : | prestigious : rubbish | | | |

Fig. 8.4. Main metaphorical domains (Hagen).

gender notions effect a partial transformation of or application of ideas otherwise framed as given (e.g. genital characteristics are innate, or the distinction between *mbo* and *rømi* itself); but the application is only partial — that is, ultimately male and female cannot stand for the *difference between mbo* and *rømi*. Where male and female do stand for a total difference is in relation to ideas about prestige and rubbishness, which are the supreme domain of Hagen creativity.

## IV  Conclusions

My reiterated comparison between certain of 'our' (empiricist) notions of nature and culture and Hagen beliefs has been made to a specific purpose. Our own concepts provide a structure so persuasive that when we come across other cultures linking, say, a male—female contrast to oppositions between the domestic and wild or society and the individual, we imagine they are parts of the same whole.

For at times, in our collectivizing idioms, we equate social order with cultural systems, rule with artefact, human nature with environment, generating pairs of contrasts related between themselves, and reproducible on paper as opposing columns (cf. Goody 1977).

| | | |
|---|---|---|
| nature | : | culture |
| individual | : | society |
| innate. | : | artificial |
| personality | : | role, etc. |

The further potent contrast between male and female symbolizes some of these oppositions, also turns them upside down, and introduces relations between them. It is the possibility of transformation from one column into the other (culture modifies nature, civilized persons revert to animal behaviour) which gives social science its problematic (how do 'individuals' become 'social' beings) and allows us in our descriptions of others to abstract culture as a human creation from the natural givens of the world. And the symbol of gender has led to further academic concerns. The imputation that our male—female stereotypes incorporate a dichotomy between subject—object stems partly from notions of property and partly from our view of the natural world as acted upon. Allied with this is the hope occasionally expressed that by eliminating culture as it is presently constituted and thereby better understanding our natures we could start anew; meanwhile, individuals can 'do their own thing', we do not have to be bound by society because society is simply an invention, and so on.[29]

---

29  Cf. M. Strathern (1976). I take these preoccupations as both popular

Ortner was absolutely to the point as far as Hagen is concerned when she suggested that women come to symbolize socially fragmenting, particularistic concerns against those integrative social interests which preoccupy men (1974:79).[30] Hageners express human relationships through things, through food which is ingested, valuables which are exchanged; and from their occupation of clan territory and their ownership of wealth, males are predominantly transactors in relationships. They define themselves against females whose lack of 'culture' (in this sense) makes them 'rubbish' — but not 'objects', not 'natural'. It is our own culture which sets up males as creators and inventors and females therefore as perilously near objects, for we define 'culture' itself as manifested in things which are made and are alienable (cf. Dumont 1977:81). For us, women emerge as objects in a double sense, either as representing a natural resource over which culture is transcendent, or as the artificial end results of men's energy.

Lindenbaum's account of the Fore (1976) makes an explicit equation between the control of natural powers in persons (primarily sexuality) and the environment. The axes of her contrast are that of regulation and management as against the uncontrolled and unpredictable. In Hagen a notion of control arises as an aspect of domesticity or humanity (*mbo*) and is thus conceptually *set against* forces outside this sphere. Hageners do not transform *rømi* into *mbo* things, though they may try to harness *rømi* power for their own ends. Settlements in new areas involve a redefinition

and academic. They stem from our formerly religious and now evolutionary vision of man in relation to the animal kingdom/natural world, from a technology which rests on the belief that all material is malleable, within certain limits, so that the definition of those limits is important, as well as from a desire common to many moral systems to give social arrangements legitimacy by proving their inevitability ('naturalness').

Mathieu points to our notions of essence (1978a). Interest in the 'nature' of things is an interest in essential identity, in the given. Culture is posed against (1) a notion of raw material, and thus the elements which are subjected to our creative, experimental, modifying control; (2) the irreducible core, the limits to our technology, defiant individualism, the 'true' character that is merely overlaid with cultural forma. In demarcating different kinds of reality, this contrast between biological and social, innate and made, provides a limitless area of investigation for several disciplines (cf. Archer 1976; Lloyd 1976).

30  I do not go into the question of notions of self-hood. The stress Hageners lay on autonomy as an attribute of the person is to be seen as part of the particularistic nature of individuals, a source of their differentiation from the givens of the social world (following specific social goals as well as diverging from them may be interpreted as acts of will). For an exploration of certain equations between self-hood and nature–culture ideas see Willis 1975.

of power (what was once only a source of *rǿmi* elements has become a source of nurture) but this is a readjustment of spheres of influence rather than a conversion of one kind of power into the other. *Rǿmi* power can be brought to bear on human activity precisely because it is constituted always in antithesis to *mbo*, and cannot therefore be incorporated by it.

Many of the Fore contrasts are repeated in Hagen. Settlement is marked off from the forest; the wild is distinguished from the cultivated as a dangerous and fertile source of power; females are represented as wild and out of control, having to be tied to men with their larger vision of the social order. But it is clear that for Hagen at least we cannot combine these oppositions into a single series. Thus women may be compared both to domestic pigs (biddable) and to wild ones (not), men be regarded both as travellers able to tap the powers of the forest and as planted agents of society. Their use of gender in the differentiation of human activity is not to be confused with our own usages of a similar dichotomy to symbolize the relationship between nature and culture itself.

Nature and culture do not exist in Hagen as categories of the order, for example, of the clearly conceptualized distinctions between prestige and rubbishness, social goals and individual autonomy, or mind, body and spirit. These abstract entities are all verbalized to some degree and involve explicit symbolic representation. Such concepts are reasonably accessible, and we need to understand them to make surface sense of Hageners' own interpretations of their behaviour. Nothing at this level corresponds to 'nature–culture'.

Nor, as far as implied content of our terms is at issue, can one specifically equate *mbo* (domestic) and *rǿmi* (wild) with culture/nature. There is no homology between environment and human nature, nor between technology and social rule. The wild includes some items we classify as 'natural', viz. uncultivated plants, as well as antisocial motivation, and these are brought into opposition with *mbo* things which include the cultivated, the sociable, the socially-oriented. But *mbo* refers to immanent conditions of growth and a given humanity, not also to technology or the imposed rule. And *rǿmi*, wild, is not a constituent of things *mbo*, neither a resource to be worked on nor elemental components of the domesticated world.

Ardener, Barth, Langness and Ortner were discussing nature–culture in the presence of images (either their own or in the ethnography) to do with themes of control. Even if we were to allow that enough of our concepts of 'culture' corresponded to *mbo* or that there was reasonable overlap between the semantic domains of *rǿmi* and 'nature', *the tension between the Hagen terms* is different. *Mbo* and *rǿmi* are in an antithetical rather than a hierarchical, processual relationship. The domestic domain is not seen as colonizing the wild; the development of social consciousness in persons is not represented as culture transcending nature. These elements are alien to Hageners' ways of thinking. They use a notion of a realm beyond themselves (*rǫmi*) to signify the characteristics of human bonding (*mbo*), but this distinction itself is innate, subject to discovery not reformulation. Thus humanity is bounded off from the non-human, but does not seek to control it. Control comes from within, a self-defining attribute of the social world.[31]

There is no culture, in the sense of the cumulative works of man, and no nature to be tamed and made productive. And ideas such as these cannot be a referent of gender imagery. Hageners do use gender idioms to talk about social as opposed to personal interests, and the cultivated as distinct from the wild. But these two domains are not brought into systematic relationship; the intervening metaphor of culture's dominion over nature is not there. On the contrary, insofar as gender is used in a differentiating, dialectical manner, the distinction between male and female constantly creates the notion of humanity as a 'background of common similarity' (Wagner 1975:118–19). Neither male nor female can possibly stand for 'humanity' as against 'nature' because the distinction between them is used to evaluate areas in which human action is creative and individuating. Thus, indeed, the whole issue of control appears to be encapsulated within the notion of things *mbo*. Representations of domination and influence between the sexes are precisely about ways of human interaction, and not also about humanity's project in relation to a less than human world.

31  I have clearly taken liberties in reducing our own ideas to a simple scheme. Of course we use things expressively, of course as Wagner notes there is a dialectic between invention and convention, individual creativity and social norm. I am simply pointing to one line of thinking which for us produces associations that very plausibly translate other people's dichotomies into schemes of our own.

Although I have been interested in this topic for a long time, its present formulation owes much to recent analyses of Hagen ethnography by Andrew Strathern and to Roy Wagner's *The invention of culture*. Additionally I thank both of them for criticism of the present paper; versions of it have been read to the Anthropology Departments of Cambridge University, the Collège de France and the London School of Economics, from whose discussions I have profited. I am grateful also for the detailed scrutiny of Patricia Hill, Debbora Jones, Carol MacCormack and Marie Reay, many of whose comments are incorporated here, and for Marianne Leach's help with the final manuscript. Girton College generously assisted with typing expenses.

## References

Archer, J. 1976. 'Biological explanations of psychological sex differences', in *Exploring sex differences*, eds. B. Lloyd and J. Archer. London: Academic Press.

Ardener, E. 1972. 'Belief and the problem of women', in *The interpretation of ritual*, ed. J.S. La Fontaine. London: Tavistock.

1977. 'The "problem" revisited', in *Perceiving women*, ed. S. Ardener. London: Dent.

Ardener, S. 1977. Introduction to *Perceiving women*. London: Dent.

Barth, F. 1975. *Ritual and knowledge among the Baktaman of New Guinea.* Yale: Yale University Press.

Benoist, J.-M. 1978 [1975]. *The structural revolution.* London: Weidenfeld and Nicolson.

Buchbinder, G. & Rappaport, A. 1976. 'Fertility and death among the Maring', in *Man and woman in the New Guinea Highlands*, eds. P. Brown & G. Buchbinder. Spec. pub. Amer. Anthr. Assoc. no. 8.

Bulmer, R.N.H. 1967. 'Why is the cassowary not a bird?', *Man* (N.S.) 2, 5–25.

Burridge, K. 1973. *Encountering aborigines.* London: Pergamon Press.

Clay, B. 1977. *Pinikindu: Maternal nurture, paternal substance.* Chicago: Chicago University Press.

de Beauvoir, S. 1972 (first pub. 1949). *The second sex.* London: Penguin.

Dumont, L. 1977. *From Mandeville to Marx.* Chicago: Chicago University Press.

Errington, F. 1974. *Karavar: Masks and power in a Melanesian ritual.* Ithaca: Cornell University Press.

Firestone, S. 1972. *The dialectic of sex.* London: Paladin.

Glennon, L.M. 1979. *Women and dualism.* London: Longman.

Godelier, M. (trans R. Brain). 1977 (first pub. 1973). *Perspectives in Marxist anthropology.* Cambridge: Cambridge University Press.

1978. 'Infrastructure, societies and history', *Current Anthropology*, **19**, 763–71.

Goody, J.R. 1977. *The domestication of the savage mind.* Cambridge: Cambridge University Press.

Hallpike, C.R. 1977. *Bloodshed and vengeance in the Papuan mountains.* Oxford: Oxford University Press.

Hastrup, K. 1978. 'The semantics of biology: virginity', in *Defining females*, ed. S. Ardener. London: Croom Helm.

Huntsman, J. & Hooper, A. 1975. 'Male and female in Tokelau culture', *Journal of the Polynesian Society*, 84, 415–30.

Langness, L.L. 1976. Discussion in *Man and woman in the New Guinea Highlands*, eds. P. Brown & G. Buchbinder. Spec. pub. Amer. Anthr. Assoc. no. 8.

Leach, E.R. 1976. *Communication and culture.* Cambridge: Cambridge University Press.

Lévi-Strauss, C. 1966 [1962]. *The savage mind.* London: Weidenfeld and Nicolson.

1969 [1949]. *The elementary structures of kinship.* London: Eyre and
   Spottiswood.
Lewis, G. 1975. *Knowledge of illness in a Sepik society.* London: Athlone
   Press.
Lindenbaum, S. 1976. 'A wife is the hand of man', in *Man and woman in
   the New Guinea Highlands,* eds. P. Brown & G. Buchbinder. Spec.
   pub. Amer. Anthr. Assoc. no. 8.
Lloyd, B. 1976. 'Social responsibility and research on sex differences', in
   *Exploring sex differences,* eds. B. Lloyd & J. Archer. London:
   Academic Press.
Mathieu, N.-C. (trans. D. Leonard Barker). 1978a. *Ignored by some, denied
   by others,* Explorations in feminism no. 2. London: Women's
   Research and Resources Centre.
   1978b [1973]. 'Man–culture and woman–nature?', *Women's Studies,*
   **1,** 55–65.
Meggitt, M.J. 1964. 'Male–female relationships in the Highlands of
   Australian New Guinea', *Amer. Anthr.* (Spec. publication) **66,** 204–24.
   1976. 'A duplicity of demons', in *Man and woman in the New Guinea
   Highlands.* Spec. pub. Amer. Anthr. Assoc. no. 8.
Meigs, A.S. 1976. 'Male pregnancy and the reduction of sexual opposition
   in a New Guinea Highlands society', *Ethnology,* **15,** 393–407.
Newman, P. 1964. ' "Wild man" behaviour in a New Guinea Highlands
   community', *Amer. Anthr.* **66,** 1–19.
Ortner, S.B. 1974. 'Is female to male as nature is to culture?', in *Woman,
   culture and society,* eds. M.Z. Rosaldo and L. Lamphere. Stanford:
   Stanford University Press.
Poole, F.J.P. 1981. ' "Sacred" and "polluting" dimensions of female
   identity among Bimin-Kuskusmin', in *Sexual meanings,* eds.
   S. Ortner & H. Whitehead. New York: Cambridge University Press.
Read, K.E. 1955. 'Morality and the concept of the person among the
   Gahuku-Gama', *Oceania,* **25,** 233–82.
Reiter, R.R. 1975. Introduction to *Toward an anthropology of women,*
   ed. R. Reiter. New York: Monthly Review Press.
Rogers, S.C. 1978. 'Woman's place: a critical review of anthropological
   theory', *Comparative studies in society and history,* **20,** 123–62.
Rosaldo, M.Z. & Atkinson, J.M. 1975. 'Man the hunter and woman:
   metaphors for the sexes in Ilongot magical spells', in *The interpret-
   ation of symbolism,* ed. R. Willis. A.S.A. studies 3. London: Malaby
   Press.
Sahlins, M. 1976. *Culture and practical reason.* Chicago: Chicago Univer-
   sity Press.
Schneider, D. 1968. *American Kinship: a cultural account.* New Jersey:
   Prentice-Hall.
Strathern, A. 1970. 'The Female and Male Spirit cults in Mount Hagen',
   *Man* (N.S.) **5,** 571–85.
   1972. *One father, one blood.* Canberra: ANU Press.
   1973. 'Kinship, descent and locality: some New Guinea examples', in
   *The character of kinship,* ed. J.R. Goody. Cambridge: Cambridge
   University Press.

1977. 'Melpa food-names as an expression of ideas on identity and substance', *Journal of the Polynesian Society*, 86, 503–11.

1979. 'Men's house, women's house: the efficacy of opposition, reversal and pairing in the Melpa *Amb Kor* cult', *Journal of the Polynesian Society*, 88, 37–51.

Strathern, M. 1968. 'Popokl: the question of morality', *Mankind*, 6, 553–61.

1969. 'Why is the Pueraria a sweet potato?', *Ethnology*, 8, 189–98.

1972. *Women in between. Female roles in a male world.* London: Seminar (Academic) Press.

1976. 'An anthropological perspective', in *Exploring sex differences*, eds. B. Lloyd & J. Archer. London: Academic Press.

1978. 'The achievement of sex: paradoxes in Hagen gender-thinking', in *The yearbook of symbolic anthropology I.* ed. E. Schwimmer. London: Hurst.

1981. 'Self-interest and the social good: some implications of Hagen gender imagery', in *Sexual meanings*, eds. S. Ortner & H. Whitehead. New York: Cambridge University Press.

Forthcoming. 'Domesticity and the denigration of women', in *Women in Oceania*, eds. D. O'Brien and S. Tiffany. ASAO publication.

Strathern, A. & Strathern, M. 1968. 'Marsupials and magic: a study of spell symbolism among the Mbowamb', in *Dialectic in practical religion*, ed. E.R. Leach. Cambridge: Cambridge University Press.

1971. *Self-decoration in Mount Hagen.* London: Duckworth.

Vicedom, G.F. & Tischner, M. 1943–8. *Die Mbowamb.* Hamburg: Friederichsens, de Gruyter & Co. (3 vols.)

Vicedom, G.F. (trans A. Strathern). 1977. *Myths and legends from Mount Hagen.* Port Moresby: Institute of Papua New Guinea Studies.

Wagner, R. 1975. *The invention of culture.* New Jersey: Prentice-Hall.

1978. *Lethal speech.* Ithaca: Cornell University Press.

Wilden, A. 1972. *System and structure.* London: Tavistock Publications.

Willis, R. 1975. *Man and beast.* London: Paladin.

# Index